CATHOLIC SECONDARY EDUCATION IN SOUTH-WEST SCOTLAND BEFORE 1972

CATHOLIC SECONDARY EDUCATION IN SOUTH-WEST SCOTLAND BEFORE 1972

Its Contribution to the Change in Status of the Catholic Community of the Area.

T A FITZPATRICK

ABERDEEN UNIVERSITY PRESS

First published 1986
Aberdeen University Press
A member of the Pergamon Group
© T A Fitzpatrick 1986

British Library Cataloguing in Publication Data

Fitzpatrick, T A
 Catholic secondary education in south-west
 Scotland before 1972: its contribution to the
 change in status of the catholic community of the area.
 1. Catholics—Scotland—History   2. Education,
 Secondary—Scotland—History   3. Scotland—
 Social conditions
 I. Title
 305.6′2′0414   BX1499

 ISBN 0 08 032439 8

PRINTED IN GREAT BRITAIN
THE UNIVERSITY PRESS
ABERDEEN

To Nora

CONTENTS

FIGURES, TABLES, MAPS

Figures

Tables

INTRODUCTION

The century of education, compulsory from 1872 at the behest of the State, has seen a complete transformation in the life of the Catholic community of the south-west of Scotland. Within that period three major Education Acts - in 1872, 1918 and 1945 - set the Scottish educational context and provided the stimuli to which the Catholic community had to respond. At first that response was concerned principally with primary or elementary education, as carried out in the parochial schools directly under ecclesiastical control; after 1918, and as a result of the Act of that year which reorganised the secondary sector for the whole nation, provision of educational opportunity at that level for Catholic children assumed greater importance. The expansion which followed posed a series of difficulties not resolved before the outbreak of the Second World War. Progress did resume in the aftermath of war, in the changed educational context set by the 1945 Act, in a world in which social, economic and technological change was proceeding at an unprecedented rate.

The work which follows - an abridged version of a doctoral thesis held in the library of Glasgow University - attempts to identify the contribution of the secondary sector of the Catholic educational system to the change in status of the catholic community. It acknowledges, without attempting a detailed analysis, the intimate bond that exists between the catholic primary and secondary sectors, and the degree of their interdependence especially in the area of religious education and formation.

At the centre of the thesis is the notion that, whatever the will of the ruling authorities, civil or religious, the formative educational process depends ultimately on the 'slow commerce of person with person'. Acknowledgement of the enormous contribution of the vast body of teachers, primary and secondary, to the spiritual, intellectual, moral and economic well-being of their pupils can only be made in the most general terms, but is none the less sincere for that.

When the First World War ended, the Catholic community was still concentrated into the most heavily industrialised areas of the south-west, relatively poor in educational, cultural or economic terms, still conscious of its immigrant past, underprivileged, and conspicuously lacking in formal secondary education. By virtue of its strong religious loyalty, ethnic origins and the prevalent concept of the nature of the Church, it lived very much as a separate and inward-looking community. Its political involvement was not commensurate with its size. The separate quality of Catholic life was emphasised by its school system, which was essentially elementary in character. Secondary education of any quality was available to only a tiny minority of the population. A wide gap in attainment and provision had grown up between the catholic and the state systems.

When after 1918 the ecclesiastical authorities decided to transfer the schools into the national system, they accepted the responsibility of providing a distinctive Catholic secondary sector conforming to the requirements of the 1918 Act. They were immediately faced with the needs simultaneously to expand the number of secondary places, to raise standards of staffing and accommodation, and to recruit a teaching cadre qualified at higher and rising levels than before.

Between the wars some progress was made. A more highly educated and professionally sophisticated teaching body began to emerge, able to draw on the educational traditions developed by the Religious Teaching Orders and in the parochial schools as well as on the model provided by the schools of the non-denominational sector. Priority was given to the senior secondary sector. The catholic presence at University level increased, and a graduate class began to emerge in which continuity with the social and cultural life of the historic community was preserved. By the latter part of the 1930's decade the expansion in the number of secondary places could not keep pace with the increase in the supply of teachers. Before the end of this phase, a surplus of catholic teachers had arisen.

Further progress was halted by the outbreak of war. Because of the excessive concentration of the catholic population in industrialised areas, evacuation and other war-time exigencies bore heavily on its educational system. Nevertheless the shared experiences of war brought the catholic body closer than before to the national community.

As in 1918, the end of the Second World War coincided with the passing of a major Education Act. This introduced a changed concept of secondary education, and led to a blurring of the distinction between primary and secondary education and ultimately to the abolition of the separate categories of junior and senior secondary schools. Thereafter educational development took place in a totally changed socio-economic-political and religious context, characterised by the emergence of the Welfare State, the spread of aegalitarian ideas, the rise to power of the Labour Party, a redistribution of population, explosion of knowledge, decline in religious belief and erosion of traditional values and attitudes to authority. Development of the national system took the form of the raising of the school leaving age, expansion of the curriculum and a reorganisation of secondary schools on comprehensive lines.

The catholic secondary sector followed in the wake of the national system, but because the historic disparities between them still persisted, its needs did not coincide with those of the national schools. Teacher-supply and the expansion of secondary places presented more acute problems than in the non-denominational sector. Difficulties arising from the breakdown of historic communities as a result of urban renewal were more deeply felt, besides which, the general decline in religious observance had profound implications for a system which accepted religious education as its raison d'être. When the revolution in secular education initiated by the 1945 Act was succeeded by a comparable upheaval in religious education as a result of the Second Vatican

Council, the crisis of confidence affecting the catholic secondary teaching body deepened.

Towards the end of the 1960's, positive responses to these pressures began to emerge. Diocesan catechetical centres were set up; full-time chaplains were allocated to some secondary schools; the catholic college of education expanded, and a Catholic Education Commission was appointed to advise on educational issues.

By 1972, improvement in the overall position of the catholic secondary sector was apparent. The number of schools had increased; reorganisation into a comprehensive system was almost complete in Glasgow, and well under way elsewhere. The shortage of secondary teachers continued, but was a reflection of improved teacher-pupil ratios, more extensive curricular choice and increased educational opportunity rather than of any inability of the community to meet the demand for teachers. The community as a whole, still over-represented relatively to its size in the most socially deprived areas, was no longer so concentrated into the most congested industrial districts; it had vastly improved access to secondary and higher education; its cultural, social and economic status had improved, a graduate and professional stratum had emerged, and a greater degree of identification with the national community was being established. Along with these changes however went a growing polarisation within it based on social divisions.

In the half-century of operation of a dual-control system, the educational objectives of State and Church seemed to have shown some convergence. By the end of that period the schools and community had been so far transformed that a reappraisal of the contribution that could properly be expected from the catholic secondary sector was required. Since the attainment of objectives emanating from whatever source would rest on the performance of the teaching body, any such reappraisal would require a fundamental analysis of the role of the secondary school and the responsibilities of the secondary teacher vis-a-vis both civil and ecclesiastical authorities.

CHAPTER ONE

THE POST-REFORMATION RENAISSANCE OF
THE CATHOLIC CHURCH IN SCOTLAND

The Protestant Reformation of the sixteenth century resulted in the almost total eclipse of the Roman Catholic Church in Scotland. Only in pockets of the north-east shoulder and in parts of the West Highlands and Islands was there any substantial continuity of the ancient faith.

By the end of the eighteenth century this situation was changing. In 1780 the Catholic Relief Bill for England was passed, to be followed thirteen years later by the corresponding measure for Scotland. Thereafter Catholic churches and chapels began to open in almost every part of the United Kingdom.(1). About the same time the failure of the 1798 rebellion in Ireland, along with the Highland Clearances of the 1770's and the beginning of industrialisation in Strathclyde together stimulated a rapid increase in the population of south-west Scotland, with a significant Catholic element from Highland and Irish sources.

With this increase the Church was revitalised. As the number of Irish immigrants grew, the predominance within the catholic community of the north-east and West Highland areas diminished, and along with this went a shift in mental attitudes. "Indigenous (Scottish) catholics, whether English-speaking in the Lowlands or Gaelic-speaking in the Highlands, were alike in that they reflected the social and political sentiments of their Protestant neighbours, ...The Catholics of the West Highlands and the Hebrides experienced the same problems and grievances as their Protestant neighbours in these areas....This cultural orientation was to change....the centuries-old homogeneity of Scottish Catholicism largely vanished."(2) The unity, albeit imperfect, of the local church was subjected to a considerable strain by the advent of a body of mainly gaelic-speaking immigrants in whose consciousness nationhood and religious affiliation were inextricably intertwined, and who tended to look to Dublin rather than to St. Andrew's or even to Rome for spiritual leadership.

In the post-Reformation period ecclesiastical control of the Scottish church was first exercised by a succession of Prefects Apostolic, whose jurisdiction extended over the whole country. In 1731, the country was divided into two districts, the Highland (Gaelic-speaking) area of the West and the Lowland (non-gaelic) area east of the Highland Line. By the beginning of the nineteenth century however Irish immigration was altering radically the demographic pattern. Whereas in 1800 there had been c.30,000 Catholics in the country, by 1827 the total had risen to 70,000 of whom some 25,000 were in the

Glasgow Region. A new administrative structure was required and this took the form of three Vicariates, East, West and North. Glasgow became the centre of the Western District, which comprised the counties of Argyll, Ayr, Bute, Dumbarton, the southern part of Inverness, Lanark, Renfrew, Wigtown and the Western Isles, and was given its own resident Bishop.(3) The structure which thus came into being differed from the norm for a national Hierarchy, in that the bishops and priests were agents for the Congregation for the Propagation of the Faith and had no formal connection with the particular area in which they served.

The first Vicar Apostolic of the Western District was Bishop Ronald MacDonald who was translated from the Highland District to Glasgow when he was already over 70 years of age. He was succeeded in 1833 by his coadjutor Bishop, Andrew Scott, who like most of the Scottish Catholic clergy of the time was a native of the Enzie in Bannffshire.(4) In the same year Bishop John Murdoch, also a Bannffshire man, was appointed Coadjutor to Bishop Scott, and in 1845 succeeded him as Vicar Apostolic of the Western District.

The division of the country into three Vicariates was administratively successful, helping to channel the benefits of the Emancipation Act of 1829 evenly throughout the country. However, the successive failures of the potato crop in Ireland in the 1840's turned the flow of Irish immigration into a variable flood. In the three years from 1847 the Catholic population of Glasgow doubled. "The catholic population of the Western Vicariate rose week by week.... the civic as well as the ecclesiastical administration was at breaking point.... the incomers needed not just churches and schools and institutions, but housing and food and the bare necessities of existence."(5)

The rapid increase in population led to friction between the native Scots and the displaced Irish, and eventually to a demand on the part of the Irish community for the establishment of a normal hierarchical structure and the appointment to it of Irish bishops. In 1864 Bishop Murdoch received an address signed by twenty-one of the Irish clergy, the tenour of which may be judged from the following terse statement:
"As the people are all Irish, they consider that Irish bishops should be appointed."(6)
Bishop Murdoch died the following year.

An Irish Coadjutor Bishop, James Lynch, was appointed to assist Bishop John Gray who had succeeded Bishop Murdoch; but this appears only to have exacerbated an already difficult situation, as has been indicated by Monsignor McRoberts. The dilemma facing the Western Vicariate, he wrote, was "Either to follow Bishop Lynch and a small coterie of Irish priests, who were bent on turning the Catholicism of south-west Scotland into an extension of the Irish Church, with Irish Bishops, Irish priests and an Irish faithful, living in a self-imposed ghetto, preserving its separate Irish identity and culture and resisting all contact with the national life around them; forming in effect an alien enclave in Scottish society ....or.... endeavour to integrate, and participate as far as possible in the general life of the country."(7) The dilemma was resolved in favour of the second alternative, as a result of the Visitation and Report of Archbishop (later Cardinal) Manning. He recommended that Bishop Gray be retired, Lynch translated to an Irish Diocese and the Scottish Hierarchy restored. Until that could be arranged, an Englishman should be appointed to reconcile the separate factions in the Western District.(8)

In 1869 Monsignor Charles Eyre, Vicar General of the diocese of Hexham and Newcastle, was sent to Scotland as Administrator Apostolic of the Western District and Apostolic Delegate to Scotland, with the twofold task of restoring ecclesiastical authority in the Western District and preparing the way for the restoration of a Catholic hierarchy in Scotland. Before long he had gained the loyalty of the Catholics of the Western District, and turned to the major task of reorganising the Church's administration. The three Vicariates were broken up into six dioceses. The Archbishopric of St. Andrew's and Edinburgh was set up as a Metropolitan Archdiocese, to which the dioceses of Aberdeen, Dunkeld, Argyll and the Isles, and Galloway were restored as suffragan sees; the Archdiocese of Glasgow was given the titular status of an archbishopric until such times as it would be provided with suffragan sees, and its jurisdiction was defined as extending over the city of Glasgow and the counties of Lanark, Renfrew, Dumbarton, part of the county of Stirling, a northern portion of the county of Ayr and the islands of the Great and Little Cumbrae. The southern portion of the county of Ayr and the remainder of south-west Scotland would make up the diocese of Galloway.

This territorial division remained unchanged until 1948, when the Archdiocese of Glasgow was raised to the status of a Province and given the suffragan sees of Paisley and Motherwell, coextensive respectively with Renfrewshire and Lanarkshire. At the same time the northern portion of Ayr and the Great and Little Cumbraes were allocated to Galloway.

The Growth of the Catholic population

Some indication of the rate of growth of the Catholic population can be gleaned from the establishment of missions in the south-west during the post-Reformation period. In the following account their locations are presented in the geographical framework of the post-1948 diocesan boundaries.

The first four decades of the nineteenth century saw a slow growth in the number of Catholic missions in the south-west. The earliest were: St. Mirin's in Paisley, founded in 1808; St. Andrew's Dumfries in 1813; St. Peter's Dalbeattie in 1814; St. Andrew's Glasgow, now the cathedral church of the Archdiocese, in 1816; St. Mary's Greenock in the same year; St. Patrick's Dumbarton in 1830 and St. Margaret's Airdrie in 1836. Of the total of 11 founded in this forty-year period, 6 were in Galloway, reflecting the long-standing inflow of Irish agricultural labour into that area.(9) Permanent immigration of the Irish into the urban areas only assumed importance after the concentration of the cotton industry in the 1830's(10)

The next twenty years, from 1840 till 1860, saw a dramatic change. 31 parishes were opened - 13 in Glasgow, 9 in what is now the Motherwell diocese, 5 in Paisley and 4 in Galloway. These were the years of massive Irish immigration after the Great Famine. Between 1841 and 1851 the population of Ireland fell from 8.2 millions to 6.6 millions. With due allowance for natural increase, it has been estimated that between 1846 and 1851 nearly one million Irish people emigrated, and approximately 1.5 million perished.(11)

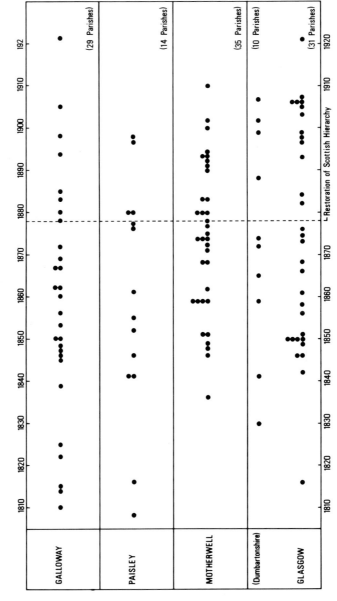

Fig. 1. Foundation of Catholic Parishes in S.W. Scotland 1800–1922 A.D.
(within post 1948 diocesan boundaries)

TABLE 1

Number of Catholic Parishes, with Populations, in S.W. Scotland in 1922

Diocesan Area (1972 boundaries)		Number of Parishes	Population	Elementary School Population	% (4 of 3)
Glasgow City		31	193,795	35,491	18.3
	Dumbartonshire	10	29,723	5,370	18.1
Motherwell		35	96,650	19,124	19.8
Paisley		14	50,668	9,415	18.6
Galloway	North Ayrshire	7	8,375		
		97	379,211		
	Remainder	22	16,000	4,873	20.0
Total		119	395,211	74,273	18.8

Source: The Archives of the Archdiocese of Glasgow.
        See also Appendix 1

By the end of the 1860's the tide of immigration had passed its flood. In the years from 1860 till the turn of the century Glasgow added 17, Motherwell 23 and Galloway 17 parishes to their respective totals. Development was less rapid in Paisley, where 7 new parishes were founded, 5 of them between 1876 and 1880. The first years of the twentieth century showed a continuation of steady progress in Glasgow, with 8 foundations in the first decade, but elsewhere activity was tapering off, to cease entirely during World War 1. From 1910 to 1920 only 3 new parishes were established in the whole of the south-west, 2 of them in Galloway.

Table 1 summarises the position reached in 1922. Therein the Archdiocese of Glasgow is subdivided into Glasgow City and Dumbartonshire, and that sector of the present Diocese of Galloway which before 1948 was part of Glasgow is listed as North Ayrshire. It gives a total of 379,211 in 97 parishes as the then population of the Glasgow Archdiocese.

Table 2 gives the Scottish Catholic Directory's estimate of the Catholic population for 1922. The figure for Glasgow is 450,000, and for the whole of Scotland 601,304. Elsewhere an estimate by Darragh (12) of the total Catholic population is 586,000, 15,304 less than the Table 2 figure. If this difference were attributed entirely to an overestimate of the population of Glasgow, a revised estimate for Glasgow would be 434,696, still considerably in excess of the Table 1 figure.

If Darragh's national total is used along with the diocesan totals in Table 1, the conclusion is reached that in 1922 south-west Scotland contained about 67% of all Scottish Catholics, and the area that is now the Metropolitan Province of Glasgow, some 63%.   The remainder was divided among the four remaining dioceses, of which the Archdiocese of St. Andrew's and Edinburgh was by far the largest with some 13.2% of the total.

Darragh further observes that by the early 1920's Scottish Catholics made up about 12% of the total population. On this basis Catholics of the south-west amounted to 8% of the population of Scotland; and those of the Province of Glasgow alone, some 7.6%.

THE DISTRIBUTION OF THE CATHOLIC POPULATION OF THE SOUTH-WEST

Perhaps of greater importance than size for its future cultural development was the distribution of the population. Two-thirds of all Scotland's Catholics lived in the south-west, and of that number the vast majority – almost 95% of them – were accommodated within the boundary of the Archdiocese of Glasgow. A study of the Strathclyde Region published in 1975 concluded that at that time parts of the region were among the most deprived in Western Europe(13) – that is, after fifty years of massive if not always successful effort to ameliorate the worst ravages of nineteenth century industrialisation. It is in this perspective that the situation of the Catholics of south-west Scotland in socio-economic and cultural terms has to be seen.

The Catholic Community in Glasgow City

In 1922 33% of all Scotland's Catholics, numbering about 200,000 people,

TABLE 2

ESTIMATED CATHOLIC POPULATION OF SCOTLAND IN 1922 BY DIOCESES

		% of Scottish Total
St. Andrew's and Edinburgh	77,804	12.9%
Aberdeen	12,500	2.1%
Argyll and the Isles	12,000	2.0%
Dunkeld	33,000	5.5%
Galloway	16,000	2.7%
Glasgow	450,000 (1)	74.8%
Scotland	601,304 (2)	100.0%

(1) Figure reached in Table 1 is 379,211.

(2) Darragh's estimate is 586,000.

were concentrated into the 31 parishes of the city of Glasgow. The programmes of municipal housing which were later to transform working–class housing in the city had not begun; and the catholic population, with little representation in the middle or upper end of the social or income spectrum, had been almost totally unaffected by the middle–class migrations to the city's periphery which had taken place during the period of Glasgow's pre–1914 prosperity, along the railway lines or tram routes westwards to Jordanhill and Bearsden or southwards to the growing residential districts of Cathcart, Shawlands and Newlands. Inevitably the vast majority of the immigrant Irish and Highland populations were domiciled in the poorest areas. "An immigrant population of labourers...went for the cheapest housing. So did any sector of the population whose economic position was unstable."(14) The catholic population was firmly based in the areas of multiple deprivation, the areas associated with the worst consequences of industrialisation, with the poorest housing conditions, declining industries and high unemployment.

Three square miles is the area of a circle of approximately one mile radius. Such a circle centred at Glasgow Cross is shown on Map 1. This is the area referred to in the Third Statistical Account of Scotland: "One seventh of the population of Scotland (i.e. about 750,000) was thus compressed into three square miles of central Glasgow."(15); but even that horrendous statistic fails to convey fully the congestion that existed. Map 1 shows in simplified form the land–use of the area, which encompassed, inter alia, a part of the River Clyde and Glasgow's then busy dockland, and the market area. Among many relatively large users of space were Glasgow Green, the Royal Infirmary, the Necropolis and Southern Necropolis, Glasgow Cathedral, the Royal Technical College and Duke Street Prison. The area occupied by the central business district was largely denied to domestic dwellings. A considerable part of the total surface area was taken up by railway property, notably the four main passenger termini, the College Goods Station and the rail sidings at Gushetfaulds. In addition there were many large industrial enterprises with much associated waste land, such as Tennant's Brewery and Dixon's Blazes, as well as numerous warehouses, whisky bonds and distilleries, and stables and smithies for Glasgow's large population of horses.

On Map 1 the locations of Catholic parish churches in the area are shown, identified by the index numbers used in Table 20 of Appendix 1A. It shows that in 1922 this part of Glasgow contained almost all of the territory of the following 8 parishes – 1, 2, 3, 4, 6, 15, 16, 30 – together with a con- siderable part of the territory of each of the following – 7, 14, 28. The population of the first group numbered more than 66,000, and of all 11 parishes, almost 95,000.

Even if the radius is extended to 1½ miles, the general pattern of land–use alters only slightly. Within the enlarged circle considerable areas in the north at Garngad and south at Polmadie were given over to industrial uses; and the major parks which might have provided some environmental relief were for the most part outwith the area. Within this larger circle there were, in whole or in part, the following parishes – 10, 17, 18, 19, 23, 26 – which accounted for approximately 40,000 more of the Catholic population of the city.

In effect, in 1922 almost one quarter of the Catholic population of all Scotland

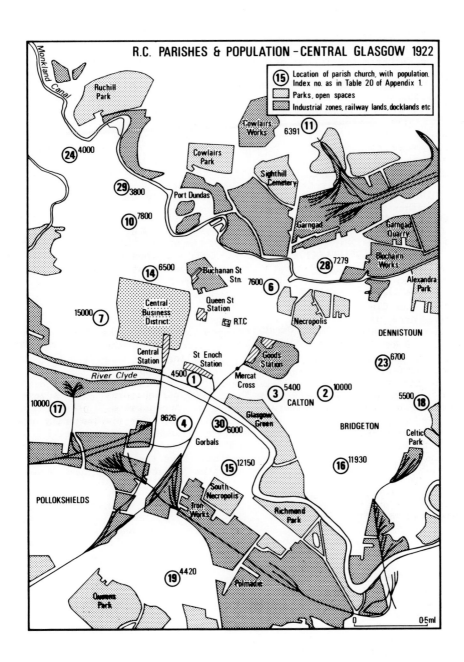

Map 1

was domiciled within 1½ miles of Glasgow Cross.

The Catholic Community in Dunbartonshire

In 1922 the Catholic population of Dunbartonshire amounted to 29,723 accommodated in 10 parishes dispersed over the two separate areas of the county. One main concentration had grown up in the Dumbarton-Vale of Leven area, where 3 parishes served 10,797 people; a second, associated with the late nineteenth century growth of Clydebank, also consisted of 3 parishes serving 12,343. The remainder were located in 4 widely dispersed parishes. See Map 2 and Appendix 1.

The Catholic Community in Motherwell

Here in 1922 almost 97,00 people were accommodated in 35 parishes, loosely grouped together as follows:

Index	Area	No. of Parishes	Population
A	Airdrie-Coatbridge	10	29,239
M	Motherwell-Wishaw	8	28,976
H	Hamilton-Bothwell-Blantyre	7	22,370
R	Rutherglen-Cambuslang	3	7,305
C	Blackwood, Carluke, Carstairs Lanark, Stepps and Strathaven	6	4,700

Index letters are used to identify these parishes in Table 22 of Appendix 1A.

Of the 35 parishes, only 6 had more than 5,000 parishioners, the largest being Our Lady of Good Aid in Motherwell and St. Augustine's in Coatbridge. The people lived close to their places of work, which for the majority were the coalmines, iron and steel works, the railways or other public works. Lanarkshire communities, being relatively small, had the advantage that their inhabitants had access to the surrounding countryside. Nevertheless housing conditions were frequently extremely poor, matching the worst to be found anywhere in Glasgow.

The Catholic Community of Paisley

Here the population of 50,668, about 8.5% of Scottish Catholics, was accommodated in two urban clusters - one, centering on Paisley, consisting of 10 parishes with 27,835 people, and the other, with 4 parishes serving 22,833, located in the Greenock-Port Glasgow area. The largest parishes - St. Mirin's in Paisley, founded in 1808 and St. Mary's in Greenock, in 1816 - each had more than 10,000 parishioners, and were comparable in size with the largest parishes of the city of Glasgow.

The Catholic Community of Galloway

In 1922 there were in North Ayrshire 7 parishes with a total population of

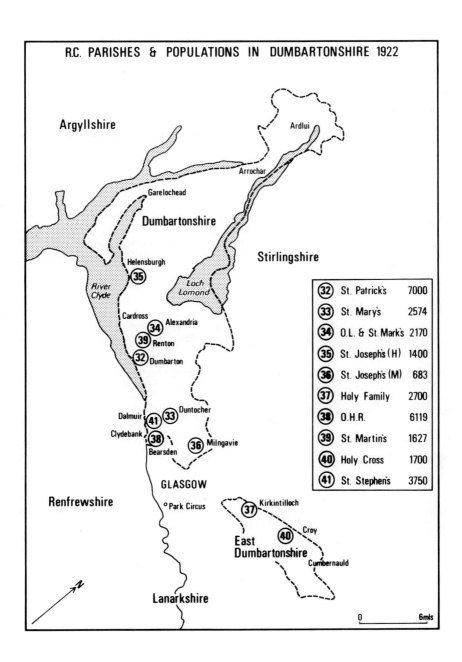

R.C. PARISHES & POPULATIONS IN DUMBARTONSHIRE 1922

Argyllshire

Ardlui

Arrochar

Garelochead

Dumbartonshire

Stirlingshire

Helensburgh

River
Clyde

(35)

Loch
Lomond

(32)	St. Patrick's	7000
(33)	St. Mary's	2574
(34)	O.L. & St.Mark's	2170
(35)	St. Joseph's (H)	1400
(36)	St. Joseph's (M)	683
(37)	Holy Family	2700
(38)	O.H.R.	6119
(39)	St. Martin's	1627
(40)	Holy Cross	1700
(41)	St. Stephen's	3750

Cardross

(34) Alexandria

(39) Renton

(32) Dumbarton

Dalmuir (41)(33) Duntocher

Clydebank (38)

Bearsden   (36) Milngavie

GLASGOW

Renfrewshire   ° Park Circus

Kirkintilloch

(37)

Croy

(40)

East
Dumbartonshire

Cumbernauld

N

Lanarkshire

0   6mls

Map 2

8,375. The major agglomeration was in the Saltcoats-Stevenston-Kilwinning area. Over the remainder of Galloway the estimated population in 1922 was 16,000 in 22 parishes. The largest centres were in Dumfries, Ayr, Kilmarnock, Cumnock and Irvine.

THE STRUCTURE OF THE CATHOLIC POPULATION

By the end of the eighteenth century the Catholic population of Scotland, estimated at c.30,000, had reached its nadir. (See Table 3) The population of the Highland Vicariate had fallen to c.16,000; the total in the Lowland Vicariate, c.14,000, was already showing an upward trend. The number increased rapidly throughout the nineteenth century, and at a decreasing rate thereafter.

The first important element in this growth clearly was the immigrant Irish population, together with their descendants. It is however worthy of note that in the early years of this century this inflow steadily reduced (16), eventually to be surpassed by immigration from other sources, including England. (See Fig.2) It was also the case that not all Irish immigrants were Catholic. According to O'Connor, "a higher proportion of Protestant-Irish emigrants from Ulster arrive...(in Glasgow) annually than to any other single conurbation in Britain."(17)

The second important element consisted of native Scots Catholics, in Dumfries, Kirkcudbright and Wigtown in the south, Bannffshire and surrounding areas of the north-east and in parts of the West Highlands and Islands.

A third element latterly consisted of relatively small groups from various parts of Europe, including Germans, Belgians and French as well as Italians, Poles and Lithuanians, whose coming was related to the nineteenth century upheavals in Europe which culminated in the Great War.

Finally, to the above categories there fall to be added immigrants from England, parts of the Empire or USA. Among those of this group who were catholic, some at least were of Irish descent.

It would seem therefore that by 1922 the Catholic population of the south-west was made up as follows: first, there was a substantial proportion who were born in Ireland. Their children, if born in Scotland, were classified as Scots. Secondly, there was a group of Highland ancestry; according to Tivy over the period from 1851-1951 the inflow of population from the Highlands into West Central Scotland maintained at a fairly constant rate around 10% of all incomers.(18) Presumably Catholics constituted a minority of this group, and it is reasonable to assume that this element accounted for not more than 10% of the Catholic population of the south-west. Thirdly there was a small group of European nationals. The remainder, a substantial number and possibly even a majority, was composed of second or third generation Irish families or families of mixed Irish-Scottish origin.

It is probable that intermarriage of the immigrants with the indigenous population, Catholic or not, proceeded to a very considerable extent, in spite of the constant and fiercely reiterated opposition on the part of the Church

TABLE 3

ESTIMATES OF CATHOLIC POPULATION OF SCOTLAND,
1680–1951

Year	Number of Catholics	% Increase or Decrease	Percentage of total Scottish Populations
1680	50,000		5.0 (?)
1745	40,000	− 20	3.0 (?)
1755	33,000	− 17.5	2.6
1800	30,000	− 9.1	1.8
1827	70,000	+ 133	3.0 (?)
1851	146,000	+ 108	5.0
1878	333,000	+ 128	9.2
1901	446,000	+ 34	10.0
1911	513,000	+ 15	10.8
1921	586,000	+ 14	12.0
1931	662,000	+ 11.4	13.7
1941	702,000	+ 6	14.6
1951	748,000	+ 6.5	14.7

From: Darragh, J. Catholic Population of Scotland
            I.R. IV,1 (1953) p. 58.

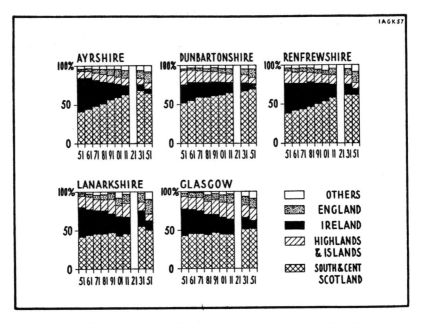

1921 is omitted because Census in this year was taken in June, when normal conditions were complicated by both absence and presence of holiday-makers.

Based on data from the *Census of Scotland*.

Extracted from Population, Distribution and Change by TIVY, J. in the Glasgow Region, – R. Miller and J. Tivy (Eds.)

Fig. 2.   Origin of Incomers in Counties of West Central Scotland and Glasgow, 1851–1951

to 'mixed' marriages.

The fact that so important a part of the strength of the Catholic Church in south-west Scotland, as indeed in the United Kingdom as a whole, derived from Irish sources has a significance going beyond the counting of heads. Irish Catholicism has been and has remained distinctive in a number of ways. Insulated by language and geography from the mainstream of continental catholicism, Ireland during the early centuries of the Christian era was able to develop its own style. Whereas in post-Reformation England one effect of the penal laws was to make Catholicism an exclusive religion for the privileged few who had access to a private chapel, in Ireland Catholics were confined to the poorer section of the population, deprived of educational opportunities and essential liberties. One consequence has been that Irish Catholicism has exhibited a greater puritanism of outlook and a greater emphasis on naive faith, as well as what is perhaps its most distinctive feature, "the fusion of religion and nationalism in the Irish mind."(19) Besides making it difficult at first for the indigenous Scottish or English Catholics to accept their co-religionists among the early Irish immigrants, these differences exercised a continuing influence on the development of the Catholic community in the south-west, and tended to exacerbate the problems of an immigrant group seeking to identify with its host community.

NOTES

1.   Jackson, J. Archer   The Irish in Britain   pp. 138-9
2.   McRoberts, Mons. D.   The Restoration of the Scottish Catholic Hierarchy
                            in 1878
                                                      IR XXIX,I.
3.   W.C.C. 1980, p.21.
4.   W.C.C. 1981.   "Bishop Scott was one of the great apostolic
                            priests.... No biographical note of this nature
                            can do justice to the debt owed...by subsequent
                            generations of catholics."
5.   McRoberts, Mons.D   Loc.cit.
6.   Ibid.
7.   Ibid.
8.   W.C.C. 1981, p.25.
9.   Handley, J.E.   The Irish in Scotland   pp.3-56
10.   Tivy, J.   Population Distribution and Change.
                            Miller, R. and Tivy, J. (Eds.) The Glasgow
                            Region.
11.   Smith, C. Woodham   The Great Hunger   pp.411-2.
12.   Darragh, J.   Catholic Population of Scotland IR IV,I (1953)
                            p.58.
13.   Census Indicators of Urban Deprivation: Working Note No.6.
                            ECOR Division, Department of the Environment,
                            Feb. 1975.
14.   Ross, Anthony O.P.   Development of the Catholic Community
                            IR XXIX,I (1978) p.33.
15.   Third Statistical Account of Scotland. Glasgow volume.
16.   Handley, J.E.   The Irish in Modern Scotland, p.246
                            Handley calculates that after 1908 the inflow fell
                            below 1,000 per annum.
17.   D'Connor, K.   The Irish in Britain   p.119.
18.   Tivy, J.   Loc.cit.
19.   Jackson, J. Archer.   Op.cit. p.137.

CHAPTER TWO

A SEPARATE COMMUNITY

Because of its size and geographical concentration, the Catholic population of the south-west of Scotland was able to exist around the turn of the century as a separate community. The people were grouped in densely populated settlements in the more heavily industrialised areas of the Clyde Valley, most of them in the city of Glasgow. These were close-knit communities, bound together by ties of blood, common origins and a common faith. Loyalty to the Catholic Church and to the Catholic way of life, however intuitively understood and accepted, was for them part of the natural order. For the most part they were housed close to the parish churches and the schools which before 1918 had been provided by the Church - in many instances the same building served both purposes - and to their work-places, since for the majority the principal mode of transport was by Shanks's Mare.

"Church and school were the centre of the local Catholic community's life, social as well as religious, and reinforced its identity and self-respect by their very existence."(1) Sharing the common lot of humble folk, which involved excessively long hours of hard physical work both for the labouring men and women coping with domestic conditions unimaginable to the modern generation, compounded by the unending battle against dirt, poverty and disease, the bulk of the catholic community lacked time, energy or other resources for social or cultural activity except at a very local level. As a result, communities tended to become inward-looking and cut off from even fairly close neighbours.

The following extract from a study of an English Catholic community affords an interesting comparison:

"What the nineteenth century church achieved...was the service of locally-based Irish Catholic communities. The parish was the principal means by which this was done. In the setting-up of territorial parishes the ideology of the Church as a counter-society and the local solidarity of the Irish exactly coincided... the schools the parish built were regarded as part of the parish.... As the teachers lived locally, they sat with the children at their special Sunday Mass.... It was a time too when people tended to do the same job as their parents, live in the same districts and not go about much between areas; there was no particular reason why anyone living in the east end of the city should ever go to the west end.... The parish was thus built around local interests

17

of a shared sort. This was one of its sources of strength and the basis of parochial pride and self-assertion. It was a base which could be extended into a sense of solidarity with the wider Catholic body."(2)

The bulk of the Catholic population was of Irish descent and carried Irish patronyms. Non-Irish Catholics and non-Catholic Irish abounded, but nevertheless in the public mind to be Catholic was to be Irish and vice-versa. "If...it is the case that being Irish is a state of mind, then the catholic community of the early 20's could be said to be still Irish. The majority were of Ireland, yet no longer living there. Now of Scotland, yet not feeling Scottish, nor British; geographically cut off from the mainspring of their own native culture, without being easily adaptable to that of the host community."(3) However, it would also be true to say that the typical pattern of settlement, consolidation and gradual accommodation to the host community evinced by Irish groups elsewhere in Britain (4) was also emerging here. The massive immigrations of the nineteenth century were over, and despite some tensions a degree of economic absorption had taken place; the shared sufferings of 1914-18, a living memory, had brought the Catholic community closer than ever before to the rest of the nation, and strengthened a growing tendency to draw slowly away from the attitudes characteristic of its immigrant origins and past.

The greatest concentrations were reached in particular localities in Glasgow. It has been argued that the basic mode of life, tenement dwelling, created conditions under which there could be a real social mix, and that this militated against the immigrant tendency to huddle together. Victorian and Edwardian Glasgow was one city.(5) Still, there is truth in the allegation that the catholic community did develop something of a ghetto mentality; and near-ghetto conditions did exist in some places long after the early 20's. About Scotland in the 1950's it was said that "(it) is most akin to Ulster in the separation of the communities. In the remnants of the Motherwell and Gorbals ghettoes the inherited siege-mentality persists."(6)

There were relatively few Catholics in business or the professions. The vast majority of the men were employed in unskilled or semi-skilled occupations, in the coal-mines, public works, iron foundries, shipyards, docks, on the railways and so on.(7) Victorian urban life made exorbitant demands on man- and woman- power, and Glasgow was no exception. Many girls from the Highlands or Ireland were attracted into domestic service in the enormous town-houses of Glasgow's Victorian hey-day, while the city's dependence on horse-drawn traffic provided occupations as carters, grooms, stable-hands, farriers, smiths and so on for men who, because of their upbringing in Irish rural communities, were skilled in the handling of horses.(8)

Although the early nineteenth century Irish incomers had made on the whole a good impression and had sought to integrate into their new environment, the situation altered as the numbers grew. Native Scots came to fear and distrust the expanded Catholic community, whose members, embittered by memories of the Great Famine, responded by retreating into their own worlds, thus making it even more difficult to adapt to what were for them the unnatural conditions of an industrialised and urbanised society. One consequence was the relatively poor educational attainment of the Catholic population, of which only a tiny fraction had been exposed, by 1918, to any secondary education beyond that of the "supplementary" classes of some elementary schools. Members of the small Catholic business class were to be found in callings in which their principal investments were native wit and energy. There were many dealers in Irish agricultural produce, a sizeable number of publicans and pawnbrokers who here as elsewhere played an important part in the social and economic life of the immigrant community, and coal merchants, hauliers and bookmakers whose activities reflected the Irish commitment to the handling and breeding of horses. There was a significant presence in the clothing industry, then a much more important activity in Glasgow than it is now, perhaps because of the stimulus given by the requirements of the Church. There were many small shopkeepers, newsagents, dealers in second-hand furniture and lodging-house proprietors who formed a stratum of society separate from the mass of labouring men. Among advertisers in the Glasgow Observer for 5 January 1918 there were 5 dealers in Irish agricultural produce, 6 in waste paper, 5 in woollen rags, 6 in clothing and 3 in second-hand furniture. There were also 12 funeral undertakers.(9)

In the professions, the better-educated section of the community had produced a tiny elite of medical, para-medical, dental and legal practitioners, a handful of minor civil servants and local government officials, a few journalists and trade union officials, some independent business men of modest standing, and a number of teachers, the majority of whom were non-graduates trained for work in the elementary schools. Many were uncertficated. During session 1917-18, out of 97 women who completed training at Downhill College, only 4 were graduates.(10) There were 4 Catholic members of staff of Glasgow University - Prof. J.S. Phillimore (Humanity), W.E. Brown (History), Prof. Grillo (Italian) and P.G. McGlynn (Humanity) - of whom only the last was a product of the local community. The professional group should also include the considerable number of priests and other dedicated to the religious life, whose number cannot easily be estimated. Although in the early 20's the Church was still dependent on a continuing supply of priests from Ireland, their number was counterbalanced by those from the local area who left to serve in many other parts of the world. The 1927 Winter issue (NO.18) of the St. Aloysius' College Magazine published a list, not claimed to be exhaustive, of those Old Aloysians known to have been ordained as priests up to that time. It contains the names of 104 secular priests and 38 members of Religious Orders. Sixty-three of the seculars were ordained for the Archdiocese of Glasgow; the remainder were scattered over England, Wales, Canada and North America as well as the other Scottish diocese. The 38 Religious were divided among 7 orders.(11)

An indicator of the low economic status of the Catholic community was its almost total exclusion from employment in banks, (12) insurance offices, drawing offices or the more skilled levels of engineering. No doubt this related in part at least to the antipathy (13) which developed between the Catholic descendants of the immigrants and the native Scots, which resulted in a measure of discrimination (14) against them. Of Irish Catholics it was said, as late as 1923, that "they cannot be assimilated and absorbed into the Scottish race. They remain a people by themselves, segrated by reason of their race, their customs, their traditions and above all by their loyalty to their Church."(15) No doubt also that the prevailing climate was affected by the presence and activities of many militant Orange groups, and by the influence of Free Masonry;(16) but it was also related to the attitudes of the Catholic people themselves. "Glasgow Catholics of Irish extraction met suspicion with resentment. They claimed full citizen status without admitting the implications of that status... Feeling that they were not accepted as first-class citizens, they tended to withdraw inside themselves, and to look for slights in all directions."(17) Above all, their exclusion from the lower ranks of the white-collar occupations was a function of the relatively low educational attainment of the community, which for almost half-a-century had lived in a kind of educational wilderness, cut off from the mainspring of development in the nation at large. Nor was there any indication of a real initiative to bring about improvement in this sphere. The 1918 Act, which was to be the most effective agent in the advancement of the community, was accepted but not designed by them. Even then, the acceptance was reluctant on the part of some.

Among commentators on the Irish immigrant community, there is a suggestion that its political impact was less than might have been expected from its size and solidarity. One early commentator, Father Eric Hansen, addressed the Catholic Truth Society in 1906 in the following terms: "Here within a small radius we have some 200,000 Catholics. In the whole Archdiocese the number is 320,000.... It is one of the greatest industrial centres in the world. How many Catholic employers of labour have we? Where are the master engineers or shipbuilders who are Catholics?.... It is a University city. Among the 2,500 students at Gilmorehill could we find a dozen catholics? Is there one reading for a degree in Arts?.... Is there a single schoolmaster in the whole Archdiocese, elementary or secondary, who possesses a University degree?.... With marvellous unanimity they are as a class the least ambitious of all, the humblest in their ideas and aspirations, the least independent and enterprising, the most willing to take back seats and to be pushed aside by others."(18).

Others refer to the failure of the community to emerge, before 1914, as a thrusting element in working class movements. In this connection it has to be recognised that the total effect of the Irish vote in the latter half of the nineteenth century is difficult to gauge, because of the uncertainty surrounding the extent to which the mainly poor Catholic electorate was able to register on the electoral roll.(19) "A ratepayer's and residential franchise ...contained built-in obstacles to the registration of the Irish poor." There was in addition the question of illiteracy, which presented problems to people whose native tongue was Gaelic.(20) Handley attributed the modest part played by the Irish in proletarian politics to poverty, indifference to the philosophy of 'getting on', and preoccupation with the question of Home Rule for Ireland. (21) Walker offers an explanation linked with the religion of the immigrants and the dominant influence of the priesthood in the community. Because of the conviction, common among the Irish laity and endorsed by their priests, that association with the non-Catholic community would lead to contamination of morals, manners, customs and religious beliefs the Irish Catholics tended to erect wherever they congregated a community within a community; and in these enclaves imbibed values, conformed to codes of conduct and submitted to patterns of subordination which, even if essential to cultural survival, acted nonetheless to cut them off from the mainstream of working-class aspiration.... "Irish Catholic parochial life was a way of life... in which religious, political, economic, educational and recreational elements were fused to form a culture.... Within their substitute society the immigrants were exhorted to the virtues of docility and resignation, while institutionally the structure of parochial organisations compelled precisely this quiescence.

The Irish in Scotland emerged as creators of arks of refuge rather than as builders of barricades."(22) Middlemass suggests that "Because...they were well-off in the first decade of the twentieth century compared to their conditions in Ireland, the fires of political indignation burned low." He also makes the point that the developing Labour movement stood condemned in the minds of many Catholic clergy more for its attitude to the Irish question than for its social policies with which many indeed sympathised.(23) Brogan (24) the son of a Gaelic-speaking Irishman and Scots-Irish mother, lays stress on the fact that "the Irish were pitifully unorganised, partly because they were not reconciled to permanent settlement in Scotland, and partly because they came from a land that had virtually no native institutions." McRoberts hints at another factor. During the years of massive immigration, the greatest problem for administrators in the south-west was the fluidity of the situations as they developed in the receiving communities. "Groups...were liable to disappear as soon as individuals had earned enough to pay their passage to the U.S.A. This...creamed off the most energetic and enterprising of the immigrants, leaving an undue proportion of the most needy and feckless...nearly a generation after the peak period of immigration, when the Irish immigrants of America and Australia and of cities like Liverpool and Manchester had provided a fair number of thriving business-men and respected civic leaders, no such development had taken place in the West of Scotland"(25) A down-to-earth view is given by McShane. "The Workers' Union tried to recruit the unskilled men in engineering and building trades.... It was very difficult...Craft unions wouldn't accept labourers, and labourers' unions were weak because the type of work they did made them hard to organise." (26) The bulk of the Catholic men belonged to the class of unskilled labourer. In consequence, their political education, which might have been advanced by participation in well-organised union life, instead was hampered and retarded.

The comments noted do not exhaust all the possibilities. The majority of the immigrants into south-west Scotland came from the north and west of Ireland, where Gaelic was widely spoken, and in many parts of which the land was poor and the agricultural base of the local society very restricted. In times of stress it was the poorest people from these areas, those least able to adapt to the cultural shock of an urban environment, who were forced to emigrate. It could also be argued that the flow of young people into the priesthood and the Religious Orders, who constituted a substantial fraction of the educated Catholic body, may have withdrawn from the local community a significant number endowed with the qualities needed for political leadership.

In these analyses the commentators quoted tend to lay emphasis on the importance of Irish traditions, and on the concern of the clergy for things Irish. But the Catholic community was not wholly Irish, nor was the Irish community wholly Catholic. Neither was the priesthood entirely Irish, nor for that matter wholly Irish and Scots-Irish. The motivation of those devoted Scottish priests who toiled for the welfare of the expanding Catholic community throughout the nineteenth century - men like Bishops Scott and Murdoch, or Father Peter Forbes - clearly did not arise from commitment to things Irish. Their case is paralleled by those whose origins were in England or the continent. As well as Archbishop Eyre, a Yorkshireman, there could be instanced Fathers Beyaert and Delbeke, both Belgians, the Italian Father Magini and the German Canon Jansen, and many others. Peter Muller "was born at Luibsdorf in 1859...the church in Germany was passing through a period of persecution. A number of priests,...offered their services to Archbishop Eyre...one of these was Father Muller."(27) Father Terken, a Dutchman, worked in Baillieston for twenty-five years,(28) and in an earlier period a number of French émigré priests, exiled as a result of the French Revolution, toiled in the Greenock, Paisley and Ayr localities.(29) Further powerful influences were exercised by priests, brothers or sisters, members of Religious Orders, many of whom were nationals of England or continental countries. The first two headmasters of St. Mungo's Academy, Brothers Procope and Tatianus, were both Frenchmen, as were Brothers Guerin and Ezechiel. For all of these, their commitment was to the tenets and practice of the Catholic Church, rather than to some political or ethnic group.

For an explanation of the quiescent attitudes of the Scots-Irish Catholics in the early years of the twentieth century, it is necessary to look beyond nationalistic, economic or political motivation without however disregarding these influences.

If the community is looked upon as Christian rather than Irish, and its priorities viewed in that perspective, then its characteristic self-affacement may be seen as the resultant in political terms of what was essentially a theological outlook. To seek first the Kingdom of God was an injunction which many if not all accepted as simple common sense, and to take without protest 'the lowest place' the practical implementation of the Gospel.(30) Encouraged by contemporary theological emphases, particularly the then prevalent concept of the nature of the Church, the Catholics of Scotland tended to see themselves more and more separated from 'the world' which, in spite of its being the work of an infinitely good God, came to be regarded as hostile and even evil. At best it was accepted as a 'Vale of Tears', a description which neither liturgical practice nor the experience of centuries of suppression nor indeed the common lot of humanity in their own material circumstances did anything to weaken. Their attitude could be summed up in the words of the Apostle James: "True religion consists in this - to help the needy in their distress, and keep oneself unspotted from the world."(31) Not surprisingly, the community grew to be suspicious of the world of the secular state and fearful of contamination by it. Secular education was seen to be one medium of that contamination.

CATHOLICS AND THE RISE OF THE LABOUR PARTY

At the turn of the century the principal focus of political interest for the Catholic community had been the question of Home Rule for Ireland, with a consequent strong adherence to the Liberal Party. "In 1900 the Catholic population tended to vote solidly for the orthodox Liberal, purely on the Irish issue."(32) But there were other reasons for this support. In Britain as a whole the more advanced working men usually voted Liberal, and in Glasgow the majority of workmen did. That party had striven for the working class to have the vote, and the few working men who were MPs went to Parliament with Liberal support.

This was a situation which would not continue for long. In 1893 the Independent Labour Party was founded. Socialist ideas began to be propagated among working people, and most of the young Catholics who were attracted to these ideas joined the I.L.P. Much socialist propaganda was anti-Christian, and in the great debate which ensued religion and politics became inextricably fused. By the beginning of the twentieth century it was becoming clear that a substantial part of the Catholic vote was going to the emerging Labour organisations.(33) A genuine working-class leadership was emerging, within it a man from the Catholic community, John Wheatley, founder of the Catholic Socialist Society and Minister of Health in the first Labour government. For Wheatley as for other politically active Catholics the dilemma to be faced was whether it was possible to reconcile the teaching of the Church with a socialist political creed. The Church's teaching was enshrined in Pope Leo XIII's encyclical Rerum Novarum, framed to meet the anti-clerical threat of European Socialism. Catholic political activists found themselves faced with a crisis of conscience in the often acrimonious debate which developed, resulting in several instances in a break with the church. The background of Free Thought against which the political argument was conducted added to the confusion. For the majority of Catholics however it was probably true that before 1914 "Home Rule for Ireland was still a far stronger call than any programme tainted with socialism...the real and vibrant divisions in Glasgow at the time were between Catholic and Protestant, Irish and Scots, Lowland and Highland, and between the various divisions of Protestantism viz. Presbyterianism in its various forms, and Episcopalianism."(34)

Before 1914 the ideological argument concerned only a small minority of the population. For the majority the main issue apart from the Irish question lay in the field of education. The events of 1914-18 brought a complete transformation. For those who had experienced the horrors of trench warfare, all other experiences paled into insignificance; for the rest, the sight of maimed and blinded ex-service men in public places was a constant reminder of the holocaust. In the light of this awesome event, even the wrongs of Ireland took on a different perspective. Unfortunately the failure of the Government to implement the pre-war promise of Home Rule, and the disastrous Partition of 1922, kept the Irish question at boiling point for years to come. Nevertheless political interest among Scottish Catholics shifted from Irish affairs towards internal problems, and support for the rising Labour Party grew, in spite of the Russian Revolution and "the burning question for many of how radical a Catholic could be and remain in good standing with the Church."

Finally, the Education Act of 1918 totally altered the domestic scene, initiating the period of greatest development of the local Catholic community.

CHAPTER THREE

THE CATHOLIC SCHOOLS BEFORE 1918

BEFORE 1847

For more than 200 years after the Reformation, no formal Catholic schooling existed in the south-west. Eventually, as the population of the Lowland Vicariate increased, the need for schools in the more populous areas became urgent.(1) In 1817 the Catholic Schools Society was formed in Glasgow, and the rudiments of education began to be provided for some Catholic children. Schools were set up in Gallowgate, Gorbals, Bridgeton and Anderston, which by 1825 were giving instruction in day and evening classes to about 1,400 pupils whose ages ranged from 6 to 20.(2)

A major stimulus came with the Education Act of 1847, which extended the system of Grants-in-aid for education that had been introduced by the Privy Council in 1834. Schools could now obtain government aid to augment the salaries of their staffs through the pupil-teacher system, in which pupils who showed aptitude could be apprenticed for teaching at the age of thirteen. Grants became available for school buildings, but would not be given where the building was also to be used for church purposes. A Poor Schools Committee was formed,(3) on which Catholic interests were represented; but in fact few Catholic schools qualified for building grants before 1872, largely because of the policy that was adopted of constructing dual-purpose church-and-school buildings.

Before 1847, the quality of any education given was very poor. Fewer than half of the Catholic children attended school at all, and of these less than half learnt to read.(4) By 1845 the population of Glasgow had rocketed to around 350,000, of whom possibly more than a quarter were Irish – this before the massive immigrations of the famine years. When Bishop Murdoch then succeeded Bishop Andrew Scott as Vicar Apostolic of the Western District, action to improve educational provision soon followed. Father Peter Forbes, pastor of St. Mary's parish in Abercrombie Street,(5) who like Bishops Scott and Murdoch was a native of the Enzie, went to Tourcoing in Flanders to invite the Franciscan Sisters, established there for over 200 years, to set up a community in Glasgow. About the same time he invited the Sisters of Mercy in Limerick to take charge of an orphanage in his parish which had been opened by Bishop Scott in 1833 to provide for children whose parents had died in the cholera epidemic of 1832.

Both Orders responded. Two Franciscan Sisters, Mother Adelaide Vaast and Sister Mary Veronica Cordier came to Glasgow in 1847 and opened a small school in Monteith Row(6), a residential area in which a small group of catholic families was well enough established to support the venture. Within a few months, however, on 17 February 1848, Mother Vaast died of cholera. She was in her thirty-seventh year.

Bishop Murdoch handed over the charge of the school to the Sisters of Mercy, who had arrived from Limerick, and in anticipation of an increased demand for places rented a house for them in neighbouring Charlotte Street. They however wished to continue with the work for which they had been invited, and on 24 September 1849 they moved to the Orphanage. The Monteith Row School reopened in the premises in Charlotte Street in the charge of Sister Mary Veronica Cordier, assisted by a Miss C. Marchand who had accompanied the Sisters from France and who incidentally had helped to defray expenses. She became the first postulant of the new Scottish community, taking the name of Sister Mary Francis.

Due to the efforts of these two Orders considerable progress in the provision of education for Catholic girls was made over the next twenty years. In 1850 the Franciscans began to take in boarders at Charlotte Street and soon afterwards took over parochial schools at St. Andrew's, St. Alphonsus', St. John's and St. Joseph's parishes. The Sisters of Mercy opened a house in St. Mungo's parish and took charge of two day and two night schools there and in St. Mary's parish in Calton, as well as organising flourishing Sunday schools. In 1866 they handed over the St. Mary's schools to the Franciscans, and opened a Convent School in St. Mungo Street, which was transferred in 1868 to premises in Rose Street, Garnethill.

The impetus given to the education of girls was not immediately matched for boys. For a decade after 1847 their only educational opportunity was that offered in the adventure schools which sprang up in various parts of the city. The scene altered in 1858, with the arrival of the Marist Brothers from France. A prime mover in bringing this Teaching Order to Glasgow was Father Archibald Chisholm, the first pastor of the parish of St. Mungo in the Townhead district, where there was a growing Irish catholic population attracted by the need for labour in the chemical and iron works then developing rapidly in the north of the city. Although burdened by the debt on his church, he bought a site in Glebe Street and built there a school for boys which was ready by the summer of 1857. M. Charles Thiebaut, a French linen merchant living in Dundee, introduced the Marist Order to Bishop Murdoch and to Father Chisholm, who at once asked for three of the brothers for his boys' school. In July 1858 he obtained the services of Brothers Procope, Tatianus and Faust, who took charge of the parochial school and also opened a fee-paying school with six pupils in their own house at 96 Garngad Hill on 23 August 1858. By the end of the first session the roll had increased to thirty-three. It reached the hundred mark for the first time in 1867.(7)

In 1859 the parish of St. Joseph in North Woodside Road was placed in the charge of the Society of Jesus. Later that year the Society opened a school at 77 Charlotte street with twenty-five boys on the roll. In 1866 they made the move to Garnethill. At first this promised well, and by 1868 the average attendance had reached seventy. Early progress however was not maintained, and the number of pupils fell to around forty.(8)

Progress elsewhere in the city was slow. By 1866 when the Argyll Commission reported on the state of education in Glasgow, there were 16 Catholic elementary schools in which 2,604 children were being taught, and 3 higher class schools attended by 186 pupils.(9) Over 1,000 others were receiving some kind of education in private adventure schools, evening schools and reformatories. Not more than one-third of the Catholic children of Glasgow were attending a school of any kind.

In other parts of the Archdiocese educational provision was even less. In Dunbartonshire, where St. Patrick's parish had been established in 1830 and St. Mary's Duntocher in 1841, there was little or no education before 1872. In Lanarkshire, where the first parishes to open were in Airdrie and Hamilton, the record is somewhat better. In 1852 St. Mary's School in Hamilton opened with 60 pupils, and in 1857 St. Aloysius' in Airdrie followed with 83 children in four classes. By the end of the 1860's there were "7 Sunday schools, at Wishaw, Shotts, Carfin, Cleland, Motherwell, Newmains and Shieldmuir, though only two elementary schools for immigrants existed."(10) The managers of the Catholic schools had not benefitted fully from the 1847 Act; "As the school-cum-chapel building was not uncommon,...the regulation cut off mach-needed support from many parishes."(11) In Renfrewshire and Ayrshire the first parishes to be established were at Paisley St. Mirin's in 1808, Greenock St. Mary's in 1816, and Ayr St. Margaret's in 1822. The first efforts to provide some form of Catholic education in these areas are to be attributed to a small number of French émigré priests, who came around the turn of the century, driven from home by the atrocities of the French Revolution.(12) Apart from these beginnings, the earliest development was in Paisley where a parochial school was opened in 1816, supervised by a committee of 12 Catholics and 12 Protestants. By 1830 the town had three Catholic elementary schools, and Sunday schools were conducted in neighbouring villages.(13) New parishes opened in Barrhead and Houston in 1841, and Johnstone in 1852; but in spite of this early start, there was no notable further advance until after 1872. St. Mary's School in Greenock opened in 1816, and a second school in Port Glasgow, in a sail loft, in 1832. "It served as a Day School, Sunday School and Infants' School, and was maintained by scholars' fees and voluntary contributions from the Catholic community. Religious instruction was taught at the Sunday School...Protestant children were not excluded on weekdays...the school was under the superintendence of the Bishop, the Parish Priest and a committee of Catholics...it had one teacher."(14) In 1836 there were 50 pupils on the roll. In 1846 a new parish of St. John the Baptist was constitut-ed in Port Glasgow, and by 1854 the school there had a roll of about 100. The following year a further sub-division of St. Mary's parish took place, and St. Laurence Parish in Greenock opened. A parochial school followed in 1857. In Ayrshire by the mid-1850's there were flourishing missions at Kilmarnock, Ayr and Dalry, and it was in these places that Catholic education initially developed. It is recorded that in Kilmarnock in 1866 "a large new schoolroom had been built...the roll in the day-school was 170."(15) In Ayr the oldest surviving log-book of St. Margaret's School dates from 1869.(16) There was however no substantial educational progress in the county until after 1872.

The Education Act of 1870 for England and Wales, the precursor of the Scottish

[Copy of First Prospectus of the College.]

A. M. D. G.

THE CATHOLIC COLLEGE, GLASGOW,
77 CHARLOTTE STREET,
September 12, 1859.

The object of this College is to afford a Religious, Literary, and Commercial Education to the Catholic Middle Classes of Glasgow.

The Professors of the College are members of the Society of Jesus.

The Religious instruction of the pupils is particularly attended to.

The course of Education, besides the ordinary elements, comprises a course of Latin and Greek Classics, French, and Mathematics.

TERMS :

For One Pupil, ...	...	...	£1 10 0	per Quarter.
For Two 'Brothers,	...	...	2 10 0	,,
For Three Brothers,	...	...	3 10 0	,,

No extra charge except for school books.

Mass is said daily in the College Chapel at Half-past Eight. The parents of the pupils are earnestly requested to secure the punctual attendance of their children at Mass, and to inspect and sign the Judgment books with which the pupils are furnished.

The Scholars living at a distance will be provided with the means of preparing any refreshments which they may bring with them.

Application for admission to be made at—

77 CHARLOTTE STREET; or at ST. JOSEPH'S,
North Woodside Road.

L. D. S.

Fig. 3. First Prospectus of St. Aloysius College

measure of 1872, sounded a loud warning to Scottish school managers. As well as announcing with withdrawal of grants for building purposes, the Act proclaimed that 'no catechism or religious formulary distinctive to any particular denomination' should be taught in maintained schools, and ominously introduced compulsory education for children of from 5 to 13 years. In Scotland immediate action was taken to improve the provision of school places. By 1872 the number of schools in Glasgow had increased to 23, catering in all for some 6,000 children in day schools and over 1,000 in night schools. Nevertheless the average attendance in 1872 was only 3,534 - less than 60% of the roll, and only about a quarter of the total of catholic children of school age in Glasgow.(17)

THE POSITION IN 1872

In 1872 in the whole of Scotland there were 130 masters and mistresses to take charge of 148 Catholic school departments; helping them were 240 pupil teachers, giving an average staff of 2.5 for each department of boys, girls, infants or mixed.(18) On the eve of the Act of 1872 most Catholic elementary schools had not yet come under official inspection. The embryonic secondary sector from which would have to come the teachers that would be needed to meet the demands of an imminent system of compulsory education, consisted of four schools, all in Glasgow. From 1847 onwards, educational matters for the Catholics of Great Britain had been handled by the Catholic Poor Schools Committee, on which Scotland was represented. Throughout the 25 years preceding the Act of 1872 it was the Committee's constant complaint that the Catholic population had not availed itself of public funds to the extent they might have done, mainly through apathy and groundless fears of government control. "In many cases the managers were too poor...to clear the debt - a pre-requisite for the grant - or were obliged to use the school for church services which likewise disqualified it for the grant. Nor was it easy...to shake off the mental shackles of centuries of persecution, especially when a large element ...consisted of Irish immigrants who had reason to doubt the sincerity of governments. But the reiterated complaints of the Catholic Committee...leave no doubt that casualness, make-do and lack of interest or effort had left Catholics short of grant-earning schools and trained teachers."(19)

It is perhaps an over-simplification to attribute the state of the schools in 1872 so readily to casualness and apathy.   The achievement of the 25 years from 1847 in Glasgow should not be underrated, particularly in the circumstances of massive immigration and grinding poverty then prevailing. It was a period of dissension at the level of responsible ecclesiastical authority, which deprived the local catholic community of firm leadership; and it was a time when the relationship between Church and State was undergoing serious change, not only in Scotland, where the struggle of the State with the Kirk was already joined, but also in England and especially in France, where the consequences of the Revolution still were reverberating. The Catholic Poor Schools Committee itself adverted to the issue of Church-State relations: "What conditions of things as to the relation of the State to the Church in the matter of primary education may be coming in the future is unknown.... The golden age is past; we stand in the silver; we may have to encounter the iron."(20)

What is clear is that the major stimulus to action on the part of the Catholic community derived from government directives. Before 1847, Catholic education scarcely existed. After 1847, Catholics were permitted, for the first time in 300 years, to share in a public grant. The Act of 1847 in fact encouraged religious education in state-aided schools, making it a condition for the reception of government help. The seminal developments which took place between 1847 and 1872 were fostered by the state's provisions. Above all, it was the threat of compulsory education which galvanised the community.

THE EDUCATION (SCOTLAND) ACT 1872

In 1869 a Bill had been introduced into Parliament to establish a non-denominational system of education, with no provision for voluntary schools. This would have meant the end of Catholic education in Glasgow, as without grants no expansion could be made, and existing schools could scarcely continue. The Bill however was returned by the Lords, and amended in favour of the voluntary schools. The Education Act for England and Wales of 1870 followed. Voluntary schools could continue to receive certain grants, but building grants would be withdrawn. A local rate was to be levied, and with this schools were to be built and maintained by School Boards with power to compel attendance of children between 5 and 13 years of age. In these Board schools "No catechism or religious formulary distinctive to any particular denomination was to be taught."(21)

In 1872 the corresponding Education Act for Scotland was passed. It provided for the creation in every parish and burgh of School Boards, by popular election, empowered to provide schools where required, to levy rates for their erection and maintenance, and to enforce the attendance at school of all children between the age of 5 and 13; also for the transfer of any inspected voluntary schools so desiring to local authorities or School Boards, any schools so transferred to be administered by the Boards under the control of a Scotch Education Department to be set up under the Act. Financial aid would come from Central Government and local rates. No grants for building would be made after the passing of the Act. It sanctioned the continuation of use and wont in religious instruction, thus allowing any school transferred to continue as a denominational school; but emphasised the separation of religious from secular instruction by enacting that religious instruction should be placed at the beginning or end of the school meeting. Parents would have the right to withdraw their children from any religious instruction of which they disapproved. Voluntary schools could continue as before with the aid of certain grants, but there would be no building grants, no aid from the rates and no exemption from them. In the terms of the Act, no Parliamentary or other grant could be given for religious education, but if the managers of a school wished to have it examined by H.M.Inspectors, and if these considered it to contribute to the efficient education of a district, a grant could be given, provided that the conscience clause was observed and that teachers were certificated. H.M.Inspectors would have no right or authority to examine in religious subjects.

It is tempting to see the 1872 Act as part of a process designed to wrest control of education away from the churches. In 1861 the Church of Scotland had given up its right to examine prospective teachers. Then in 1869 there had been an attempt by Act of Parliament to introduce a non-denominational system with no place for voluntary schools. "The Act of 1872 completed the work of 1861. Religious education was not compulsory. It made explicit the principle that religious teaching and secular teaching were things apart.... the conscience clause was the only consideration paid to religious teaching which it neither commended nor forbade, but merely permitted the continuance of the custom."(22)

Scottish Catholics petitioned against the Bill. They held that denominational schools should be entitled to support both from parliamentary grants and local rates; they objected to the fact that no compensation would have been paid if schools were transferred, although most of the Catholic schools had been built with no aid from public funds; and to the principle explicit in the Act that religious and secular teaching were separate exercises.(23)

This move was unsuccessful. Along with other voluntary boards, notably the Episcopalians, the Catholic authorities decided not to transfer their schools. In their judgment, the schools would have lost their denominational character had they acted otherwise.

Although in Scotland the School Boards were free to approve of Catholic or Protestant instruction in the schools, in practice it was a Protestant system that emerged. "The question of religious instruction in schools was one of the issues at the first elections for School Boards held after the passing of the Act, and in view of the Protestant majority instruction was given naturally in accordance with their beliefs. In some parts of the Highlands and Islands.... Catholic Boards were elected and the Catholic religion taught in the schools under their jurisdiction. But every School Board elsewhere ignored the fact that the Act allowed them to maintain, if they so chose, to maintain schools in which the Catholic religion could be taught. The only exception was in the case of Glasgow which maintained two special schools for Catholic children."(24) In effect, in spite of the flexibility permitted by the Act, mutual lack of trust resulted in the polarisation of the community.

"With negligible exceptions the School Boards of Scotland resolved to provide religious instruction in all their schools at the cost of the rates in a form acceptable to Protestant Churches generally, but refused to make corresponding provision for the Catholic minority among their ratepayers."(25)

DEVELOPMENT OF CATHOLIC SCHOOLS 1872-1918

As a consequence of the decision to remain outside the national system, the history of Catholic education in Scotland for almost half a century after 1972 is the story of its survival in an era in which the educational advances of the national system would constantly outstrip the most strenuous efforts of the Catholic community. By the turn of the century a well-articulated national system was developing. The primary sector catered for children up to about 12 years of age. In 1901 the leaving age was raised to 14, and in 1903 the Qualifying Examination was instituted, and supplementary courses were introduced for the majority of children - those expected to leave school at 14. The 1899 Code had brought in the category of Higher Grade or Intermediate schools or departments, in which courses extending over 3 years would be given by a special staff of duly qualified teachers. The result was the organisation of post-primary education into the three categories of Supplementary, Higher Grade (or Intermediate) and Secondary sectors. A pass in the Qualifying Examination was necessary for entry to post primary work. "The supplementary courses were for the majority group of pupils who left school at 14; the higher grade school was for pupils who remained in school until 16, sometimes to the leaving certificate stage; and the higher class school was intended for pupils who continued in school long enough to prepare for the leaving certificate examination and university entrance at about 18 years of age."(26) This pattern continued until the reorganisation of post-primary education in 1918.

To meet the requirement of compulsory education introduced by the 1872 Act, an enormous expansion of the existing provision in the Catholic sector was necessary. The Catholic authorities had to find resources to build and staff schools of a standard sufficient to attract those government grants that were open to them. The key to the grants was efficiency in schools, since the awards depended on the attainment of acceptable educational standards as well as on the average attendance. For both of these a supply of capable teachers was essential. The dilemma was obvious and would persist. The priority had to be an increase in the efficiency of the primary schools, at a time when there was no adequate secondary sector to stimulate the supply of teachers and provide their basic training. The situation was further complicated by the fact that an increase in grant resulting from any increase in the number of teachers would be offset by the resulting increase in salaries. The solution seemed to lie in the provision of more trained teachers who would attract a larger grant, improve the quality of the education provided and at the same time remain satisfied with a more or less stationary salary.(27)

So long as elementary education meant no more than a grounding in basic literacy and numeracy, the initial enthusiasm of the Catholic community allowed it to cope with the situation, even at a time of rapid increase in the number of children of school age. In a decade from 1875 the number of parochial schools in Scotland rose from 92 to 150; and by 1894 the number was 180, with accommodation for 60,000 children. But, as the curriculum expanded at the urgings of the Scottish Education Department to include the physical, emotional and vocational needs of the pupils, new problems of supply and training of teachers were raised for the voluntary sector.

The need for improvement in the teaching strength was commented on by the S.E.D.,(28) who advocated the establishment of a Catholic teacher-training college in Glasgow. In 1894 Dowanhill Training College for women was opened under the control of the Sisters of Notre Dame, who had been since 1854 responsible for Mount Pleasant College in Liverpool.(see Appendix 2)

From 1894 till 1900 the total number qualified was a mere 143. Progress was slow, and when the pupil-teacher system was replaced in 1908 by the Junior Student system new problems arose for the voluntary sector. Had the Religious Orders not borne the main burden of secondary education at this time, it is difficult to see how the Catholic system could have survived. By 1913-14, in the whole of Scotland "of 99,400 Catholic pupils, 9,000 were taught in supplementary classes, but only 1,278 were receiving higher education. These were taught in 14 schools, 12 of which were conducted by Religius Orders."(29)

DEVELOPMENT OF SCHOOLS IN GLASGOW 1872-1918

This was a time when the Catholic population was increasing rapidly. 15 new parishes were opened. "In the first 7 years of the 20th century the average attendance in Glasgow Catholic schools showed an increase of 4,000...by 1918...a further 12,500...some classes...contained over 100 pupils...between 1900 and 1918 6 new elementary schools were opened to relieve congestion...extensions were erected in 8 schools...the demands of the developing post-primary courses were the greatest challenge...only one of the Glasgow Catholic schools had a supplementary class in 1903, but by the next year there were 8, and by 1906 there were 226 pupils in such classes in elementary schools, together with 196 in higher grade schools."(30)

These figures show the pressure on the Catholic authorities to increase the provision of primary places. As a result, for a considerable period after 1872 there was no substantial advance at the secondary level. As early as 1856 the premises originally acquired by the Franciscan Sisters in 1849 for the school in Charlotte Street had been outgrown. Adjoining properties were acquired and a new building erected in the garden, but by 1872 these arrangements were again inadequate. In 1878 Elmwood House in Bothwell was purchased. "In 1872 these arrangements were again inadequate. In 1878 Elmwood House in Bothwell was purchased. "In 1892 an addition was built to Elmwood. A few years later the Diocesan Authority made it a Pupil Teacher Centre...when the Pupil Teacher system was abolished, the school was recognised as a Higher Grade School... In 1920 Elmwood was raised to a Secondary School with a Junior Centre."(31)

In 1894 the Convent School at Charlotte Street came under government inspection, and more advanced work was undertaken. The roll then was about 70. It was at first impossible to find Catholic graduates for the staff, and the assistance was obtained of a number of masters from Glasgow High School who came after hours. In 1899 the school was recognised as a Higher Grade School, and a Pupil Teacher Centre instituted. Thereafter pupils were presented for the Intermediate Certificate, and later for the University Preliminary examination.(32)

During this period the work of the Convent of Mercy School in Garnethill also prospered. In 1894 the neighbouring Buccleuch House was purchased, and a start was made on studies beyond the elementary level. However, as there was little inducement for pupils to remain at school after age 14, the numbers in the upper classes were not sufficient to justify the grant for a higher grade School.(33)

1894 was an 'annus mirabilis'for Catholic education. Glasgow Corporation Tramway Company began operations, and city centre schools became accessible to the far-flung inhabitants of Parkhead, Springburn, Crosshill, Shettleston and Maryhill. That year a Teacher Training College was established in Dowanhill,close to the University and with ready access to schools. Two years later its first group of diplomates, 22 in number, were ready to start work in the schools. By 1918 these pioneers had been followed by more than 1,400 others. In 1897, the Notre Dame Sisters opened a High School for Girls on a site adjoining the college, and set up there a Junior Training Centre for prospective teachers. The school opened with 24 pupils, a Principal, 1 certificated Assistant and 2 pupil teachers.

In any of the years from 1896 to 1899 the number of diplomates qualifying at Dowanhill T.C. was never as much as 30. In 1900 it jumped to 37, and rose continuously thereafter. The sudden increase can be attributed to the fact that former pupils from Notre Dame High School were then beginning to come forward to increase the numbers already on stream from the two older Convent schools in the city.

For some years after 1872, progress in the provision of secondary education for boys was slow. In session 1871-72 the roll of St. Mungo's Academy had reached about 140-150. Four years later it had fallen back to 122. In 1884, as pressure on accommodation showed signs of increasing, a house in Parson Street with an adjoining piece of land, formerly part of the glebe of the Barony Church, was acquired. The Brothers moved into the house, and a new school was built on the adjoining plot. The roll remained fairly stationary for the next ten years, but by 1896 it had jumped to almost 200, and had started on a pattern of growth which continued without interruption for the next half-century. In 1908 a Junior Students Department was instituted, with 30 prospective teachers enrolled.(34)

In 1872 the fortunes of St. Aloysius College were at a low ebb. With a roll of only 40, the school was on the verge of being closed. The turning point came with the appointment of the Rev. Francis E. Bacon as Prefect of Studies. He came with strict orders from his superior Rev. Peter Beck, General of the Society of Jesus, to close the College if he could not make it function successfully. Five years of incessant toil followed, during which the number attending increased from 47 to 170, and the foundations of future progress were truly laid.(35) As with the other Catholic schools, the College benefitted enormously from the advent of the Tramway system. More significant however, for Catholic education generally as well as for the College was the appointment of Father Hanson SJ in 1901 as Prefect of Studies. Eric Hanson was born of English Protestant parents in 1860. On leaving school he studied at the Protestant Missionary College in Canterbury, but left there for Oxford where he continued his studies in Theology, taking a B.A. in 1885 and M.A. in 1888. In 1886 he had been received into the Catholic Church. In 1888 he entered the Society of Jesus, and was ordained in 1899. When he took up his appointment in Glasgow he was 41 years of age. He soon perceived that his main task was to educate the Catholic parents, who were in the main indifferent to education, rather than their sons. Not long after his arrival he was asking: "Among the 2,500 students at Gilmorehill could we find a doxen Catholics?...is there a single schoolmaster in the whole diocese, elementary or secondary, who possesses a University degree?" Largely due to his efforts there was awakened in the Catholic community a consciousness of the benefits that higher education could confer on their children.(36) The results soon showed. In 1909 five students of the College were placed on the University Bursary list, including the First Bursar; and by 1914 former pupils had gained the Snell Exhibition three times in four successive years.(37)

The advances made at secondary level in Glasgow were however far from meeting the full needs of the situation. By 1918 the 22 parochial schools of the city had a total roll of 32,785 pupils, but the five senior schools between them accommodated only 1,201.(38) Since all of the latter had primary deparments - in 1914 S.M.A. had 100 pupils in its primary division - it is clear that less than 3% of the school population were receiving a full secondary education. "In 1918...nearly 5,000 pupils were accommodated in our schools in excess

TABLE 4

Catholic Schools in Glasgow in 1917–18 with Rolls

CATHOLIC ELEMENTARY EDUCATION   69

(5) 1917-1918

School	Roll	School	Roll
St Andrew's	936	St Aloysius'	1300
St Mary's	2400	St Francis'	3096
St John's	1603	Bridgeton	2670
St Alphonsus'	1250	St Michael's	1107
St Conval's	868	St Agnes', Lambhill	850
St Joseph's	2489	St Charles'	650
St Patrick's ⎫		St Anne's	1320
St Martin's ⎭	3185	St Paul's	620
St Mungo's	2092	St Luke's	1380
Maryhill	1313	St Columba's	1080
St Aloysius', Springburn	1136	St Roch's	1440

From Report of the Religious Examination in the Archdiocese of Glasgow,
1917-18, pp 9 and 10.

(6) CATHOLIC INTERMEDIATE AND SECONDARY SCHOOLS IN GLASGOW

	1911-1912	1913-1914	1917-1918
Charlotte Street Convent Higher Grade	157	181	269
Garnethill Convent Higher Grade	*	96	128
Dowanhill Convent Higher Grade	175	188	220
St Mungo's Academy	70	262	350
St Aloysius' College Secondary	202	239	234
TOTAL	604	966	1201

* No separate figures given of those receiving Higher Education.

From Report of the Religious Examination in the Archdiocese of Glasgow,
1917-18, p 13.

All the above schools presented candidates for the Higher Leaving
Certificate except Garnethill Convent School, which presented for the
Intermediate Certificate only.

Extracted from: SKINNIDER, Sister M.   Catholic Elementary
Education in Glasgow 1818-1918,   SCRE No. 54

of effective places for them. Only two of the supplementary centres had adequate science equipment. Of the schools following a full secondary course, only two measured up to the standards required for accommodation, and only 300 pupils were in post-Intermediate classes."(39) "In the Archdiocese of Glasgow in 1918 there were 449 untrained assistants compared to 763 trained...it was obvious that by 1918 the catholic schools of Glasgow were fighting a losing battle."(40) Table 4 gives a detailed picture of the situation. It is difficult to decide which are the more startling figures – the enormous size of some primary schools with more than 3,000 pupils, or the combined total of 1,201 pupils in the Intermediate and Secondary schools.

DEVELOPMENT OF SCHOOLS OUTWITH GLASGOW 1872 – 1918

Dunbartonshire

In Dunbartonshire, catholic communities developed first in the town of Dumbarton itself, in the Vale of Leven, in Duntocher and in the Kirkintilloch area in the eastern portion of the county. Clydebank was a comparatively late development. Settlement there on any notable scale began about 1872, when the Clydebank Foundry moved downstream from Finnieston in Glasgow to a greenfield site on the north bank opposite the confluence of the River Cart. For some time Duntocher was larger than Clydebank. Growth however was rapid, spurred by the opening of Singer's factory in 1884. Two years later the population had reached c.5000 and Clydebank acquired Burgh status. Thereafter its growth rate was phenomenal, with the population doubling in each of the two following decades.

Before 1918, catholic education in the county was conducted almost entirely at the elementary level in the parochial schools. There was little or no post-primary education, except at Notre Dame High School in Dumbarton, founded by the Sisters of Notre Dame in September 1912 with six members of staff and 73 pupils, all girls, which in any case was virtually inaccessible from the Kirkintilloch area, and even from the large population of Clydebank by reason of transport costs.

The first parochial school opened in Kirkintilloch in 1871, with 55 pupils, in premises which later reverted to their original use as a hay loft. In 1874 a dual purpose Chapel-School was opened, when the parish of St. Ninian and the Holy Family came into being. In Clydebank the parish of Our Holy Redeemer was founded in 1888, and an elementary school opened the following year. By 1895 a new building with accommodation for 900 pupils had been provided; by 1913 further accommodation was needed and an annexe for 600 pupils was added.(41)

By 1917-18 the total number in attendance at the parochial schools of the county was of the order of 5,000, of whom virtually none went on to any form of post-primary education apart from that offered in the supplementary classes. When as a result of the 1918 Act the Ad Hoc Authority came into being, "it became responsible for eleven more or less unsatisfactory catholic schools."(42) Inspectorate Reports point to the extent to which the parochial schools had fallen behind the Board Schools. There was a shortage of staff; absenteeism was rife; far too few pupils made use of the supplementary system. "A great many pupils beyond primary age were still sitting in primary classes owing to their lack of progress...three classes entirely without teachers amounted to 185 pupils...by 1918 only 6% of the school roll ever reached the supplementary class, and most reached the age of 14 while still sitting in classes lower down the primary school." Most catholic parents...were of the working class... any many were reluctant that their children should stay at school until the age of 14, far less that they should complete a full course of senior secondary education."(43)

Lanarkshire

Before 1845 only one catholic parish existed in Lanarkshire - St. Margaret's Airdrie, founded in 1836. Between 1847 and 1872 fourteen more were opened, and by the turn of the century a further seventeen. St. Patrick's Coatbridge was founded in 1845, and from it arose St. Mary's Whifflet, (1874) St. Joseph's Cardowan, (1875) Our Lady and St. Joseph, Glenboig (1880), and St. Augustine's Langloan, Coatbridge (1882). Under the spur of the 1872 Act, a number of parochial elementary schools were founded - in Whifflet in 1874, in Motherwell and in Coatbridge in 1875, in Blantyre in 1877, in Lanark and Carstairs in 1878, and Uddingston in 1883. The first post-primary department was instituted in St. Augustine's in 1894. "1894 saw the opening of the new school...and a section was devoted to secondary education. On the opening day there were 38 on the roll." The Inspectorate Report for the first session comments: "The classics were well done in all stages. French is particularly good. I regard this departure on the part of the catholic body as a most promising one."(44) Secondary provision in Motherwell is first mentioned in 1895. Motherwell R.C. Higher Grade School evolved from the parochial school of Our Lady of Good Aid. Separate secondary accommodation was not acquired until 1905, when three classrooms in the parochial hall were brought into use. These continued to be occupied by both primary and secondary pupils until 1923.

The institution of a secondary department in Motherwell was an important step for the Archdiocese, in that it was an attempt to provide free secondary education for the catholics of the county. From the outset an effort was made to look on the secondary school as the responsibility of all the parishes served by it. Every parish priest was expected to pay a levy for the new school in proportion to the number in Standard V in his own parochial school; and also to be responsible for providing, where necessary, a railway ticket to Motherwell for the fortunate few in his parish destined for secondary education in the Motherwell school. School books were to be similarly provided.

George Bennett occupied the post of Head Teacher from 1902 till 1931. Throughout this period he had to cope with the problems of a developing secondary school, beset with endemic problems of poor and insufficient accommodation and inadequate staff, compounded by his having for more than twenty of those years the added responsibility of the headship of the primary school. On November 22 1904, a note in the log book reads: 'The weather today is exceptionally cold and something like 300 children are off - a few have no boots.' 12 Dec. 1904: '50 - 60 children are in need of boots.' The roll was 852. For this there was a staff of 5 certificated teachers, supplemented by 13 pupil teachers. Pupils were gaining the Intermediate Certificate enabling them to secure a place either in St. Mungo's Academy or in Elmwood Convent.

With the extension of the powers of the School Boards, the catchment area of the school also expanded. In 1908 children in country areas could be conveyed to school or boarded nearby. Parents could be prosecuted for non-attendance of their children. In 1911 facilities were provided for practical training in woodwork and domestic science. In the elementary school, 10 classes had rolls of between 65 and 70. The official Report of 5 Dec. 1913 states:" 14 classes were in excess of the Code, 10 of these being over 65...Mr. Bennett is overweighted by the duties which fall on him as a teacher in the Higher Grade School and responsible Head of the two schools." The full payment of the grant was endangered, as always, by the lack of accommodation. In 1918 the smallest class was 39, and the largest, in a room suitable for 59, was 92."(45)

Renfrewshire, Ayrshire, Dumfriesshire

Development of education in Renfrewshire was centred at Greenock and Paisley. In Greenock and Port Glasgow the parochial schools of St. Mary's and St. John's expanded. A new building for St. Mary's was opened in 1878; a chapel-school, St. Ninian's, was founded in Gourock in 1880, and St. John's School in Port Glasgow moved into a new building in 1884. The familiar pattern of accommodation lagging behind population continued through the turn of the century. "Large classes and small salaries were the lot of the Catholic teachers.... When St. Mary's Higher Grade School was established in 1909...a course of secondary education was available for Catholic children."(46) In Paisley, the first major advance after 1872 came with the arrival of a Teaching Order, the Faithful Companions of Jesus, who set up St. Margaret's Convent School there in 1889. It began with 15 pupils as an Independent Junior School for girls only.

Progress was rapid and by 1896 the top classes were recognised as a Secondary Department. No comparable provision for the secondary education of boys was made until after 1918. The demand for higher education for males seems to have been small: here as elsewhere the aim of many boys, not seriously disputed by their parents, was to leave school at the earliest possible moment.

In Ayr, "it was not until the turn of the century that the Catholic schools began, as it were, to rise from their knees. Until 1918 the struggle for existence and survival never really ceased." The first mention of any provision of post-primary education occurs in 1909 in St. Margaret's School, in a reference in a log-book to work in a supplementary class. The development there of a secondary department was a post - 1918 phenomenon.(47) The situation in the Kilmarnock district was somewhat similar. A parochial school had been founded at St. Joseph's Kilmarnock in 1866, and chapel-schools at Galston and Crosshill in 1885 and 1891. In 1901, the Inspectors warned that St. Joseph's School did not merit their approval, and that the grant would be stopped if the accommodation was not increased. There were then about 400 children on the roll. St. Joseph's School did not achieve Higher Grade status until after 1918. In 1883 the Catholics of Irvine, with the help of the third Marquis of Bute, a convert to the Catholic faith, built a church-school, which provided primary education only.

In Dumfries the parish of St. Andrew had been founded by 1810, but it was not till 1873, when the Marist Brothers founded St. Joseph's College that there was any local provision of secondary education for catholic boys. For most of its existence the College combined the functions of a boarding school

for boys and a training centre for entrants to the Marist Order. Great emphasis
was placed on religious observance, and on sport and games in the life of
the school.

THE OVERALL POSITION IN 1918

By the end of the First World War, the Catholic schools system of the south-west
of Scotland was near to breaking point. From 1872 there had been a massive
increase in the number of children, and in provision for them at primary level,
but this had not been matched by a corresponding increase in the number of
post-primary places. The pattern of education which had evolved was essentially
of a primary nature, carried out in poorly-equipped, overcrowded and under-
staffed schools, often in circumstances of considerable physical hardship.
In St. Peter's School in Partick in 1918 the school was gas-lit by fish-tail
burners, rather than by the more efficient gas mantles. Conditions were so
bleak that the additional hardships of rationing imposed by the Great War
went almost unnoticed. Teachers everywhere had to cope with enormous numbers
of pupils. A class of 102 infants in St. Francis' School was handled by one
teacher. In many cases the training teachers had received was minimal. Some
of those described as trained may have had no other training than that provided
by the pupil-teacher system. There was a shortage of male teachers.(48) Poverty
was widespread. There are several references in the Notre Dame sound archive
to the numbers of children who came barefoot to school, and to the small numbers
who went on to secondary education.

There was a prevailing tendency among catholic boys to leave school at 14.
"For many the notion that schooling should continue beyond the compulsory
term of years seemed preposterous." "The respective purposes served by
Supplementary Courses and H.G. departments do not seem to be perfectly
understood as yet by our people."(49)

In the curriculum there was a great emphasis on the 3 R's, and in spite of
the difficult conditions a high standard of literacy seems to have been
achieved. Discipline was firm - the cane was then the instrument by which
punishment was administered - but nevertheless the picture emerges of primary
schools as happy places which provided a secure and stable environment for
their inhabitants. Religious instruction and religious life were obviously
important parts of the school experience: "Everything seemed somehow to be
reflected from the Church...somehow school and church were the same thing."
The teachers were highly regarded, possibly because they were closely identified
with the local community and with the religious upbringing of their charges.(50)

In spite of their considerable achievements there can be no doubt that by
1918 the Catholic schools were fighting a losing battle. Having opted out
of the national system in 1872, the Catholic community received no share of
the school rates to which nevertheless they had to contribute. They had also
to provide, build and equip their own schools, for only after a school was
built did it receive government assistance. "There could be only one result...an
increasing dead-weight of debt, and this, in conjunction with the current
expanding notions of education and the consequently growing demands of the
Education Department, made the burden well-nigh intolerable."(51) The Glasgow
Herald summed up the position: "They (the voluntary schools) have done good
work in their day, but the demands of modern education have subjected to an

intolerable strain their equipment and salary funds."(52)

There was however another important aspect, identified in a Report of the Scotch Education Department more than a quarter of a century before: "There is a point beyond which the work, especially in the senior classes, will not rise, a point considerably lower than that attained in the Board schools.... It is a deficiency which no industry of the teachers, no skill of the managers, no stimulus of inspection can remedy; for it arises solely from the intellectual defects of a staff who have not received a regular and thorough training...not merely in the method of teaching, but a training in intellectual study."(53)

A pre-requisite of any substantial improvement in the Catholic educational system therefore was a greatly increased supply of more highly trained teachers at all levels of the primary and secondary schools; persons who, by sharing the motivation, dedication and religious commitment of the earlier generation of Catholic teachers, could preserve the character and traditions of the Catholic sector while raising its educational standards.

NOTES

1.	Bro. Kenneth	Catholic Schools in Scotland 1872-1972.
2.	Handley, J.E.	Irish in Scotland pp.279-281.
3.	Skinnider, Sister M.	Catholic Elementary Education in Glasgow 1818-1918 Studies in the History of Scottish Education 1872-1939 (Ed. Bone, T.R.) SCRE No.54.
4.	Handley, J.E.	Irish in Modern Scotland p.192
5.	Ibid.	p.90.
6.	A Franciscan Sister	The Franciscan Nuns in Scotland 1847-1930. Pamphlet published by the Glasgow Observer 1930.
7.	Handley, J.E.	History of St. Mungo's Academy 1958-1958.
8.	Anon.	D.B.J. Vol.2 No.3 Dec.1949.
9.	Skinnider, Sister M.	Loc.cit.
10.	Handley, J.E.	Irish in Modern Scotland, p.191, footnote.
11.	Ibid.	pp.217-8.
12.	McGloin, J.	I.R. XVI,1, p.31 et seq.
13.	Handley, J.E.	The Irish in Scotland p.282. See also The Navvy in Scotland pp.54-55.
14.	Centenary Brochure	of the Church of St. John the Baptist, Port Glasgow 1845-1954.
15.	Church of Our Lady	of Mount Carmel Souvenir Brochure 12 May 1963.
16.	McGloin, J.	Catholic Education in Ayr 1823-1918. IR XIII,1 1962.
17.	Skinnider, Sister M.	Loc.cit.
18.	Brother Kenneth	Catholic Schools in Scotland 1872-1972.
19.	Ibid.	Catholic Education in Scotland 1878-1917; in Scottish Survey 1878-1955, pub. G.O. and SCH.
20.	Handley, J.E.	Irish in Modern Scotland p.220.
21.	Skinnider, Sister M.	Loc.cit.
22.	Robertson, J. Grant	Education(Scotland)Act 1918. CTS of Scotland 1937 p.11.
23.	AAG.	Resolution of Catholic Education Meeting 12/3/1872.
24.	Robertson, J. Grant	Loc.cit. p.18.
25.	Struthers, Sir John	Draft Memo. on Amendments to the 1918 Act. SED/ED/14/129.
26.	Wade, N.A.	Post-primary education in the Primary Schools of Scotland 1872-1936. SCRE, p.105.
27.	Brother Kenneth	Loc.cit.
28.	Inspectorate Report	1891. Quoted by Skinnider.
29.	Barry, W.	DBJ 1955.
30.	Skinnider, Sister M.	Loc.cit.
31.	A Franciscan Sister	Loc.cit.
32.	Ibid.	Anne Conway, the first former pupil of the Charlotte St. School to enter Glasgow University, graduated with First Class Honours in Classics in 1911. See NDSA 14.
33.	Sister Mary Gertrude	Sometime Headmistress of Garnethill Convent School, DBJ Feb. 1949.
34.	Handley, J.E.	History of St. Mungo's Academy 1858-1958.
35.	St. Aloysius College	Magazine Vol.1, No.1.
36.	Anon.	DBJ, Vol.2, No.3, Dec. 1949.
37.	St. Aloysius College	Magazines, Dec. 1920 and June 1935.
38.	Skinnider, Sister M.	Loc.cit., p.69.
39.	Bro. Kenneth	DBJ, May 1962.

40.   Skinnider, Sister M.   Loc.cit.

41.   Paterson, A.C.   Educational History of Clydebank.

42.   Roberts, A.E.B.   The Operation of the Ad Hoc Education Authority
                            in Dunbartonshire.
                            In Studies in the History of Scottish Education
                            p.279 SCRE No.54.

43.   Maguire G.T. and Murray, S.V. The   Story   of   a   School   1874-1974.
                            pub.   Deacon   Bros.   Kirkintilloch   1974.

44.   St. Augustine's Parish Golden Jubilee Brochure 1984.

45.   White, J.   Our Lady's High School, Motherwell. Unpublished
                            manuscript, made available by Mr. James Breen.

46.   St. John the Baptist Church (Port Glasgow) Centenary Brochure 1854-1954.

47.   McGloin, J.   Catholic   Education   in   Ayr   1823-1918.   IR   XIII,1
                            1962 and IR XIII,2.

48.   NDSA 2 and NDSA 12 refer.

49.   Handley, J.E.   History of St. Mungo's Academy 1858-1958.

50.   See NDSA Nos. 2,5,6,8,12,18.

51.   Robertson, J. Grant. Op.cit.

52.   Glasgow Herald Editorial 18/12/1917.

53.   Education (Scotland) Report 1891, p.257.   Scotch Education Department.

CHAPTER FOUR

A NEW ERA

THE EDUCATION (SCOTLAND) ACT, 1918

From the Slough of Despond into which they were in danger of sinking the
Catholic schools were rescued by the Education (Scotland) Act of 1918. This
generous measure initiated major developments at every level of the formal
educational structure, and provided a framework for advances, to be implemented
over following decades, into which the Catholic schools were transferred,
and with the support of which the system, particularly its secondary sector,
expanded.

The Act, described as "a statesman-like measure for broadening, deepening
and strengthening Scottish education", aimed at furthering the development
of an educated community marked by religious toleration and equal opportunity
for all. A central motivation was its concept of secondary education, to
be provided for all children at varying levels suited to their capacities,
in periods of compulsory school attendance which would be increased as the
system developed. In the administrative structure which it instituted, schools
would be classified as Junior or Senior Secondary, and with the advent of
these categories supplementary classes in primary schools would disappear.

Its more important ordinances were as follows: The county became the basic
administrative unit; the education authority would be an Ad Hoc body elected
specifically to control education. The powers of the Authorities and their
relationship to the Department, renamed the Scottish Education Department,
were established. A minimum salary scale for teachers was laid down. The
continuance of religious instruction, the provision of nursery education,
the relations between Authorities and Independent Schools, school leaving
age, continuation classes, the transfer of voluntary schools, the establishment
of an Advisory Council and the strengthening of the Education (Scotland)
Fund were all dealt with in detail. It became lawful for an Authority to
grant financial assistance to young persons for attendance at an intermediate
or secondary school, and similarly to assist any duly qualified person to
attend a university or training college or central institution. For the
voluntary sectors then controlled by the Episcopalian and Roman Catholic
authorities, the major issue at stake was whether or not to transfer their
schools into the national system. For them, the most important sections of
the Act were Section 7, concerned with Religious Instruction, and Section
18, which dealt with the Transfer of Voluntary Schools.

Section 7 reads as follows:

"Whereas it has been the custom in the public schools of Scotland to give instruction in religious subjects to children whose parents do not object to the instruction so given, but with liberty to parents, without forfeiting any of the other advantages of the schools, to elect that their children should not receive such instruction, be it enacted that education authorities shall be at liberty to continue the said custom, subject to the provisions of Section 68 (Conscience Clause) of the Education (Scotland) Act, 1872."

The Conscience Clause states:

"Every public school, and every school subject to inspection and in receipt of public money as herein-before provided, shall be open to children of all denominations, and any child may be withdrawn by his parents from any instruction in religious subjects and from any religious observance in any such school; and no child in any such school shall be placed at any disadvantage with respect to the secular instruction given therein by reason of the denomination to which such child or his parents belong, or by reason of his being withdrawn from any instruction in religious subjects. The time or times during which any religious observance is practised or instruction in religious subjects is given shall be either at the beginning or at the end, or at the beginning and at the end of such meeting, and shall be specified in a time-table approved by the Scotch Education Department."

Section 7 therefore made it possible for Catholic schools, if transferred into the national system, to function as denominational schools, if the parents of the pupils concerned so wished and if the other conditions laid down were observed. Further safeguarding of their religious character was provided for in Section 18 which guaranteed the continuance of religious instruction or observance according to the use and wont of the former management of the schools. The relevant sub-sections are as follows:

Section 18, sub-section 3

Any school so transferred shall be held, maintained and managed as a public school by the education authority, who shall be entitled to receive grants therefore as a public school, and shall have in respect thereto the sole power of regulating the curriculum and appointing teachers: Provided that:-

(i)   The existing staff of teachers shall be taken over by the education authority and shall from the date of transfer be placed on the same scale of salaries as teachers of corresponding qualifications appointed to corresponding positions in others schools of the same authority;

(ii) All teachers appointed to the staff of any school by the education authority shall in every case be teachers who satisfy the Department as to qualifications, and who are approved as regards their religious belief and character by representatives of the Church or denominational body in whose interests the school has been conducted;

(iii) Subject to the provisions of Section 68 (Conscience Clause) of the Education (Scotland) Act 1872, the time set apart for religious instruction or observance in any such school shall not be less than that so set apart according to the use and wont of the former management of the school, and the education authority shall appoint as supervisor without remuneration of religious instruction for each such school, a person approved as regards religious belief and character as aforesaid, and it shall be the duty of the supervisor so appointed to report to the education authority as to the efficiency of the religious instruction given in such school. The supervisor shall have the right of entry to the school at all times set apart for religious instruction or observance. The education authority shall give facilities for the holding of religious examinations in every such school.

It was further enacted in Section 18, sub-section 7 that

"a school established after the passing of this Act to which this section would have applied had the school been in existence at that date may with the consent of the Department be transferred to the Education Authority, and the provisions of this section shall, with the necessary modifications, apply to any such school so transferred."

Sub-section 8 made it lawful for an Education Authority to erect a new school where the Department were satisfied "upon representations made to them by...any Church or denominational body" that a new school is required.

These provisions made possible the evolution of a system of denominational schools supported by public funds. The denominational body concerned would have a measure of control over the education provided through its statutory power to grant approval as regards religious belief and character to duly qualified teachers, and to approve supervisors of religious instruction. The appointment of teachers would rest with the education authority, who would also retain the power to regulate the curriculum. Implicit in these ordinances was the separation of religious and secular instruction. Further important considerations for the denominational bodies were that future development was safeguarded by the sections relating to the provision of new schools, and by the appointment of the Scottish Education Department as arbiter in any dispute between an education authority and a denominational body.

For the Catholic sector, the question of the appointment of teachers was a matter of primary concern. In the voluntary system the teachers were the key to the working of the system, and in the circumstances envisaged under the operation of the Act, would be the principal guarantors of the religious character of the schools.

Section 18 also dealt with the conditions under which voluntary schools could be transferred into State control. Sub-section 1 states:

Section 18 (Transfer of Voluntary Schools)

(1) It shall be lawful at any time after the first election of education authorities under this Act for the person or persons vested with the title of any school which at the passing of this Act is a voluntary school...with

the consent of the trustees of any trust upon which such school is held, to transfer the school, together with the site thereof and any land or buildings and furniture held and used in connection therewith, by sale, lease, or other- wise, to the education authority, who shall be bound to accept such transfer, upon such terms as to price, tent, or other consideration as may be agreed, or as may be determined failing agreement by an arbiter appointed by the Department upon the application of either party.

This was acceptable to the Catholic authorities. The buildings and properties involved had been provided by them without aid from public funds. Any grants received had been for the maintenance of schools already built.

Sub-section 8 dealt with the vitally important issue of the provision of new schools, making it lawful for an authority to erect these where the Department considered they were required. A strong body of catholic opinion had favoured the alternative of providing their own new schools at need with the approval of the Department, holding that it should be mandatory for authorities to accept transfer of such new schools, and that explicit reference should be made to them in the relevant clauses of the Act, making it absolutely clear that the education authority concerned would be bound to accept such schools, or alternatively provide them themselves. In the event, a measure of ambiguity was allowed to remain by the inclusion of the statement that "a school established after the passing of the Act...may with the consent of the Department be transferred..." which was not resolved until the decision in the Bonnybridge case in 1928.

THE DEBATE

Throughout the negotiations leading to the formulation of the Bill, represent- atives of the Glasgow Archdiocese had held that Catholic schools when trans- ferred should be managed by school Management Committees with power to nominate the teachers who might be appointed and to dismiss when the grounds of dismissal were connected with religious belief and character. They further held that the supervisors of Religious Instruction should be appointed by the Catholic authorities, and that the building of future schools should be undertaken by the local Catholic committee. These they regarded as the irreducible minimum conditions for the handing over of the Catholic schools to the national system. (1) The chief proponents of these views were Archbishop Maguire of Glasgow and Bishop Henry Grey Graham, Auxiliary Bishop of Edinburgh. In his Lenten Pastoral Letter of 1918, Bishop Graham - a son of the Manse and former minister of the Church of Scotland - made a characteristically forthright statement of his stance on the schools issue: "I am utterly opposed to handing over our schools, no matter what conditions and safeguards are secured..I have the gravest fears that...under the new system the catholicity of the schools will be interfered with.... To make them state schools is the first step on the downward path towards secularising them...I consider the threat of starvation contained in Clause 20...which stops all grants if we do not enter the scheme within two years...a piece of coercion very much to be resented.... Our Catholic schools are impoverished; the strain on them is certainly growing more severe every year on account of the pressure of new educational demands, and also of higher salaries for our teachers, to which I think they are perfectly entitled.... My view is that there is nothing to prevent the government equalising our schools with the other schools of the country by increasing our Treasury Grants, a source from which we now receive and have for long received a measure of State support. This alternative has not been offered to us."(2)

Theirs was a minority opinion. The general view of the Hierarchy, the Catholic teachers and a considerable body of the clergy, particularly its younger members, was that the Bill offered a solution to the problems of the Voluntary schools.

Not surprisingly, Catholic teachers as a body were in favour of the Bill, which provided that existing staffs would be retained on equal terms with others in the employ of the education authority, and for the introduction of a national minimum salary scale. The improved status which would result would be of even greater benefit to the underpaid Catholic teachers than to their colleagues. The Glasgow teachers made their position known through a deputation to the Department in February 1918, where it appears to have been more sympathetically received than at the office of the Archbishop.

The Bill was being prepared for its Third Reading when a resolution was passed by the Cathedral Chapter and Senior Priests of the City of Glasgow(3) declaring that without the minimum conditions as outlined above, they could not accept the Bill. A majority of the Standing Committee of the Catholic Education Council and of the Bishops' Conference had already approved the final agreement reached by the principal negotiator, Monsignor Brown. Disagreement of this magnitude and at this time within the Catholic body might well have led to the abandonment by the government of that part of the Bill dealing with the Voluntary Schools. The danger was averted by the matter being referred to the Holy See, who decreed that the minority must abide by the decision of the majority of Bishops, clergy and laity and accept the Bill as a settlement of the education question.(4)

On 21 November 1918 the Bill received Royal Assent.

In the process of hammering out the details of the Bill, the ecclesiastical authorities, in their anxiety to safeguard the religious character of the schools tended to overlook many of its beneficent measures, particularly those most closely affecting the pupils. Likewise the interests or opinions of the parents, who in the eyes of the Church are the first educators, were given rather scant consideration; it was the politicians and administrators who displayed the greatest foresight and widest vision. One of the principal architects of the Bill, Lord Skerrington, who acted in an advisory capacity to the Scottish Hierarchy, commented: "I was never more astonished in my life when I was informed in the spring of 1918 that in the opinion of the Bishops the then existing Education Council possessed no independent powers of any kind, but was absolutely under the control of the Hierarchy."(5)

An examination by Brother Kenneth of the stages by which the Catholic body was led to reverse the decision of 1872 to remain outside the national system, concludes:

"No summary account can convey adequately the slowness of retreat of many from entrenched positions, and the extreme reluctance with which they accepted the inevitable in the end.... Had they been able to see the Bill...as a Children's Charter, restoring to so many their birthright of equal educational opportunities of which they had been deprived for social or religious reasons, their opposition would have been softened, for Catholic children generally came into both categories. Their parents or grandparents had been channelled by a caste system into civic insignificance. Today the Catholic community has emerged and shares increasingly in the full national life while retaining its identity."(6)

IMPACT

Ten days after the Armistice, the Education (Scotland) Act 1918 was passed; it became effective as from May 1919. Two hundred and twenty-six Catholic as well as other Voluntary schools transferred to the new Ad Hoc Education authorities. The Act was of the nature of a concordat between Church and State in respect of education, "the most sensitive nerve in our Catholic organisation. it is the closest...point of contact between the Church and the modern State. The solution...as at present conceived in Scotland is in essence an adjustment between these two age-long, necessary, formidable and often rival institutions." (7)

At a stroke the situation of the Catholic schools was altered from decline and near despair to expansion and hope. The status, prospects and morale of the teachers were immediately raised, and the whole community was able to look forward to a greatly enriched future. Some of the beneficial consequences of the Act were very soon apparent, and would increase with the passage of the years. "For Catholic teachers it meant the removal of the long-standing disparity between their own salary levels and those obtaining in the state system. For the Hierarchy it guaranteed the continuation of distinctive doctrinal instruction within Catholic schools, and gave them an indirect influence over teaching appointments. For catholic pupils there was a better chance...of enjoying the fruits of a free post-elementary education. And for the laity...grounds for hoping that the financial pressure to which they had hitherto been subjected...would be eased."(8)

Nevertheless, some sections of the community looked to the future with uncertainty. This was especially the case in Glasgow, which contained the largest grouping of Catholic schools, and among the clergy who managed these there continued to be support for the view that too much control had been surrendered. A hankering persisted for something akin to the English solution, whereby the Church retained responsibility for providing school buildings and complete control over the appointment and dismissal of teachers. This attitude was not shared by Monsignor Brown, who recognised that the Bill offered the possibility of developing a fully Catholic educational system, if the opportunities which it presented were seized. "All we desire can be given us by the Bill if the local education authority is friendly."(9)

A conglomeration of massive and inter-locking problems had to be resolved if the potential benefits of the Act were to be fully realised. These had their roots in several quarters - some in the attitudes of the community to the educational process; some in the existing conditions in the schools them-selves;(10) and some in the very nature of the new educational challenge that had to be faced, namely the setting up of a system meeting the requirements of the State, satisfactory to the Church, and capable of operating at the secondary level for a much broader spectrum than ever before of the Catholic population. Although by the early Twenties there was a growing awareness on the part of the Catholic community of the benefits that might follow the raising of its own educational standards, and that the financial provisions of the Act made their aspirations more possible of realisation, nevertheless profound distrust of State interference or control still existed, which extended to a State-ordered system of education, seen in many places as a harbinger of a totally secular and materialistic society. There was no widely-held vision of the form a Catholic secondary system should take. The concept of education that prevailed, in which the spiritual formation of children was seen to lie at the heart of the exercise, was essentially one of elementary education designed for pupils who would leave school without any aspiration for higher education. As such, it offered an inappropriate model for the secondary schools that could be expected to develop after 1918. It was one in which the schools were essentially part of the parochial structure, managed by the clergy with all the backing of ecclesiastical authority. They were the chosen medium through which instruction in the Catholic faith was given, once and for all, and to them was entrusted the preparation of children for initiation into the Church through the sacraments of Penance, Eucharist and Confirmation. What was taught in the schools was designed to last for a lifetime. Concentrating as it did on the practice of the Catholic religion, it was not structured to provide its pupils with the equipment for reflection within an ecclesiastical context on the meaning of their religion. Within the system there had developed a special relationship between the clergy and the primary teachers, who constituted an important executive sector of the Church's educational effort. The teachers' authority to teach derived essentially from the ecclesiastical authority, which was also the paymaster.

Whatever the merits of this system - and they were many - it had suffered some distortion, partly through the practice of early leaving which was widespread in the community, and partly because of the material deprivation in the schools, and their separation from the educational advances currently taking place in the state schools.

TRANSFER

Once the decision to transfer the schools had been taken, the Diocesan Education Board in 1919 instituted a Schools Transfer Board to advise the Archbishop on the conduct of the operation and to supervise its working. Within the ranks of the clergy, and especially the members of these two bodies, deep concern as to the form of a new Catholic secondary sector was expressed, as is clear from their records.(11) Throughout the inter-war period repeated attempts were made to grapple with the problems of an expanding secondary sector.(12)

In the overall strategy which emerged, two major strands can be identified. First, there was a need to develop a common policy towards the various Ad Hoc Committees with regard to the disposal of existing school properties and the provision of new accommodation. Secondly, a supply of suitably qualified teachers had to be achieved. In each of these areas, the proceedings of the Diocesan Board were dominated by the needs of the primary sector. Elementary schools were by far the major part of the voluntary system, and their school buildings often intimately linked with Church property, whereas with few exceptions Catholic Higher Grade schools were managed and their buildings owned by one or other of the Religious Teaching Orders, and therefore excluded from negotiations as to transfer of property. "All Convent schools and St. Mungo's Academy are excluded from the negotiations as we have no control over them."(13) With regard to the supply and training of teachers, no substantial distinction was made between the primary and secondary sectors.(14)

Under the Act it was open to the Catholic authorities to transfer schools property "by lease, sale or otherwise" to the Ad Hoc Committees. A meeting of the Catholic Education Council held on 27 July 1919 in Edinburgh decided by 6 votes of 3 that "unless in exceptional cases it is expedient that schools should be sold."(15)

In the view of the leader of the Glasgow delegation, Canon Ritchie, Vicar General of the Archdiocese, the vote was of questionable value in that those in favour represented a population in Edinburgh and Argyll of 82,000, while those dissenting spoke for Glasgow's 400,000 Catholics. Glasgow decided to adopt a policy of lease rather than sale. The reasons he averred for this decision show on the one hand a wish to preserve the degree of clerical control which characterised the pre-1918 arrangement, and on the other a lack of confidence in the good faith of the newly-formed Ad Hoc Authorities. If the ownership of the schools were to be relinquished, he believed, "Catholic teachers and pupils would be at the mercy of the Education Authorities...in the event of education being secularised how could the Catholic clergy and teachers retrace their steps?" By retaining ownership a policy of 'wait and see' could be followed which, while leaving open the option of sale to be considered at some later date, would in the meantime exercise a salutary disciplinary effect. "By holding possession...tenants are more likely to observe to the letter the regulations of the Bill with respect to Religious Education and the atmosphere of the schools."(16)

The implications of this decision for the secondary sector prompted a heated debate within the Schools Transfer Board. Its chairman, Rev. Hugh Kelly of Dumbarton, wrote: "It is quite impossible to say how many Higher Grade schools will be required throughout the diocese...in all probability the present accommodation will have to be doubled at least. As to the question upon whom should fall the onus of building these schools, my Board is of the opinion that, in the light of the Bishop's decision enjoining that we must retain ownership of the schools, we cannot with any shadow of consistency come to any other conclusion than that we must at our own expense provide for the Higher Grade pupils as well as those in elementary stages."(17)

Nevertheless Glasgow went ahead with its policy to lease rather than sell it schools, although in the remainder of the south-west, the Diocese of Galloway, being a suffragan see of St. Andrews and Edinburgh, waived her right to build in favour of the Ad Hoc Authority. The sequel was that "the Diocesan Education Board emerged with new duties to perform and a considerably enhanced status.... It was to collect the rental income from the school leasing arrangements which had been concluded...and expend it upon the erection of post-elementary schools.... Higher Grade schools, and after 1923, Advanced Division Centres...the building of elementary schools was still left as a responsibility of the individual mission affected."(18)

Thenceforth the D.E.B. sought to discharge its duties within the constraints imposed by this decision. Leasing arrangements were made with the Ad Hoc Committees in Lanarkshire, Dumbartonshire, Renfrewshire, Ayrshire and Glasgow: a Central Fund for educational purposes, fed by the rentals accruing from the Authorities, was instituted; the needs of the community for an expanded secondary sector were examined, possible sites for new secondary schools were sought and in some instances negotiations for purchase were begun; loans for expansion at secondary level were made to the Religious Teaching Orders; loans were also made available to students in training for teaching, and regulations for the training of catholic teachers were promulgated.

Within a decade the policy of leasing was reversed. A letter from Archbishop Mackintosh to the chairman of the D.E.B. dated 3rd January 1927 runs as follows:

Dear Fr. Cush,

From now onwards, instead of letting its schools to the various Education Authorities, the Archdiocese, as the leases now in force expire, will negotiate with those Authorities for the sale of the said schools. It must not be a sale at any price, but a sale to be arranged by suitable negotiation or arbitration.

Please communicate this decision to the D.E.B. so that it may carry it out as for occasion arises.

I am, Yrs. sincerely,
(signed) D. Mackintosh, Archbishop of Glasgow (3/1/27) **(19)**

This volte-face was forced upon the Church authorities primarily by the demand for secondary education resulting from the financial provisions of the 1918 Act, and the impossibility of meeting the costs from their own resources; but it also related to the element of ambiguity which had been allowed to remain in the terms of the Act itself. By that dispensation, responsibility to provide for expansion devolved jointly on the D.E.B. and the Ad Hoc Authority, and sub-sections 7 and 8 of Section 18 were not clear as to where the prior responsibility for the provision of new buildings would lie. This ambiguity lay at the heart of a protracted dispute between the Board and Lanarkshire Authority regarding new accommodation needed in 1921-22 at St. Mary's School Whifflet to provide for its upgrading to Higher Grade status. This was partially resolved in favour of the Board in 1924, largely through the good offices of the Scottish Education Department, but the fundamental issue at stake was not fully put to rest until the Bonnybridge judgement was announced in May 1928. Thereafter the Board announced that subject to certain safeguards the Archdiocese would waive its right to act as sole provider of catholic school premises, in favour of the Ad Hoc Authority.

The second major concern of the D.E.B. was the training of a teaching force and its certification for work in the Catholic schools. By 1921 detailed regulations had been approved.(20) In effect, the prospective Catholic teacher had to satisfy the requirements of two masters. For the State he had to have a good basic general education assessed in terms of the Scottish Leaving Certificate, a recognised qualification in the subject to be taught (for secondary teachers) and certification as a trained teacher; for the Church, to be approved as to "religious belief and character" by the Bishop of the diocese in which he resided. Since every Catholic teacher in a Catholic school was expected to share in the work of religious instruction, the Church's approval was a recognition not only of his suitability as a Christian believer to hold authority over children, but also of ability and training as a catechist.

The Church's regulations of 1921 were as follows:

MALE TEACHERS

1.   All catholic male teachers must live in the Hostel (St. Kentigern's) during their course of training.
2.   Exemption from residence to be given only for special reasons.
3.   Those exempted must attend lectures on Religious instruction.
4.   Male students at the University intending to graduate in Arts or Science must be present during their first year at the Hostal classes in Religious Instruction and at the end of that year pass the written examination in Catholic Doctrine. They must attend the course of lectures in Psychology and Education for two years. After graduating they must reside at the Hostel during their year of training and while there pass the second Religious Examination.

FEMALE TEACHERS

No female teacher trained in Scotland shall be eligible for employment in any Catholic school who has been trained in whole or in part in any but Catholic centres and Training Colleges.

No approval to be given to teachers male or female from outwith Scotland who had not been trained in a Catholic Training College, unless a written guarantee was given by them that they would present themselves for the Religious Examination and thus qualify for the Religious Certificate.

This policy replicated the system in Hammersmith where many male Scottish Catholic teachers had been trained pre-1918. St. Mary's College, which drew its students from a nation-wide catchment area, provided a residential training course for non-graduate teachers. While this approach might have been appropriate for the training of primary teachers in England, it was not so for the majority of Scottish secondary teachers, whose entry to teaching had to be by graduation at a University; and after 1924, when graduation became necessary also for male primary teachers, it was no longer suitable for them. Besides, the vast majority of candidates for training in the west of Scotland lived within an easy tram-ride of Hostel and University - a goodly number of them in fact within easy walking distance.

As in the case of disposal of property, the policy could not endure for long. Cases soon occurred of men students seeking exemption from hostel residence on grounds of health or inability to meet the cost.(21) Some female students incurred the displeasure of the Board by residing at the Hostel at Jordanhill (7/5/22).(22) In 1923 one expulsion from St. Kentigern's Hostel is noted and 7 other students were warned. In June 1923 the Marist Brother in charge wrote to the D.E.B. condemning the system: "Students are compelled to come into residence...their attitude is one of continuous protest...residence should be optional and students not living in should be obliged to attend a course of lectures and to pass the examination required by the Diocesan authorities." (23)

Nevertheless, the ideal of residential training continued to be upheld for some time. "Until compulsory attendance is enforced for at least a year, possibly during the post-graduate year at Jordanhill, the full beneficial effects of the Hostel will not be felt."(24)

As a consequence of the Local Government Act of 1929, the Ad Hoc committees were abolished, to be replaced by Education Authorities of the County Councils and Burghs, and the Church Authority had to set about the task of building its relationship with these new bodies. By the early 1930's this relationship had decisively altered, and the development of the Catholic secondary sector had moved some distance further from Church control.

NOTES

1. Bro. Kenneth. The Education (Scotland) Act 1918 in the Making. IR(1968) XIX,2 p.110.
2. McEwan, Mons. H.G. Bishop Gray Graham pp.136-7. J.S. Burns 1973.
3. Bro. Kenneth. Loc Cit.
4. Ibid. P.124.
5. Bro. Kenneth. Loc Cit. p.116.
6. Ibid.
7. Long, J.C. Memorandum of the Education System in Scotland p.35
8. Treble, J.H. IR XXIX,2 p.123.
9. Skinnider, Sister M. Loc Cit. P.124.
10. NDSA 1, 2, 4, 5a, 6 contain references to the state of the Catholic schools before 1918.
11. AAG MSS. Ed. Records.
12. Treble, J.H. The Working of the 1918 Education Act within the Glasgow Archdiocese. IR (1980) XXXI No.1.
13. DEB minutes 5/12/1927.
14. DEB 5/12/21.
15. AAG Ed. Records.
16. AAG Letter from Canon Ritchie to Mons. Brown 29/7/19.
17. AAG Letter from Rev. H. Kelly to Canon Ritchie 25/3/20.
18. Treble, J.H. The Working of the 1918 Education Act in the Glasgow Archdiocese. IR (1980) XXXI No.1.
19. AAG MSS. Education Records.
20. DEB Minutes 5/12/21.
21. DEB Minutes 3/10/21.
22. DEB Minutes 7/5/22.
23. AAG Letter to the Diocesan Education Board June 1923.
24. DEB Minutes 5/7/27.

CHAPTER FIVE

THE SCHOOLS 1918-1939

The 1918 Act set in train a complete reorganisation of the educational system. The conduct of the Qualifying Examination was transferred to the new Education Authorities; supplementary classes were replaced by Advanced Divisions to be conducted under the Primary Schools Code; the Merit and Intermediate Certificates were abolished; the separation of secondary from non-secondary post-primary pupils was emphasised, with provision to be made for the latter in separate schools; and the regulations governing the Higher Leaving Certificate were modified to allow the secondary curriculum to be planned on a unified basis without reference to the Intermediate curriculum.(1)

In August 1923 primary and secondary Codes came into operation. Two and three-year Advanced Division courses, recognised under the Primary Code, might be offered in secondary schools, leading to the award of the Day School (Lower) or Day School (Higher) Certificate respectively. Three-year Higher Grade schools would operate under the Secondary Code.

The system of Teacher-training was also reviewed. In 1920 a National Committee for the Training of Teachers was instituted which through its Provincial Committees would supervise the two Catholic colleges. In 1924, graduation at University was required for all male teachers, primary and secondary, except specialists in Art, Music, Physical and Technical Education; and for women the Junior Student system was abolished and the Higher Leaving Certificate made a compulsory requirement for entry into teacher training.

Taken together, these enactments presented a fresh set of problems for the embryonic Catholic secondary sector. The ecclesiastical authorities had to establish a system, which would meet the needs of the community for secular education and at the same time provide a satisfactory completion of the religious education given in the primary schools. The principal safeguard for the religious character of the schools lay in the control the church authorities could exercise over the appointment of teachers. A key element therefore in the new era would be the training and religious commitment of secondary staff, but the relationship of managers and staff that had been a feature of the pre-1918 structure no longer applied. Secondary teachers did not stand in the same de facto relation to the Church authorities as their primary colleagues.

TABLE 5

Catholic Secondary Schools in 1922

Area	Name	Date Founded	Status	Religious or Lay	Sex	Approx. Roll	
GLASGOW	Convent of Mercy Garnethill	1847	Intermediate	R	G		
	OLSF Convent School Charlotte St.	1849	Sec. J.S.C.	R	G		369
	St. Mungo's Academy	1858	Sec. J.S.C.	R	B	(1922) (P & S) (1924)	615 1030
	St. Aloysius College	1859	Sec.	R	B	(1922)	453
	Notre Dame Convent School, Dowanhill	1897	Sec. J.S.C.	R	G		414
DUMBARTON	Notre Dame Convent, Dumbarton	1912	Sec. J.S.C.	R	G		290
	St. Patrick's H.S.	1920	Sec.	L	B	(1920) (1922)	80 219
	St. Ninian's H.S. Kirkintilloch	(1923)	Intermediate	L	M	Prim. Post-Pr.	671 135
PAISLEY	St. Margaret's Convent	1896	Sec.	R	G		218
	St. Mirin's Academy	1922	Sec.	L	B		112
	St. Mary's H.S. Greenock	1909	Intermediate	L	M		233
	St. Michael's Academy Kilwinning	1921	Intermediate (Early records destroyed by fire – 1939)	R	M	(1921)	7
MOTHERWELL	Elmwood Convent	1878	Sec. J.S.C.	R	Gb		163
	Our Lady's H.S.	1898	Sec.	L	M	Prim. Sec.	1544 443
	St. Mary's Sec.S. Whifflet	1920 (1874)	Intermediate	L	M		239
GALLOWAY	St. Joseph's Dumfries	1873	Sec.	R	Bb		
	Sacred Heart Convent Girvan	1875	Intermediate	R	Gb	70 – 80	
	St. Joseph's School Kilmarnock	1920	Intermediate	L	M	(1925) Prim. & Sec.	715

G – Girls only   Gb – Girls boarding   M – Mixed boys and girls
B – Boys only   Bb – Boys boarding   Sec. – Recognised by SED at Sen.Sec. Level
R – Managed by a Religious Order   Int. – Recognised by SED at Intermediate
L – Managed by Lay Staff   level
                              JSC   – Junior Student Centre

In practice the preparation of children for initiation into the sacramental life of the Church was carried out by primary teachers in co-operation with the parochial clergy; the part to be played at secondary level in the religious education of their pupils would indeed be a secondary one of reinforcing that primary commitment. After 1918, the existing bond between the parochial schools and the clergy could continue, but an expanded secondary sector was bound to cut across the parochial structures.

The problems of accommodation which had to be faced everywhere were enormous. In Glasgow in 1918 it was calculated that there was a shortfall of 5,312 places (2) in the Catholic sector but worse was to follow, because of the upsurge in demand for secondary places as a result of the financial provisions of the Act. When Brother Germanus was appointed Headmaster of St. Mungo's Academy in 1918 - a position he held for 26 years - he had to deal with an application of 160 pupils from 35 schools for 20 places. The roll of the school, previously 350, leapt to 580. Similar increases occurred in the other senior schools, due in part to an influx of pupils from Stirlingshire,(3) Clackmananshire, West Lothian, Renfrewshire, Ayrshire and Dunbartonshire as well as from the local area. By 1922 the rolls of the five senior schools were as follows:

Our Lady and St. Francis Convent School	369
Convent of Mercy School Garnethill	208
St. Mungo' Academy	615
St. Aloysius College	453
Notre Dame High School	414

a total of 2,059. At the same time the primary roll in the city stood at 35,409. Outwith Glasgow the position was even worse. In Lanarkshire, in 1918-1919, 14 out of the 39 schools transferred had an average number of pupils on the register in excess of the recognised seating accommodation. The 1922 Report of the SED on Motherwell RC Higher Grade School called attention to serious congestion and unhygienic conditions in the school: "In the elementary school, where the roll was 1,544, there was accommodation for 1,384.... In the Higher Grade School the roll had risen from 209 to 443, and these were accommodated in 7 classrooms where the rolls ranged from 31 through 59, 76 and 79 to the incredible total of 95."(4) In Dunbartonshire in 1919, the position in St. Ninian's Kirkintilloch can be adduced as exemplifying the state of the Catholic schools there. There were 693 pupils in 12 classes for which there were 19 teachers. By 1922 the roll had risen to 806, with 135 of these in the post primary sector.(5)

In general, in the Catholic schools, existing accommodation was poor in quality, woefully inadequate in quantity; fully trained, well-qualified Catholic teachers were in short supply; there was a pronounced shortage of male teachers, and of well-qualified secondary staff. The relatively poor attainment of Catholic elementary schools vis-a-vis the State schools - the result of half-a-century of lagging behind in educational development - provided only a restricted base for substantial advance at secondary or higher level, and yet any considerable improvement in the secondary schools would require a corresponding but prior raising of standards at the primary level. The existing number of secondary places, totally insufficient for immediate needs, gave no room for the expansion in pupil numbers to be expected.

The central issues were the interlocking shortages of teachers and secondary

TABLE 6

SCHOOLS HAVING SUPPLEMENTARY TOPS

Area	School	Date of Foundation
MOTHERWELL	St. Patrick's R.C. School Coatbridge	1875
	St. Mary's R.C. School Lanark	1878
	St. Joseph's R.C. School Blantyre	1877
	St. Aloysius R.C. School Chapelhouse, Airdrie	1857
	St. Augustine's, Langloan	1882
	St. John the Baptist R.C. School, Uddingston	1883
DUMBARTON	Our Holy Redeemer Clydebank	1889
	St. Mary's R.C. School Duntocher	1873
GLASGOW	St. Mary's R.C. School Abercrombie Street	1850
	St. Patrick's R.C. School Anderston	(Parish – 1850)
	St. Francis' R.C. School Cumberland Street	(Parish – 1868)
	Holy Cross R.C. School Crosshill	1882
	Sacred Heart R.C. School Bridgeton	1874
	St. Paul's R.C. School Shettleston	(Parish – 1850)
	St. Paul's R.C. School Whiteinch	1903
	St. Peter's R.C. School Partick	(Parish – 1858)
	St. Anthony's R.C. School Govan	(Parish – 1861)

school places. Although the half century since the introduction of compulsory education had seen the emergence nationally of a considerable network of Catholic elementary schools, in which the total rolls rose from around 12,000 in the 1870's to about 94,000 in 1918, there had been no corresponding increase in secondary places. Fewer than 5% of the Catholic school population went on to any form of post-primary education. Any expansion at the secondary level would require an increase in the number and quality of the teaching force, as well as a simultaneous increase in accommodation, precisely at a time when national standards in each were being forced upwards through the efforts of the SED, and by pressures from within the teaching profession itself. The call for an all-graduate profession was already being voiced, supported by the mood of the whole nation which looked to education to help overcome the malaise of the aftermath of war.

The dilemma for the Catholic authorities therefore was to bring about simultaneous advances at all levels to match the attainment of a national system with which it was already out of phase.

Beyond these apparently intractable difficulties lay a problem of a different order. The expansion of Catholic secondary education entailed the development of what was, in effect, a new model of secondary education - one that could meet the academic and other demands of the secular authority, and simultaneously provide a formative educational and spiritual experience to a much broader cross-section of the community than had previously been served.

In spite of all difficulties, some progress was soon apparent in the provision of school places. In Paisley, Dumbarton, Ayrshire and Lanarkshire new secondary foundations were made, while in Glasgow existing establishments expanded. The SED Report for 1922 comments:

"(the provision of new accommodation) is most marked among the R.C. schools, in respect of provision for Intermediate and Secondary education;.... In nearly all cases the additional provision is made in the form of hutment or other more or less temporary annexes. The earlier specimens of this type of building were sometimes barely satisfactory and certainly far from beautiful... Among the Glasgow schools there sppears to be a great, in some cases urgent, need for a larger and better supply of school places...energies have mainly directed to meeting the demand for Intermediate and Secondary education...large additions have been completed at Garnethill Convent Intermediate School, Our Lady and St. Francis Secondary School and St. Mungo's Academy Secondary School.... In Lanarkshire...almost every Catholic school is overcrowded, several intolerably so.... Mossend and Motherwell schools are probably the worst examples. The new building at Bothwell Elmwood Convent Secondary School is approaching completion and 4 additional rooms have been found for Hamilton R.C. School by the reconstruction of a neighbouring house; but on the whole little has been done despite the urgency of the need...(In Ayr)...the only case of extension reported is at Kilmarnock St. Joseph's R.C. School where a large addition has been made.... In Paisley an important advance has been made by the completion of the new St. Margaret's Secondary School..."(6)

DEVELOPMENT IN GLASGOW 1918-1939

The development of Catholic secondary education during this inter-war period falls into two phases, before and after 1929. For a decade after 1918 the provision of additional accommodation was the responsibility of the Diocesan Education Board. By 1928 it could no longer sustain this role, and in that year the parochial schools passed into the ownership of the Corporation of Glasgow (7); thereafter all new schools would be provided by the Education Authority. Under the Local Government Act of 1929 the Ad Hoc Committees were abolished, and their functions transferred to the town and county councils. For the first time local authorities were compelled to make provision for post-primary education on anything like an adequate scale. Schemes for all forms of primary, intermediate and secondary education, without payment of fees, had to be prepared and put into operation.

Before 1929

In this first phase, the major advances at the secondary level were effected by the Religious Orders themselves, who were not involved in the leasing arrangements made between the Church and the Ad Hoc Committees in respect of their secondary schools. At the Franciscan Convent School in Charlotte Street two additional buildings were added. Garnethill Convent School enlarged its premises in 1922, and the next year acquired in addition Garnethill House (formerly the Glasgow Sick Children's Hospital). The Marist Brothers acquired from Bow's of High Street a neighbouring building formerly used as a stable and store. While this was being adapted, accommodation was made available by the Education Authority in St. David's School in Cathedral Street, and in the former Stow College building in Cowcaddens, which had been vacated when the new college was opened at Jordanhill. For the first time St. Mungo's Academy had a gymnasium; coal stoves were removed from the classrooms, and gas lighting was replaced by electricity. In 1924 the Archdiocese purchased the vacant Alexander's School in Duke Street, and this opened as an annexe with the name St. Kentigern's School in 1925. By session 1927-28 the roll of St. Mungo's Academy had risen to 1,147.

In 1926 the supplementary classes in primary schools were transferred to new Advanced Division Centres. The six classes of St. Mary's School in Calton, where the roll was over 2,000, were transferred to West Street Advanced Centre. In 1928 St. Roch's Advanced Centre in Garngad and St. Anthony's in Govan (incorporating the Advanced Divisions of St. Anthony's, St. Saviour's, St. Constantine's and Our Lady of Lourdes primary schools) were opened, followed by others in Kinning Park, Bridgeton, Carntyne and Oatlands.

After 1929

The Local Government Act of 1929 operated greatly to the benefit of the Catholic population. From this time forward more rapid progress in the provision of secondary places was evident.

In session 1929-30 St. Mungo's Academy began to phase out its Primary Department (roll 175) to make room for the increasing number of secondary pupils.

By 1932-33 there were 39 secondary and 1 primary class; 22 at Parson St., 13 at St. Kentigern's and 4 at Kennedy Street Annexe.(8)

The major advances however were elsewhere in the city. In 1936 Holyrood Senior

Secondary School opened in Crosshill, and the following year St. Gerard's S.S. School in Govan, also under a lay head teacher and with an entirely lay staff. These were the first Catholic schools providing full secondary courses to have opened in the city for fifty years, and the first for boys for almost eighty years. In new, well-equipped and well-sited buildings, they offered an exciting prospect of a richer educational and cultural life to the Catholic young people of the growing residential areas of the south and south-west of the city. At the same time pressure on the older institutions was relieved, and career prospect for teachers significantly expanded.

Advanced Centres at Calton and Garngad were upgraded to become St. Mary's and St. Roch's Junior Secondary School respectively. A new school, St. Mark's Junior Secondary, opened in 1937 in a new housing area at Carntyne, was followed in rapid succession by St. Columba's J.S. in Maryhill in 1938 and St. Bonaventure's in Oatlands in 1939.

This substantial progress was halted by the outbreak of war. "St. Bonaventure's J.S. was opened in August 1939 with a primary roll of 570 and with 244 pupils in the first year of the secondary course. On September 1st evacuation of some 400 pupils took place to Wigtownshire, and during the autumn term groups of 20 pupils, attending voluntarily, were taught in school."(9)

The position in Glasgow in 1938 is shown in Table 9, which shows that the umber of pupils following the full senior secondary course had almost doubled between 1922 and 1939. The number of schools offering the full Leaving Certificate course had increased from 5 to 7. The two new schools served both boys and girls, and were managed and staffed by lay teachers. The 5 old-established secondaries remained under the control of the Religious Orders. They were all single-sex establishments, 3 or them for girls only. Even with the addition of two mixed schools, only four of Glasgow's seven Catholic senior secondary schools provided for the education of boys. Prior to the abolition of the Junior Student system, three of the five older schools operated as Junior Student centres.

DEVELOPMENTS IN LANARKSHIRE

Before 1929

Some Catholic girls were able to receive a full secondary education at Elmwood Convent School in Bothwell, and adjunct of Our Lady's and St. Francis' School. Elmwood had been acquired to provide accommodation for boarders at Charlotte Street and had gradually developed as a separate school. Motherwell RC Higher Grade School was the only other school in the country offering courses leading to the Intermediate and Higher Leaving Certificates. Only a tiny minority of the children of school age accepted the opportunities offered. In session 1919-20, 41 pupils in total were enrolled in the Third Year of the Intermediate Division of these these two schools; between them they could muster only 19 candidates for the Leaving Certificate examination that year.(10)

Before 1923, Motherwell R.C. Higher Grade School presented candidates for the Intermediate Certificate; those who reached a sufficient standard and were otherwise able went on to St. Mungo's Academy or St. Aloysius College, or to

Elmwood House. Conditions improved in 1923 when accommodation shared with Motherwell Central School was provided for secondary pupils in a building formerly occupied by Dalziel High School, and as a result the course was extended to four years. Further relief came in 1925 when the Higher Grade School was separated from the Primary division, and 1926 saw the first presentation for the Higher Leaving Certificate.(11)

Throughout the county the existing school buildings, in many cases antiquated and run down, were already hopelessly inadequate for immediate needs, far less for the demands presented by an inexorbly growing population. When increased accommodation was required at St. Mary's Whifflet in 1921-22 to provide for its upgrading to Higher grade status, a protracted dispute broke out between the Archdiocesan Authorities and the Ad Hoc Committee, not resolved until 1924.(12) By then the number of pupils in the three Intermediate years had risen to over 1,000. The most pressing need was a new secondary school. For years the DEB whose responsibility included the vast array of overcrowded, dilapidated and unsuitable buildings of the primary schools struggled to meet the demand by resorting to a series of temporary expedients, such as the erection of temporary buildings often in the form of wooden huts, turning church halls into classrooms, hiring space from non-catholic institutions, or occupying on a mutually agreed basis schools vacated by the Ad Hoc Authority.(13) Although some overall progress was made, the impact on the post-primary sector was small, consisting mainly of the upgrading, eventually, of Motherwell Higher Grade School, renamed Our Lady's High School, to senior secondary status.

After 1929

In 1931 Thomas Lynch was appointed head teacher there, in succession to George Bennett who died in office. The curriculum expanded to include Music, Greek, German, Dynamics and Domestic Science. The academic performance of the school rapidly improved, and its catchment area was enlarged to include pupils from Lanark, where St. Mary's had been accorded three-year secondary status in 1929.

In spite of all the hardships of the time and the failing local economy progress continued until the outbreak of the Second World War. In 1937 a new three-year Junior Secondary school, St. Joseph's, was opened in Motherwell; two years later Holy Cross School in Hamilton followed, displacing St. Mary's School, which continued to operate as a primary school with an Advanced Division. Further relief at Our Lady's High School was provided by the phasing out of girls' classes there.

By 1939 a three-tier system of Catholic secondary education had emerged in the county. The top tier consisted of two senior secondary single-sex schools, Our Lady's High School in Motherwell and Elmwood Convent School in Bothwell. The second tier contained three-year Higher Grade schools at St. Mary's (Whifflet), St. Patrick's in Coatbridge, St. Mary's (Lanark) and Holy Cross (Hamilton), which sent on those of their pupils seeking further education either to Motherwell or Bothwell; while the third tier consisted of a number of Advanced Division or Junior Secondary Departments located in the largest and oldest primary schools in the most populous areas of the county.

DEVELOPMENTS IN DUMBARTONSHIRE

Before 1929

The first Ad Hoc Authority elected in Dunbartonshire in April 1919 had 26 members
- 5 Labour, 8 who described themselves as representatives of the whole community,
8 Protestant ministers one of whom was elected chairman, and 5 Catholic priests,
one of whom, Rev. Dean Kelly of Dumbarton, was elected vice-chairman.(14)
Dunbartonshire became one of the foremost authorities in Scotland to provide
the full range of services permitted by the 1918 Act, and this progressiveness
of outlook is attributable in part at least to the influence of the minority
groups. Already it was noted in 1922 that "the characteristic feature (in
Dunbartonshire) is the combination in one organisation of all the post-qualifying
instruction, with a consequent obliteration of the distinction between Supplementary and Intermediate Courses..."(15)

In August 1920 St. Patrick's High School in Dumbarton opened with a roll of
80 and a staff of 4. The first headmaster, a layman, was Thomas Mulgrew. "The
school buildings consisted of part of the old primary school and a converted
dwelling house. To these were later added a reconditioned church, a hut, part
of the old Dumbarton Academy buildings and part of the Burgh Hall." From its
beginning it was comprehensive in nature, in that all the Catholic boys of
secondary age from the surrounding area - i.e. Balloch, Helensburgh, Alexandria,
Renton as well as from Dumbarton Burgh itself-attended St. Patrick's High School,
and along with them the 'top stream' from Our Holy Redeemer's School in Clydebank.(16) Also in 1920 Notre Dame High School Clerkhill came under the control
of the Education Authority. By 1922 progress was also evident in the provision
for secondary education at Kirkintilloch, in the eastern sector of the county.
The post-qualifying sector of St. Ninian's School had increased to 135 in a
total roll of 930. The school began to develop as a centre for the whole of
East Dunbartonsire, and the Inspectorate Report looked upon the prospect of
secondary development as "entirely hopeful". "Since 1921, the supplementary
class had been discontinued.... The facilities made available by the 1918 Act
and fully used by the Education Authority after 1921 made possible for the
first time full secondary education for Catholics in Kirkintilloch...the
efficient operation of the school would not have been possible without the
presence, help and co-operation of substantial numbers of non-catholic teachers
...these were particularly essential in the technical and other practical
subjects."(17)

By the mid 1920's there were three schools in the county presenting pupils
for the Higher Leaving Certificate, two in Dumbarton and one in Kirkintilloch.
The large Catholic community of Clydebank however was less well served. Pupils
there seeking the full secondary course had to travel to Dumbarton, or into
Glasgow, or be content with the Advanced Division courses offered locally in
Our Holy Redeemer's School, or in St. Mary's School in Duntocher.

In 1923 the Archdiocesan Authority erected a new building for O.H.R. School
with special provision for Science, Handwork, Domestic Subjects, Art, Music
and Physical Education, but in general priority in the provision of accommodation
went to the three secondary schools. In 1927 St. Patrick's took possession
of a new building at Castlehill, where the facilities included technical and
engineering rooms, three science laboratories, gymnasium, dining hall and kitchen.

After 1929

In Kirkintilloch the Education Authority acquired Westermains House, and its grounds were set aside as the site of a new school planned to accommodate 1,100 primary and secondary pupils. This came into use on 27 November 1931, with 518 primary and 540 secondary pupils on the roll, including 270 from Stirling-shire - 50% of the secondary department. On 16 Feb. 1932 "the SED decided to grant the school official status and title as a secondary school...such recognition had formerly been withheld...because of the lack of suitable premises ...no longer was it to be known as Kirkintilloch (Town) R.C. School but as St. Ninian's R.C. High School, Kirkintilloch."(18)

In 1933 the opening of St. Modan's High School in Stirling has far-reaching consequences for St. Ninian's. The roll dropped below 900, resulting in empty classrooms at a time when its neighbour Townhead Public School was grossly overcrowded. The Education Authority, not wishing to provide a new building, directed that four classes be accommodated at St. Ninian's while remaining under the direction of their own headmaster.

In 1935 another class was added. Although the accommodation at St. Ninian's was still in excess of immediate needs, the local Catholic community believed that all of it would be needed when the school leaving age was raised to 15 in 1936. Once it became clear that this was not going to happen, their fears that their new building would be taken over by the Public School and St. Ninian's transferred to the vacated old building, became acute. On 17 Jan. 1937 an assembly of interested persons petitioned the Diocesan Board to request the Education Authority to remove all the non-catholic pupils from St. Ninian's on the grounds that their presence was resented by the Catholic community. At the same time similar representations were made to the Secretary of State. By summer 1937 the Townhead pupils had been withdrawn, and in due course the Townhead School was altered and extended.

In Dunbartonshire by 1939 the Catholic population of 30,000 or thereabouts were served by three schools offering the full secondary course (which could better be described as comprehensive schools). Clydebank was an area of difficulty. There Our Holy Redeemer's School, in 1939 one of the largest schools in the county, with a roll of approximately 1,600, was of Junior Secondary status only, contrasting sharply with the position in Kirkintilloch or Dumbarton.

DEVELOPMENTS IN RENFREWSHIRE 1918-1939

In 1918 in Paisley the only Catholic school offering Higher Grade courses was St. Margaret's Convent School, for girls only. In 1922, when the roll was 260 with 50 in post-intermediate classes, the school moved to a new building at Netherhill, and a period of expansion began. In the same year St. Mirin's Academy opened as a secondary school for boys only, with a roll of 200 and a staff of 10 lay teachers under a lay headmaster Gilbert Cameron Mowat. The schools developed relatively slowly. In 1935 when St. Mirin's moved to a new building, it was able to accept also Junior Secondary boys and girls; senior secondary girls continued to attend St. Margaret's High School.

In the Greenock and Port Glasgow areas for ten years after 1918 the only post-primary education for Catholic children was that in the supplementary (later

Advanced Division) courses of St. Mary's School in Greenock. Serious overcrowding existed, without alleviation until 1931, when the Education Authority provided an annexe with accommodation for 630 pupils. Further relief came with the opening of a new primary school, St. Mungo's at Ladyburn, Greenock in 1932. In the same year the Education Authority commissioned a new school for Catholic secondary pupils of Greenock and district. The building in Gourock was completed in less than a year, and in June 1933 all the secondary pupils and the Advanced Division classes of boys of St. Mary's School took posession under the headship of Brother Bonaventure, a Marist. The school was named St. Columba's High School, and St. Mary's continued as a mixed primary with a Junior Secondary Department for girls only.

DEVELOPMENT IN GALLOWAY 1918-1939

Between 1918 and 1939, the main centres of post-primary education for Catholic children were in Kilmarnock and Irvine. In Kilmarnock, St. Joseph's High School had been given Higher Grade status in 1920. By 1925 the total roll (primary and secondary) had reached 715. The school continued to grow, and a new building was provided by the Education Authority on a site beside the old one, but it was not till 1944 when the roll was about 1,100 that it was elevated to full senior secondary status. Before that date, Catholic children in the district who sought full secondary education travelled to Glasgow.

In 1918 the parish priest of Irvine, Canon Hogan, brought the Sisters of the Order of the Cross and Passion to his area, to staff a primary and a secondary school. He hoped to persuade the Education Authority to build and maintain these schools in the terms of the 1918 Act. He succeeded, and in 1921 St. Michael's opened with 7 pupils. By August 1923 a new building was ready. The school expanded, taking pupils eventually from as far north as Largs, as far east as Kilbirnie and south as Galston and Ayr.

On 25 October 1939 the school was burned down and all its records destroyed. A proper replacement was out of the question because of war conditions. By moving the primary department into the gymnasium and dining room, and the secondary into what had been the primary building, the school was functioning again within a week. Huts were erected by the Education Authority in 1941 and 1942. These were needed not only for the growing number of local pupils but also to provide for refugees from London, Liverpool, Glasgow and Clydeside.(20)

Elsewhere in Galloway developments in the provision of secondary education were on a small scale. In Girvan in 1875 the Teaching Order of Sisters of St. Joseph of Cluny had established a primary school for 50 children. This developed into a boarding school for 80 girls, run on a five-day week basis with most of the boarders returning home at weekends. After 1918 the total roll reached about 100 served by 5 members of staff. Until 1927 the school had no post-intermediate pupils. As a result of wartime evacuation, the roll expanded to between 200 and 300, mainly evacuees from Glasgow area, taught by 13 teachers, many of them from Glasgow.(21) St. Joseph's College in Dumfries was founded in 1873. During the greater part of its existence it combined the functions of a Catholic boarding school for boys and a training school for entrants to the Founding Order, the Marist Brothers. In the life of the school, great emphasis was placed on religious observance and on sport and games. In organisation it followed the English Public School system, and looked towards England and the English examination system rather than to Scotland. Its pupils were drawn from families resident in many parts of the United Kingdom or over-seas, with England and Scotland about equally represented. Those who belonged to the south-west of Scotland were probably a minority.(22)

THE CATHOLIC SECONDARY SCHOOLS IN 1939

The considerable progress made in the expansion of the Catholic secondary sector in the inter-war period is summarised in Tables 5,6,7 and 8. The total number of schools places had increased enormously, supplementary classes had been replaced by a system of Junior Secondary schools, and there had been a substantial advance at the post-intermediate level. There was still a considerable shortfall in provision for the higher education of Catholic boys. The smaller communities of Dumbarton and Paisley were relatively better off in that respect than either Glasgow or Motherwell, and in the latter area in particular provision for both boys and girls was still grossly inadequate.

The information given in the Tables has to be treated with caution, in that it fails to distinguish accurately between categories of secondary pupils. In Paisley for example in 1939 St. Mirin's Academy included Junior Secondary boys and girls; in Motherwell, schools such as St. Mary's Whifflet or Holy Cross Hamilton provided only the first three years of the full secondary course; in Dunbartonshire, the secondary total comprises all post-primary pupils whether qualified or not; and the Glasgow total does not distinguish between senior and junior secondary pupils. What can be deduced from Table 8 is that in a period during which the primary population remained remarkably stable, the percentage of Catholic children attaining to some kind of secondary education increased by more than three times.

TABLE 7

Primary and Secondary Pupils in Glasgow, Dumbarton,
Motherwell and Paisley in 1922 and 1939

| | 1922 | | 1939 | |
	Primary	Secondary	Primary	Secondary
Glasgow	35,490	2,059	32,236	7,809
Dumbartonshire	5,370	377	4,927	1,624
Motherwell	19,124	658	20,251	1,664
Paisley	9,415	563	10,876	1,500
	69,399	3,657	68,290	12,597
		5.3%		18.4%

TABLE 8

Secondary and Junior Secondary Pupils in Glasgow
in 1922 and 1939

Secondary	1922	1939 (June)
St. Mungo's Academy		1,044
Notre Dame High School	414	365
St. Aloysius College	453*	138
Convent of Mercy	208	395
Our Lady of St. Francis	369	429
Holyrood Senior Secondary		786
St. Gerard's Senior Secondary		671
*Includes primary	2,059	3,828
Calton Advanced		611
St. Mark's		328
Sacred Heart		550
St. Columba's		
Our Lady and St. Margaret's		1,894
St. Roch's		598

NOTES

1.   SED Circulars 44 (1921) 60 (1922) 62 (1923) 63 (1924).
2.   Treble, J.H.   IR XXIX(19) 2 p.123.
3.   NDSA 10
4.   White, J.   History of Our Lady's High School Motherwell.
                              n.p.
5.   Maguire G.I. and Murray S.V.   History of a School.
6.   SED Report   Education in Scotland 1922.
7.   City of Glasgow Archives   D-T.C.6/486.
8.   Handley, J.E.   History of St. Mungo's Academy.
9.   Inspectorate Report 27/10/43.
10.   Treble, J.H.   IR XXXI,I   p.29.
11.   White, J.   Op.cit.
12.   Treble, J.H.   Loc.cit.
13.   Ibid.
14.   Roberts, A.F.B.   The Operation of the Ad Hoc Authority in Dunbarton-
                              shire. SCRE No.54.
15.   SED Report   Education in Scotland 1922.
16.   DBJ Vol. 3 No.1, Dec. 1950.
17.   Maguire G.T. and Murray, S.V.   Op.cit.
18.   Ibid.
19.   Souvenir Brochure of the Church of Our Lady of Mount Carmel, Kilmarnock
        12/5/63.
20.   Sister Dominic Savio C.P.
21.   Contributed by Mr. Haig Reid, then Deputy Head of Sacred Heart Secondary
        School Girvan.
22.   DBJ Vol.4, No.4 October 1954.

CHAPTER SIX

THE TEACHERS

After 1918 the demand for teachers, primary and secondary, for the Catholic schools was insatiable. The new secondary schools for years after their foundation were teacher-consuming rather than teacher-producing, while at the same time requirements of the expanding older institutions grew faster than they could be supplied. In the primary schools an enormous backlog of qualified staff had to be overtaken to mitigate endemic overcrowding and to raise academic standards. Since their need was principally for men, and therefore, after 1924, for graduates, the difficulty of supply for the secondary schools was increased, to be further exacerbated by the natural increase of the Catholic population.

Standards in the national system were rising. A full secondary education for all was seen to be a high priority in the post-World War 1 period, and in Scotland this led to an urgent demand for an all-graduate teaching profession. As a result the schools of the national system set a very smart pace in academic and pedagogic attainment, which the struggling Catholic secondary sector was hard pressed to match.

The Catholic schools, faced with this prime task of stimulating a sufficient flow of capable and well-qualified teachers, found their efforts assisted in no small measure by the prospect of improved career opportunities of a nature hitherto unknown to the Catholic community. This combined with the limitation of opportunity in other directions and the distasteful aspects of the occupations with which the majority were familiar, enhanced the considerable attractions of teaching as a profession.(1) Furthermore, the financial assistance now available for those aspiring to higher levels of education enabled many working-class Catholics to embark on a lengthy professional training which formerly most would not have contemplated.

Nevertheless, in all the circumstances a shortage of Catholic secondary teachers was inevitable. From the outset this limiting factor, which compounded the handicaps of poor accommodation and disparity of attainment at the primary level, was built into the Catholic system. Its results would include a restriction of the curricular range in the secondary schools as well as on average a poorer teacher-pupil ratio than the national norm over a prolonged period.

THE SUPPLY OF TEACHERS

To meet the shortage the Catholic Authorities had to rely at first on the
increased efforts of the Religious Teaching Orders already established in
the area. Table 6 shows that by 1922, 11 of the 18 secondary or intermediate
schools in the south-west were managed by the Orders. The education of boys
was undertaken by the Marist Brothers at St. Mungo's Academy and the Society
of Jesus at St. Aloysius' College; of girls, at the convent schools of the
Franciscan Sisters at 'Charlotte Street' and Elmwood, the Sisters of Mercy
at Garnethill, the Sisters of Notre Dame at Dowanhill in Glasgow and Clerkhill
in Dumbarton, and the Faithful Companions of Jesus in Paisley. St. Michael's
Academy Kilwinning was the first 'mixed' secondary to be managed locally by
a Religious Order, the Sisters of the Cross and Passion. In addition the Sacred
Heart Nuns looked after a Convent Boarding School at Girvan, and the Marists
a boarding school for boys at Dumfries and a preparatory school at Largs.

Much of the strength of the Orders came from members whose place of origin
was furth of Scotland. The Sisters of Mercy and the Marist Brothers had strong
links with Ireland, the Society of Jesus and the Sisters of Notre Dame less
so. The two latter had come to Scotland from England, and within them English
traditions were strong, as may be seen from some of their outstanding
personalities - Sister Dr. Monica Taylor and Sister Marie Hilda of Notre Dame,
and Father Eric Hanson of the Society of Jesus, among others. In 1921-22 the
staff of St. Aloysius' College was made up of 2 Oxford, 5 London and 2 Glasgow
University graduates, 1 Diplomate of the Glasgow School of Art and 7 non-
graduates, including the 2 ladies who staffed the primary division. The other
major Order, the Franciscan Sisters, were by the 1920's so well established
locally that much of their strength did derive from Scotland, though not only
from the south-west.

Influences from outwith the British Isles existed in all the Orders and were
reflected in their membership. (1) The Franciscan Sisters had come to Scotland
from France, and the Marists and Notre Dame Sisters, who came here via Ireland
and England respectively, were French and Belgian by origin. Within all there
was a leavening from continental countries, particularly France, which enriched
the children of this area.(2)

A second input of qualified teachers consisted of the small but significant
number of non-Catholic teachers who came to serve in the transferred schools.
The History of St. Mungo's Academy refers to "that band...who came to our
aid in the difficult times that followed the passing of the 1918 Act."(3)
It is probably true that every Catholic secondary school in the Archdiocese
had its quota. A specific reference to the position in Kirkintilloch states
that "then (in the 1920's) as now (1974) the efficient operation of the school
would not have been possible without the presence, help and co-operation of
substantial numbers of non-Catholic teachers; in the 1920's these were particularly essential in technical and other practical subjects where the scarcity
of Catholic teachers seems to have been greatest."(4)

It is clear that the need to employ non-Catholic teachers persisted throughout
the inter-war period, albeit on a fairly modest scale. According to one estimate
there were in 1935 50 non-Catholic male and female teachers in the Secondary
and Advanced Division Schools of the Archdiocese of Glasgow. Such evidence

as there is shows that while the contribution of this group was made at first in a broad range of curricular areas, there soon developed a particular dependence on them in the practical subjects of Art, Music, Domestic, Physical and Technical Education. This reflected the circumstance that the schools from which the supply of Catholic teachers principally came generally lacked these subject Departments. Only with the development of Junior Secondary schools after 1928 and the opening of Holyrood and St. Gerald's Senior Secondary schools in the late 1930's did the emphasis on practical and aesthetic education increase in the Catholic sector.(5)

A comment by Colm Brogan, himself a member of staff of St. Mungo's Academy in the mid-20s, may be of interest: "When...it became necessary to send a number of non-catholic teachers of specialist subjects to Catholic schools, some education officials thought it would be tactful to send teachers who had refused to take the Protestant training course in religious teaching, believing they would be less hostile or prejudiced....But the Catholic authorities would have none of them. If it was not yet possible to staff the schools with believing Catholics, then the deficiency would be made up by believing Protestants, but on no account by unbelievers."(6)

The main source of supply of teachers however had to be the local community itself, and after 1918 there was a sustained campaign to increase the number, especially of men, in the Catholic schools.(7) This coincided with the national effort to find staff for the general expansion of secondary education brought about by the Act, and benefitted from the arrangements put in force to that end. Students of the immediate post-1918 years, among them returned veterans of the Great War, were able to follow a concurrent course of study and teacher training by which an academic qualification and the teaching certificate could be gained together. At the same time entry qualifications for many other professions were raised, and this, combined with the greater expense of these courses, acted as a deterrent to those few Catholic students who might have considered following them. Catholic graduates began to move towards the teaching profession in steadily increasing numbers. Some comments of individual involved in this movement are of interest:

"(Teaching) was the only profession that was really open to (Catholic) boys... it was the cheapest degree." "I was one of a family of 12...5 of us became teachers."

"Catholics were slow in entering professions other than teaching...Fr. Hanson and Bro. Germanus directed as many students as possible into teaching."(8) "Teaching was the only way up for people moving out of the...formally uneducated class...this was the first generation move into the professions..."(9)

As the schools expanded in size and number, teaching presented ever greater career opportunities. The notion became widespread that it was the only way for educated Catholics to put their talents at the service of the community, and Catholic girls tended to think of teaching, especially primary teaching, as the only opening available to them; one Headmaster comments: "When I used to speak to the girls in Our Lady's High School to persuade them to go on to the universities, they used to say "but I don't want to be a teacher."(10)

Another commentator remarks: "the pressure was to enter teaching...the assumption was that any girl who...got Highers was going into teaching. The broad assumption was that she would go straight to the training college."(11)

Parenthetically it could be said that it was perhaps not surprising that primary teaching exercised the attraction it did. Throughout the south-west, and in Lanarkshire in particular, the secondary sector remained an under-developed part of the Catholic school structure during the inter-war and war years. Secondary schools were few and the promotion ladder short, leading only as far as Principal Teacher of a subject, if indeed it reached that level. Beyond that, opportunity was largely blocked due to the established position of the Religious Orders who in Glasgow held in 1937 five of the available seven headships, as well as many principal teacher posts. On the other hand in the primary sector many headships as well as other promoted posts were open to lay staff. For all that, for "first generation" graduates the nature of the career structure was not a prime consideration. For the majority, the step to a university education and teaching career was enough for themselves and their families to face, and a clean job and secure economic base in the familiar environment of a Catholic school a sufficient guarantee of job satisfaction. For many however the attitude that developed was one of restricted vision, and satisfaction with a relatively low level of academic attainment.

There can be no doubt that for the desired development of the secondary sector to come to pass, and for the emergence of a suitably educated teaching cadre, a pre-condition had to be a raising of the level of academic attainment in the primary schools. The key to this lay in the education and training of the primary teachers. Dowanhill Training College, from its foundation in 1894 until the opening of Craiglockhart College in 1920, had fulfilled a solitary role in the training of Catholic women teachers in Scotland. During the first three decades of its existence only a tiny minority of its trainees held university degrees or other qualifications entitling them to teach at secondary level. Up to and including session 1924-25, in no one year was the number of trained graduates greater than five. The following session however the number leapt to 20, to remain at or above that level thereafter. In 1920-31, an exceptional year, the figure leapt again to 57, and remained at a high level until the war years.(See Table 9 and Appendix 2.)

A proper assessment of the contribution of the Catholic women teachers of the first half of the century has yet to be made. As well as carrying the burdens of oversize classes in sometimes unspeakably difficult conditions, they were instrumental in raising cultural standards generally while at the same time accepting the responsibility of preparing their charges for initiation into the life of the church. Beyond this, it was frequently the case that it was the economic security provided by sisters, aunts and sometimes mothers in the teaching profession which triggered the upward mobility-economical and cultural - which marked the Catholic body of the inter-war years. "Without the women teachers there would have been no teachers. They were the basis of the primary school, and the primary school is the basis of all education."(12)

The number of men qualifying as teachers in the '20's and '30's is not easily ascertained. For some years after 1918, many returning ex-service men entered the teaching profession. Thereafter, the supply was drawn at first almost entirely from the former pupils of St. Mungo's Academy and St. Aloysius College. No substantial flow of university students could emerge from the post-1918 foundations in Dumbarton, Renfrew or Lanarkshire until the later 1920's, if then. By the mid-1930's however the numbers of Catholic graduates were being swollen by the former

TABLE 9

GRADUATES TRAINED FOR TEACHING AT NOTRE DAME
COLLEGE 1921-1939

| | Arts. | | Science | | |
	Hons.	Ord.	Hons.	Ord.	Total
1921-22	-	-	-	-	-
22-23		1	-	-	1
-24	-	-	-	-	-
-25	-	2	1	-	3
-26	1	14	3	2	20
-27	1	15	2	2	20
-28	6	13	-	1	20
-29	-	20	-	3	23
-30	2	16	1	-	19
-31	3	51	-	3	57
-32	3	42	-	1	46
-33	3	33	2	6	44
-34	4	42	-	1	47
-35	6	37	-	6	49
-36	2	42	1	2	47
-37	2	42	1	8	53
-38	4	36	-	3	43
-39	4	36	-	9	49
	42	441	11	47	541

In the same period a total of 19 diplomates in Art and Music were trained as teachers. This supply began to appear in session 1932-33.

pupils of Our Lady's High School (Motherwell), St. Patrick's (Dumbarton), St. Mirin's (Paisley) St. Margaret's High School (Paisley) St. Michael's (Kilwinning) St. Ninian's (Kirkintilloch) St. Columba's (Gourock), St. Josephs's (Kilmarnock) and Elmwood Convent, all of which had by then been in existence long enough to be suppliers of University entrants. Even then, the majority of Catholic students were the products of the old-established city schools, which continued to attract into their orbit many of the more able young people from outwith the city of Glasgow.

One source of information about the movement into teaching during this period is the St. Aloysius College Magazine which appeared regularly throughout the 'Twenties.' This occasionally contained information about former pupils who had gone on to further study. The lists are not exhaustive, but do give an indication of trends. The December 1922 issue names 7 F.P.s who graduated in Arts at Glasgow that year, of whom 6 entered teaching. That year 11 F.P.s passed the Third Professional Medical examination. Earlier issues make few if any references to graduates entering teaching. In 1923 however there were 13 graduates in Arts and Science, along with 7 in Medicine, 2 in Veterinary Surgery, 2 in Dentistry and 1 in Law, this last being James D. Scanlan, scion of a well-known Glasgow family who later became Archbishop of Glasgow. The trend was noted in the 1925 issue, which names 25 former pupils engaged in teaching, with the faintly surprised comment that "quite a large number of Old Aloysians have devoted themselves to teaching."(13)

The flow of male graduates into teaching matched and eventually surpassed that of women. By 1924 the non-graduate route to teacher-qualification had been closed to men. All aspirants then had to seek a university degree, except those specialising in the practical or aesthetic subjects. The non-graduate route remained open to women, and it continued to exert a strong attraction for Catholic girls for a lengthy period. Salary scales were better for men than for equally-qualified women, their promotion prospects were good, and in addition the economic depression of the time added to the attraction of teaching as a career for men.

An indication of the growth in numbers of Catholic graduates may be gleaned from the history of the Catholic student societies of Glasgow University (see Appendix 3). Although clearly not all Catholic students were destined to become teachers, "It was indeed in Arts that Catholic students concentrated...and even more clear that in Arts they were destined for teaching."(14).

By the middle and late 'Thirties the supply of teachers, in the Catholic as well as in the national system as a whole, had grown faster than the rate at which school places could be provided, and many newly-qualified teachers found themselves surplus to immediate requirements of the service, in spite of the continuing need for more secondary places, especially in Lanarkshire. Other circumstances contributed. The current high rate of unemployment made it unlikely that children would stay on at school beyond the earliest legal leaving date. The established tendency within the Catholic community, largely concentrated in the most severely deprived areas, towards early leaving was thus reinforced. According to Treble the Third Year of Advanced Division classes in Scotland's Catholic schools in 1932-33 accounted for only 1.16% of the average total enrolment.(15) The same trend appeared in the secondary schools. Paradoxically, when a more buoyant demand for labour developed immediately before and during the Second World War, this also had the effect of causing boys to leave school at the earliest opportunity.

The number of graduates entering teacher-training began to decline, and the academically well-qualified products of the Catholic secondary schools sought entry to other professions in greater numbers. This tendency was strengthened by the assistance which could now be given by the older members of large families to their siblings, in the form of guidance based on experience of higher education, and in the more practical form of financial aid.(16)

As the confidence of the schools in their own potentiality increased particularly as the record of successful presentation at the Higher Leaving Certificate grew, young lawyers, accountants, doctors, dentists,vets, engineers and civil servants began to emerge from among the ranks of their former pupils.

THE TRAINING OF CATHOLIC TEACHERS 1918-1939

As a result of the 1918 dispensation, ecclesiastical control over the schools diminished. Priorities were set by the State, and formal religious education no longer stood so firmly at the centre of the educational process. The Church became more dependent on the teachers to preserve the denominational character of the schools, especially in the secondary sector in which the link with the parochial unit was less strong and the relationship between teachers and clergy on a different footing than in the primary schools.

To meet this situation, and to fulfil the dual requirements of Church and State, a rather sophisticated system of teacher-training evolved. For the State, the aspiring teacher had to obtain a Higher Leaving Certificate, proceed to a university or college to obtain a higher educational qualification, and then attend a Training College to obtain a Teacher's Certificate. The Church's requirement although different in kind, resulted in a similar demand on the student. Since every Catholic teacher was expected to share in the work of religious instruction, the Church's approval recognised not only suitability to hold moral authority over children, but also training as a catechist. Catholic students therefore were obliged to follow a course in religious education, to be taken concurrently with their university or college qualification, covering Ethics, Moral Philosophy, Scripture, Liturgy, Doctrine, Church History and Catechetics. Satisfactory performance, assessed by a written examination in each subject, led to the award of a Religious Education Certificate which was a pre-requisite for appointment to a post in a Catholic school. Entry to the course was controlled by the Prospective Teachers Religious Examination taken by senior pupils at the end of their secondary school career. It was supervised by the Diocesan Board of Religious Inspectors, who set the examination papers and arranged for their correction and the publication of results.(17)

The system operated differently for men and women. Women trainees attended one or other of the two Catholic colleges, both of which were residential and managed by Religious Teaching Orders, and students whether following the one-year post-graduate course or the diploma course of two - or three years duration were under college discipline for a long working day. For them the full Religious course was completed during their period of teacher-training. Male students on the other hand attended a series of extra-mural lectures which took place in evenings or Saturday mornings throughout their student career. All who sought to teach in a Catholic school, whether primary or secondary, were required to follow the same course.

Because the prime resource available for operating this system lay in the staff of the seminary, then at Bearsden, or in the ranks of the clergy themselves,(18) the resultant training took on a distinctive theological, doctrinal and authoritarian character. Emphasis was laid on the cognitive aspect of the religious educational experience, which tended to be seen as a catechetical exercise carried on under the gaze of a benign authority whose dictates there was no need to question. A further characteristic derived from the linguistic style in which it was conducted, in which terminology and concepts of latin origin dominated. On the whole there was a failure to take sufficient account of the different roles in religious education of the primary and secondary teacher. The training given was suitable enough for teachers of the more academic type who would work in schools where the majority of pupils were possessed of relatively high linguistic ability, but it failed adequately to prepare its students for the problems which would arise when the secondary schools enlarged their curricula and broadened their intake of pupils. As a system however it did possess considerable strength. In the few Catholic secondary schools of the inter-war period, pupils, teachers and parents had shared educational objectives. Pupils had for the most part a shared religious and educational experience at primary level, and between staff and pupils a powerful bond existed, the product of their common faith and baptism, which had an immensely unifying effect on the secondary school population. The system of training took cognisance of these factors. It recognised the central role of Religious Education in the formation of young people and went a long way towards reinforcing this attitude in the minds of teachers. It served also to maintain in students in training a consciousness of the importance of the role of the teacher, and an awareness of the immense responsibilities that go with that office. "Catholic students at the time who contemplated becoming teachers, accepted the fact that if they were going to teach in a Catholic school they should be convinced Catholics."(19)

NOTES

1.   O'Hagan, A.   NDSA 9, p.13. "The professional classes in the early days were the sons of labourers and tramway men, of whom there was a great number of Catholic Irish." See also NDSA 1 and NDSA 12 and others.

2.   The first three headmasters of St. Mungo's Academy Bros. Procope, Tatianus and Faust were Frenchmen, Sister Chantal SND and Father Annacker SJ are other examples among many.

3.   Handley, J.E.   History of St. Mungo's Academy 1858-1958   p.175 Eight members of staff of S.M.A. are named, among them R.A. Houston, a distinguished Scottish colourist, Alan Barr (Classics) later Professor of Divinity at Trinity College, and Neil McCormick (Classics) a staunch Scottish Nationalist related to 'King' John McCormick. These personalities, and others, contributed in special ways to the widening of horizons.

4.   Maguire, G.T. and Murray S.V.   The Story of a School

5.   An important contribution to the number of qualified music teachers was made by the Ommer School of Music, managed by three sisters Julia, Maria and Elsa Ommer members of a German Catholic family residing in Glasgow. During the '20's and '30's many teachers, among them several Catholics, gained their basic teaching qualification at the Ommer school.

6.   Brogan, C.   The Glasgow Story,   p.181

7.   Treble, J.H.   I.R., XXIX 1978 (2) p.128, footnote.

8.   McKee, J.J.   NDSA 2 and NDSA 3, p.3

9.   Murray, Mary P. NDSA 16 p.11. See also Murray, James NDSA 6, p.10 and 15.

10.   Breen, J.   NDSA 12, p.9.

11.   Murray, M.P.   NDSA 16, p.9

12.   Murray, James   NDSA 6, p.31

13.   St. Aloysius College Magazine 1925. See also Montague, Dr. A. NDSA 18, p.17

14.   Montague, A.   NDSA 17, p.5

15.   Treble, J.H.   Loc. cit., P.131

16.   In many large families then the rule, it became a fairly regular pattern for the oldest child to train for teaching; younger members with the requisite academic potential could then enter other professional spheres.

17.   The name of this examination was changed in the post-war period to the Final Religious Examination of Secondary Pupils. In most Catholic secondary schools all pupils being presented for the Higher Leaving Certificate were expected to sit this examination whether they intended to enter teaching or not. (See NDSA 2, pp.3 and 15) With the expansion of post-intermediate pupils after 1960, adequate resources to administer this examination were not available, and it was discontinued.

18.   Lecturers involved in these courses included Drs. Treanor and Flood of the seminary (St. Peter's College, then at Bearsden) and Dr. W.E. Brown, chaplain to the Catholic students of Glasgow University.

19.   Bayne, J.   NSDA 18, p.17

CHAPTER SEVEN

A CHANGING COMMUNITY

AN EMERGING CATHOLIC SECONDARY SYSTEM

By the end of the inter-war period, a distinctive Catholic secondary sector was emerging. For the Church authorities, the need had been to set up a system in which both secular and religious education could be provided in ways satisfactory to Church and State authorities as well as to the Catholic community. Schools were required in fact to render tribute both to God and Caesar, at a time when educational standards were being raised to meet growing expectations, and when the Catholic secondary sector was expanding at an unprecedented rate through the availability of financial resources from the public purse. In the process of transformation to a dual-control system, it was essential that the schools should retain their distinctive character. "There can be only one justification for church schools, the conviction that they have benefits to confer which can be had nowhere else."(1)

In this evolution the Catholic secondary system was subject to several powerful formative influences.

By virtue of the transfer into the state system, it had accepted the standards and to some degree the aims of the State secondary schools, at least in the secular area. The State schools would set the standard which the Catholic system had to try to match. In the inter-war period the Scottish secondary schools were securely based. They had a firm foundation on an efficient system of primary education; they were able to demand a high standard of entry assessed by the Qualifying examination; they maintained a clear distinction between primary and secondary education, and accepted a further distinction, based on academic ability, between junior and senior levels of secondary work. They offered a curriculum academic in content, geared to the requirements of the universities and the national examination system. They recognised to a limited extent the need for religious education, but saw this as the responsibility of the parents and the Church, with both of which the schools had traditionally a sound relationship.

For some of the aims of the Catholic system the model thus presented seemed very appropriate, and the Catholic schools took on something of the aspect of the state schools. For most of the inter-war period a high priority had to be the production of a steady supply of graduates to staff the expanding secondary sector and to meet the clamant need for more highly qualified teachers in the primary schools. To this end an academic curriculum and demanding examination system was necessary. Additionally, it accorded with their selective nature, in that historically they had been able to provide for only a small minority of the Catholic population, and with the restricted curriculum which traditionally was all that they were able to offer. It was also an appropriate model for their second aim, which was to fit the Catholic community to take its place in those areas of commerce and industry where a higher standard of education than it had previously attained was required, and more generally to raise its educational and cultural standards.

However, there were two important respects in which the Catholic schools differed from their state counterparts, apart from those differences in accommodation and resources which were to be expected in a smaller system in the early stages of its development – namely, its attitude to religious education, and its ability to develop a junior secondary sector. With regard to the first, although the State schools historically had adopted a religious basis for their educational programme, the de facto situation was profoundly different from that acceptable to the Catholic community. "Religious teaching was not inspected by the Department. It had no place in the Leaving Certificate. The climate of opinion was changing, especially in appalled disillusionment brought by the massacres of the First World War. By the 'Thirties, Religious Instruction was allowed two periods a week in every Protestant school, but much of the teaching was superficial and unenthusiastic. The situation in Roman Catholic schools was different; spiritual matters were the reason for their existence."(2) With regard to the second, viz the development of a junior secondary sector, the Catholic schools were at a considerable disadvantage. During the 'Twenties and 'Thirties Catholic teachers came in the main from those longer-established secondary schools where the curriculum on offer was essentially academic. Neither St. Mungo's Academy nor St. Aloysius College had departments of commercial or technical education; St. Mungo's Academy did not have a gymnasium until session 1922-23. None of the major girls' schools had departments of Domestic Science or Commerce. Although Music and Art were taught, they were on the periphery of the curriculum and not in such a way as to lead to the pursuit of these subjects at higher levels. There was therefore at first no substantial flow of aspirants to teaching in these subject areas. Technical education was in no better plight. Although in the west of Scotland engineering in its many aspects occupied a very important place, Catholics were singularly absent from its more highly skilled ranks. There was thus no pool of skilled labour within the Catholic community from which a technical teaching force might have developed, or whose members might have given a lead to younger men to enter that field. When, after 1929, the Catholic sector began to expand at junior and senior level, a wider range of practical subjects was introduced into the schools. Departments of Art, Music, Commercial and Domestic Subjects, Technical and Physical Education appeared. When in the new buildings rooms and equipment for specialist subjects were provided on a scale far beyond anything previously available, the consequent demand for teachers was met to a very considerable extent by the employment of staff from the non-transferred schools.

The second model was that provided by the pre-existing Catholic secondary schools. In 1924-5, there were only 14 recognised Catholic secondary schools in the whole of Scotland,(3) 11 of them in the south-west. Of these 11, 9 were managed by Religious Teaching Orders. Most were single-sex schools(4), reflecting the constitution of the Orders themselves. Perhaps as a practical consequence the single-sex model was maintained for a time in the Catholic system. The new schools which opened in Dumbarton and Paisley after 1918 were set up as boys' schools, balancing the existing girls' schools in these towns; and in Lanarkshire, when Elmwood Convent attained full secondary status Our Lady's High School phased out its girls' classes. The religious schools were fee-paying, with a selective intake. Fees were low, reflecting the generally low economic status of the Catholic community. Competition for places was high. The education provided was academic in content, with a rather restricted curriculum in which language and literature, particularly the classical languages, were given greater emphasis than the natural sciences. The classical tradition in education was still generally strong in the 'Twenties, but was reinforced in the Catholic sector by the status of Latin in the life of the Church. It was also the case that because of limited human and material resources and restrictions of space, the schools had little capacity to develop practical subjects within the curriculum. (5)

The religious schools accepted it as axiomatic that a fundamental aim of education was the spiritual formation of the child. "To be worthy of the name, education must be directed to the development of the moral character of the child more than to the development of its intellectual faculties. 'Manners makyth Man', and the Catholic Church knows no other means of moral development than the christian religion with its motives, its sanctions and its practices." (6) An important implication of this aim was that teachers accepted a responsibility for the moral and spiritual welfare of their pupils extending far beyond the satisfying of their intellectual needs.

By 1939, the number of catholic secondary schools in the south-west had increased to 17, of which 11 were managed by the Orders, if St. Columba's High School Gourock where the headmaster was a Marist Brother is included. By that time there had been a great increase in the number of lay teachers, especially of men, at the secondary level. In addition to the new senior secondary schools which were mostly mixed and were staffed by lay teachers under lay headmasters, there was a considerable number of junior secondary schools the majority of which were similarly staffed. The schools managed by the Orders themselves had increased in size, but were more dependent than formerly on lay teachers.

Overall the dominance of the Religious Teaching Orders was diminishing, but their influence remained very great. Throughout the inter-war period the main source of supply had lain in the former pupils of the old-established secondary schools.(7) The basic intellectual and spiritual formation of the teaching body was therefore largely the work of the Religious Orders. Out of this body were to come the future principal teachers and head teachers of the developing catholic secondary sector. For many of them, it was the model of the catholic school and of catholic education presented to them in their own schooling that would guide them when charged with the responsibilities of establishing a new system.

The presence of the Orders in the schools was reassuring to parents and teachers alike. To the former they provided a guarantee of continuity in the content and manner of achievement of a christian education; and for the latter, a daily contact which was for many a source of inspiration or guidance, and a substitute at secondary level for the link with the clergy which their primary colleagues enjoyed. Members of Orders dedicated to the art and labour of education were able to devote themselves more completely than could most lay staff to the general welfare of their pupils, and were thus able to bring to the area of religious instruction a concern for christian formation which might otherwise have been lacking in the secondary sector.

The third major formative influence on the secondary schools was the relatively much larger Catholic primary sector, from which they drew their pupils and much of their staff, and with which they shared a basic concept of the fundamental aim of the educational process. This was the concept with which the adult population had grown up before 1918. In it, school, home and parish were firmly linked under the paternal leadership of the clergy; and although the official teaching of the Church regarded parents as the prime educators of their children, in this approach the responsibility of the teacher tended to become almost co-extensive with that of the parent. It was a system of community education having as its basis the parish unit.(8) The secondary system developed out of this pre-existing structure, and shared many of its attitudes. One practical consequence was that the distinction between primary and secondary education was less clearly marked in the Catholic sector than in the developing national system.

As the Catholic schools system expanded, particularly at the secondary level, the responsibility for preserving the religious character of the schools and for the religious education given in them devolved more and more on the lay teachers who constituted the majority of the staffs. New problems arose. In the senior secondary schools, teachers were faced with the problems of religious formation of increasing numbers of older pupils who were reaching to ever higher educational standards while in the junior secondary sector problems of a different order, associated with children of lower academic ability resident mainly in very socially deprived areas were also multiplying.

By the end of session 1938-39, the secondary system was coming under increasing pressure, particularly in the area of religious education.

A CHANGING COMMUNITY

The educational revolution set in train by the 1918 Act had to take place during a period of stress in the economic, political and cultural life of the community. Throughout the 'Twenties there was never less than 14% of the insured labour force of Scotland out of work. In the West Central belt in the 'Thirties unemployment averaged 25%.(9) World trade virtually collapsed, and with it sent what was left of the prosperity of the Clyde docks and ship-building industry, with reverberations throughout the heavy engineering industries. Lanarkshire in particular "had all the hallmarks of a depressed region, with a high out-migration rate, chronic structural unemployment and few growth points...during the 1920's the living standards either fell drastically or levelled out at a point where there was little or no margin left to spend on goods or services that were not part of the basic necessities of life."(10)

Because of the concentration of the Catholic population in the industrial areas and its disproportionate representation in the ranks of the unskilled and semi-skilled, the impact on it of the industrial depression was severe, with profound consequences for the cultural advance of the whole Scottish

Catholic community.

In the political arena, the Catholic body seemed not to have found its true voice by the mid 'Twenties. Although the shared sufferings of 1914-18 had helped to unite the nation, and although there had been a shift in interest towards the internal problems of poverty, unemployment, housing and education, the Irish question was still in 1922 the most emotive political issue in the west of Scotland. The events of Easter 1916, followed by Partition and civil war in Ireland, had unfortunate repercussions in Glasgow, and served to heighten the sectarian tensions which were never very far below the surface. There resulted deep disillusionment on the part of the Catholic community with the Liberals, the party of Government, and a consequent movement into the growing Labour Party, seen as its only alternative.In the aftermath of war the influence of the Labour Party had steadily increased, particularly in Glasgow where the Independent Labour Party gained 10 of the 15 seats in the General Election of 1922. Nationwide Labour votes doubled, almost entirely at the expense of the Liberal Party.(11)

Nevertheless there was for a time considerable hesitancy on the part of many Catholics about accepting the tenets of the Labour Party. The more politically active groups within the Church based their thinking on the teaching of the papal social encyclicals. In their attempts to give practical expression to their ideas they were greatly influenced by those English Catholic intellect-uals, among them such powerful personalities as Chesterton, Belloc, Ronald Knox, Christopher Dawson and Eric Gill, who sought to propound a christian rather than a socialist solution to the political and economic problems of the day. Between this southern group and the radical socialists of the I.L.P., with whom many of the active Scottish Catholics were in sympathy, there yawned a cultural divide of cosmic proportions. Those who aligned themselves with the southern influence were in fact in the main stream of the Church's social teaching. In the eyes of successive Popes Communism was the enemy to be opposed above all others. "The burning question for many was how radical can a Catholic be and remain in good standing with the Church?" Opposition to socialist theory was based on the right to private property, seen by some to be absolute and inalienable, a view supported by "highly edited quotations from Thomas Aquinas, recommended by Pope Leo XIII as setting theological criteria for the church's members."(12)

This uncertainty, combined with the emotiveness of the Irish situation which inhibited Catholic support for the Conservative Party, resulted in a continua-tion of the tendency already strong in the community, to hold itself aloof from deep involvement in political developments, and to relate its activities to particular issues immediately relevant to its own life. "There is reason to suspect that then, as often later, the political positions of the Catholic community were pragmatic rather than ideologically based. The main issue apart from the Irish question was in the field of education."(13)

Tension related to the sectarian divisions in society occasionally surfaced. The possibility of conflict existed at three levels - theological, political and physical - and was often stimulated at each of these by the fierce commitment of the Orange Order and the predictable Green reaction. On the one hand, "many Orangemen do not fulfil the requirement of the Order that they be practising Christians, and fewer still would care to pay attention to its condemnation of foul language, but none would be unaware of its attitude to catholics"(14); and on the other, "in the Ancient Order of Hibernians there was a strong political affiliation, which was a kind of cement too, because however lax they might be in the practice of their religious duties they never flagged in their loyalties to their political stances."(15)

The 1918 Act itself was a source of alarm to a section of the Protestant community, and one cause of the rise of the Protestant Action movement which became strong enough to be represented on both Glasgow and Edinburgh Corporations. In 1934 Councillor Alex. Ratcliffe proposed at a meeting of the Education Committee in Glasgow that the Corporation "make representations to all the Town and County Councils in Scotland....with a view to ending the present sectarian school system."(16) Opposition led by P.J. Dollan, supported by Rosslyn Mitchell, eventually carried the day, but a significantly large minority (35 out of 79) had supported the motion.(17)

Nevertheless there were signs of some weakening of tension between the religious communities. The Roman Catholic Relief Act 1926 received powerful support on its passage through Parliament from the Rev. J. Barr, M.P. for Kilmarnock (18); and the Catholic bishops were able to win the support of some sections of the Protestant community in their attempt to achieve a non-violent reaction to the Protestant Action campaign.(19) Above all, the operation of the 1918 Act went a long way towards reducing the mistrustful attitude of the Catholic minority towards their protestant neighbours.

Housing then was possibly the most intractable of all the problems facing Glasgow. Piecemeal industrial over-development in Victorian times followed by prolonged failure to conquer the ensuing blight had produced a social problem unmatched elsewhere in the United Kingdom. By the mid-Twenties the major industries around whose sites the conglomerations of tenement houses had grown were in decline, and the local economy was in the grip of deep-rooted structural unemployment. In the absence of an effective policy of industrial re-development, the local authority channelled its efforts into education and housing. Through the Wheatley Act it gained the power to tackle the housing problem on an increased scale, and developed a heavy commitment to subsidised house-building long before the advent of a Labour-controlled Council.   "...Glasgow built several housing estates on the periphery of the city (Mosspark, Knightswood, Riddrie among them) as well as building on sites within the city. The theoretical basis ....was that by beginning well up the social and income scale, the new estates would add to the amenity of the city while releasing houses vacated by the more fortunate for occupancy by those who were less so. The Corporation ruled by the 'Moderates' took its tenants....on a selective basis; they were largely skilled and semi-skilled men and white-collared workers.... In other areas the policy followed was quite different....Blackhill ....exemplified the problem.... In part Blackhill came to represent....the segration of the socially difficult.... There were thus two principal kinds of development....new and well-furbished estates....around the perimeter, and other sites where no real new beginning was possible, and where old problems were ominously perpetuated and compounded...."(20)

The selective policy for tenants in the "new and well-furbished" estates operated unfavourably in respect of the Catholic community, which was under-represented in the ranks of the skilled or semi-skilled men or of the white-collar workers. One result was an emphasising of its existing tendency to settle firmly into its own enclaves usually close to the historic parish churches.

Between 1918 and 1939 only 14 new Catholic parishes were instituted in the whole of the south-west (see Fig. 4) despite the hiatus during the years spanning the First World War. Three of Glasgow's five new parishes were in new suburban areas (Riddric 1924, Knightswood 1927, King's Park 1934) the others (Possilpark 1932, Royston 1939) in re-housing areas. Remarkably, in view of the current high birth rate in the Catholic community, there was relatively little change in the population of the older city parishes, where the total declined from about 194,000 to 192,000 by 1939 (Appendix 1). Figures for the primary school population reflect the same situation. A similar stability in numbers and geographical location existed also in Dumbartonshire where no new parishes were founded, and in Motherwell where there were three (Harthill, Biggar, Viewpark) to accommodate a slight increase in total population from about 96,000 to around 100,000. The position in the Paisley diocesan area was not substantially different. The number of parishes increased from 14 to 17 (Bishopton 1926, Greenock 1924 and 1934), and the total population by some 15%. The very large parishes in the Paisley and Port Glasgow-Greenock districts rivalled in numbers the largest parishes of Glasgow.

These figures conceal the effect of emigration on the Catholic body. "...from 1871 to 1976 the net emigration from Scotland exceeded 2 million. This...reached its peak in 1921-30. At the census of 1930 and 1931 in U.S.A., England and Wales, and Canada, there were just over 1,000,000 people enumerated in these countries who had been born in Scotland.... the emigration of 1921-30 from Scotland was principally to other parts of the United Kingdom. It is a reasonable assumption that catholics were at least proportionately represented in this great movement, and ...because of their circumstances .....may have been proportionately over-represented."(21) "The great depression of the 1920's resulted in 128,000 Catholics leaving Scotland for the fresh woods and pastures new of America, Canada, Australia and New Zealand. More than half of them were from the Archdiocese of Glasgow."(22) It may well have been the case that the natural increase in the population was closely balanced by emigration losses.

THE CONTRIBUTION OF THE EVOLVING SECONDARY EDUCATION SECTOR TO THE CHANGING COMMUNITY

The image of Glasgow and the industrialised south-west in the inter-war period often emerges as an amalgam of poverty, unemployment, social and political unrest, sectarian bitterness, decaying housing and domestic squalor. Yet it was a time of great educational advance, lively exploration of political and social ideas, and vigorous local politics. In Glasgow seven daily and four principal weekly newspapers were produced and read;(23) live theatre flourished in the city's eleven playhouses, and cinemas abounded. The gramophone and 'wireless' were potent factors in the extension of cultural horizons. Amateur athletics and drama also flourished. If a major quality of a civilised community is, as has been said, energy,(24) Glasgow and the west could lay claim at least to that attribute.

In spite of the hardships and turbulence of the times, the Catholic community

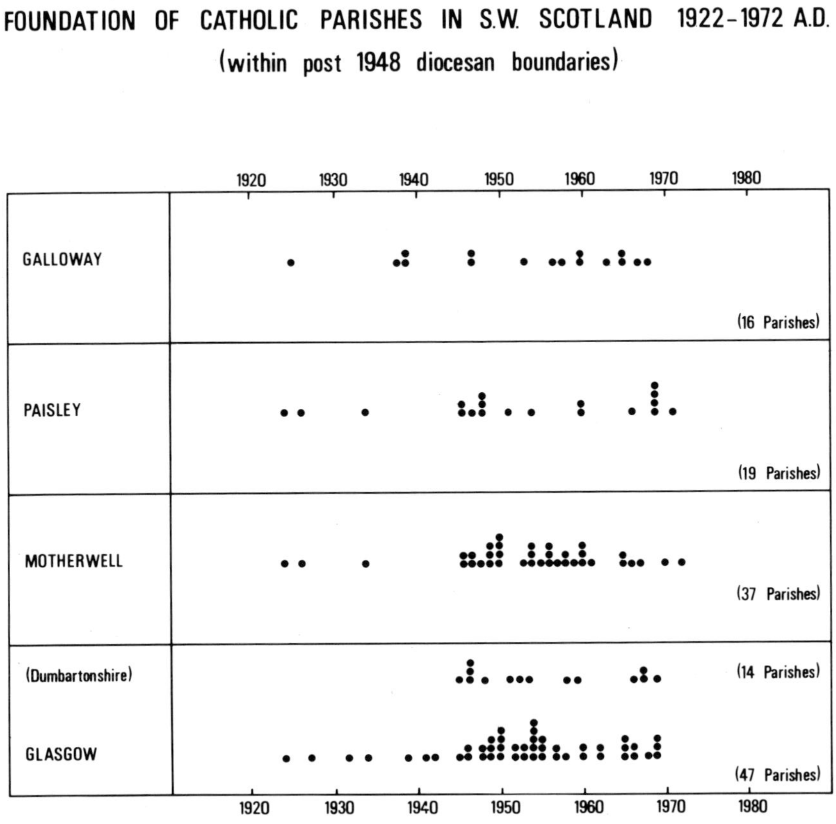
FOUNDATION OF CATHOLIC PARISHES IN S.W. SCOTLAND 1922-1972 A.D.
(within post 1948 diocesan boundaries)
1920
1930
1940
1950
1960
1970
1980
GALLOWAY
(16 Parishes)
PAISLEY
(19 Parishes)
MOTHERWELL
(37 Parishes)
(Dumbartonshire)
(14 Parishes)
GLASGOW
(47 Parishes)

Fig. 4

gained in status. "The period between 1918 and 1939 was one of growing activity in all directions.... a new degree of social mobility was being experienced by the Scots-Irish community."(25) In this advance there can be no gainsaying the importance of the Education (Scotland) Act of 1918. The financial incentives for pupils to remain at school beyond the statutory leaving age brought an immediate and sustained rise in the rolls of the Catholic secondary schools, with a consequent demand for more teachers. Parents were relieved of a financial burden they had carried since 1872, and teachers found themselves in a position of security and affluence undreamt of by their predecessors. Secondary teachers in particular, a small minority in a teaching force of more than 2,000, were accorded a very high standing. A new spirit of confidence began to grow in the community at large, fostered to a considerable degree by the teaching body.(26)

Some indicators of the influence of the teaching profession in the general life of the community are to be seen in the increased involvement of Catholics in university life, in the expansion of and in their participation in lay Catholic action as well as in a wide range of cultural activities.

Once the flow of ex-servicemen of World War 1 into the University had subsided, a period ensued in which the number of Catholic students appears to have been very small indeed. "In 1926 the number of Catholic students you could almost count on your fingers... It would certainly be less than twenty, and that would include all the Faculties."(27) By the end of that decade that situation was changing, and thereafter numbers steadily increased to the extent that in 1930 a chaplaincy for Catholic students was set up and the Rev. W.E. Brown installed as the first post-Reformation Catholic chaplain.(See Appendix 3) The majority pursued their university career in circumstances of extreme financial hardship. "There were many who stood uneasily between two worlds, the first in their family to have received a higher education, aware of the financial sacrifice their higher education required from their families, sometimes showing in their bodies the affects of poverty and unemployment....the great majority took little part in the life of the University. They usually lived at home.....using the chaplaincy centres....as shelters ....in which those who had the strength might attempt to integrate the various elements in their life, and those who lacked it might rest."(28) Student grants in the modern form did not exist. The vast majority of catholic students could not afford to join the Students' Union, and travelling expenses left them little to spend on lunches; most had to make do with 'pieces' consumed furtively in obscure corners. Indeed the Catholic student was an inheritor of the Scottish tradition of low living and sometimes high thinking characteristic of an earlier generation; but these products of the industrial revolution carried no sacks of meal.(29)

Most of these pioneers in higher education were destined for the teaching profession, and as their numbers increased their influence and example became ever more important, especially in those many cases where an older member of a family, having gained a teaching post, was able to give financial as well as moral support to younger siblings. In time many were able to undertake the more expensive training needed for entry into other professions, supported by older relatives in teaching. The fact that the average age of marriage was then considerably later than now also helped. Towards the end of the 'Thirties the trend into other occupations became more marked, assisted by the circumstance that the supply of teachers for the catholic schools had begun to outstrip the rate of provision of new posts.

Gradually a stratum of more highly educated Catholics emerged. As a result, many of the existing Catholic organisations were revitalised, and others came into being. In almost all of them the new breed of Catholic teacher played a leading part. Where the organisation was parochially based, the historic partnership between clergy and teachers remained strong; but there also came into being others pursuing secular rather than religious objectives, whose origins were often the result of lay initiative and whose management remained in lay hands. Among these were athletic and dramatic societies, professional associations, F.P. associations, and coteries whose interests were primarily literary or political.(30) Altogether a new dimension of social life was brought to the catholic community. While it could perhaps be said that in these groups something of the ghetto mentality appeared to linger on, they manifested also a consciousness of the richness and power of their christian heritage, and a growing conviction that the Catholic community had a specific contribution to make to the cultural and social life of society at large. This was an attitude which reached out to and drew strength from the life of the church in other parts of the world. It was independent of any political ideology, but had practical implications for the political sphere.

Overall the dominance of Catholic social life by the clergy began to diminish, but the traditional relationship between teachers and clergy established before 1918 remained as strong as ever.

It was in this context that there emerged, for a time at least, a new political ideal which seemed to be particularly attractive to the Catholics of the west of Scotland. Distributism was an attempt to find a middle way between Liberalism and Socialism, both of which had come under the strictures of the Vatican. It looked for a solution to contemporary problems of political and economic organisation, rejecting equally the more fashionable alternatives of Capitalism and Communism. "It stood for the individual in an increasingly collectivist age; ...demanded a more equitable distribution of property and even of land.... advocated support for the small shopkeeper and small businessman....insisted that industrial organisation should be based on the principles of profit-sharing and co-ownership rather than on monopolistic capitalism or nationalisation and were perhaps early advocates of industrial democracy..."(31)

The principal expression of the Distributist ideal is to be found in Belloc's seminal work "The Servile State", published in Edinburgh in 1912, the theme of which was repeated by Hayek thirty years later. Distributism had a strong attraction for the emerging Catholic graduate class, possibly because of its relationship with Liberalism as well as from the fact that it offered an alternative to Socialism which presented difficulties of conscience to many. Its basis of abstract principles appealed to a community with little or no practical experience of large scale control of property or industrial enterprises, and seemed to point towards an integrated approach to social organisation consonant with the social teaching of the Catholic Church.

Although there were other signs in Scotland as elsewhere in Britain of an awakening of intellectual activity within the Catholic community, it is clear that the stimulus here came from the assimilation of a number of distinguished converts, among them Compton Mackenzie, J.S. Phillimore, Sir Edmund Whittaker, Halliday Sutherland and many others. Of those from within the community itself who were able to make some contribution to its intellectual enrichment, most were members of the teaching profession.(32)

Increased involvement in tertiary education during the relatively short inter-war period led on the one hand to a greater awareness of the challenges to the orthodox Catholic outlook that were emerging from revolutionary advances in science and politics, and on the other to a more informed interest in traditional modes of religious thinking and practice. Among educated Catholics loyalty to the institutional church remained strong, and was possibly their most marked characteristic. Although clerical domination diminished, there was in the educated elite wide acceptance and even appreciation of the Church's authority as much or even more than in other sections of the community. Lay organisations dedicated to the defence or exposition of the Church's teaching in theological or socio-political matters proliferated, and in them the new breed of graduates was dominant.(33)

Towards the end of the 'Thirties however signs of dissatisfaction with the 'ancien régime' emerged. "Fideism was being challenged as experience of tertiary education increased....not only by the middle class, but by politically involved members of the working class, both groups being less and less disposed to accept the old type of clerical authoritarianism.... The challenge was muted however even during the tension created by the Spanish Civil War and its fuller expression delayed until after the Second World War."(34)

NOTES

1.   Scotland, J.   History of Scottish Education Vol.2 p.42
2.   Ibid   p.82 See also NDSA 19
3.   Treble J.H.   IR (1978) 2 p.130
4.   See NDSA 11, p.3 and NDSA 16 p.16 for comments on single-sex schools.
      Also Pope Pius XI Christian Education of Youth
5.   For comments on the curriculum of the catholic secondary schools,
      see NDSA 5a pp.10-12; NDSA 2 p.5; NDSA 12 p.3; NDSA 17 p.2
6.   S.N.D.   Sister Mary of St. Philip 1825-1905. Longmans
                            1920
7.   See Appendix 5
8.   NDSA 2, 5 and 6 have considerable references to the pre-1918 catholic
      primary schools
9.   Checkland, S.G.   The Upas Tree p.35
10.   Treble, J.H.   IR XXXI(1) p.39
11.   Middlemas, R.K.   The Clydesiders p.179
12.   Ross, A.   IR XXIX p.43
13.   Ibid
14.   Murray, W.   The Old Firm p.78
15.   Murray, J.J.   NDSA 5a p.15
16.   Education Committee Minute 2418 17/8/34. Also Ross, op. cit. pp.48-49
17.   O'Hagan, A.I.   NDSA 9, p.13 and Murray, W. op. cit. pp.136-8
                            also refer
18.   McGhee, S.   IR XVI(1) Carfin and the Roman Catholic Relief
                            Act 1926
19.   Ross, A.   Loc. cit.
20.   Checkland, S.G.   Op. cit. pp.38-39
21.   Darragh, J.   IR XXIX(2) Table 4, p.231
22.   Observer Centenary Supplement   Special Correspondent
23.   Glasgow Herald, Bulletin, Daily Record, Daily Express, Evening Times,
      Evening News, Evening Citizen, Sunday Mail, Sunday Post, Weekly News,
      Glasgow Observer. There were also at least two local papers.
24.   Clark, Sir Kenneth   Civilisation
25.   Ross, A.   Loc. cit.
26.   Ibid
27.   McKee, J.J.   NDSA 2 p.7
28.   Ross, A.   IR XXIX p.45.
29.   See also Shanks, Islay D. College Courant Vol. 25 Martinmas 1953 for
      an account of the experience of students in the 'Thirties.
30.   The Apostleship of the Sea was founded in Glasgow, as was the Knights
      of St. Columba. St. Peter's Amateur Athletic Club, St. Christopher
      Wheelers, The Marian Players Amateur Dramatic Society, Aquinas Society
      are examples of other groups.
31.   Bayne, I.O.   Scottish Catholic Observer 9/5/1980
32.   Among the teachers could be mentioned journalist and pamphleteer Colm
      Brogan, novelist George Friel, playwright Paul V. Carroll, composer
      John McQuaid and especially J.E. Handley, who was Brother Clare of
      the Marist Brothers. His scholarly work was carried out while he
      was a fully active member of staff of St. Mungo's Academy as Assistant,
      later Principal Teacher of English and finally as Headmaster. His
      published work includes The Irish in Scotland (1945) The Irish in
      Modern Scotland (1947), Scottish Farming in the XVIII Century (1953)

The Agriculture Revolution in Scotland (1963) The Navvy in Scotland (1970) A History of St. Mungo's Academy (1958) and A History of St. Mary's Boys' School, Calton.

33.   Particularly the Catholic Truth Society, Catholic Social Guild and Catholic Evidence Guild.

34.   Ross, A.   Loc. cit. p.50

CHAPTER EIGHT

INTERLUDE: THE WAR YEARS 1939-45

During session 1938-39 ominous shadows were being cast by events which were to come. In May 1938 a Government Committee had been set up to look at the problems of moving the population from areas likely to be exposed to air attack in the event of war. After the signing in September of the non-agression pact at Munich its work took on a new urgency, and by January 1939 local authorities had received details of an evacuation scheme to be put into operation in the event of an emergency. The country was divided into sending, receiving and neutral areas. Sending areas, presumed to be specially vulnerable, were Edinburgh, Rosyth, Glasgow, Clydebank and Dundee, with a total population of 1.76 million and an average density of 14,000 per sq. mile; receiving areas, regarded as relatively safe from aerial attack,contained a population of 1.8 million at an average density of 100 per sq. mile. Glasgow's receiving areas were in Aberdeen, Argyll, Ayr, Bute, Dumfries, Kinross, Kirkcudbright, Lanark, Perth, Renfrew, Stirling and Wigtown; and Clydebank's, in Argyll and Dumbarton. Neutral areas within these counties were excluded. After May 1941, Greenock, Port Glasgow and Dumbarton also became sending areas.

Evacuation arrangements were to be made for children of school and pre-school age, teachers, helpers, mothers, expectant mothers and adult blind persons. It was estimated that half of those evacuated would be school children, and that responsibility for their education would rest on the Education Authorities of the receiving areas: "It was expected that...the double shift system would suffice to absorb the incoming children, but that in many districts full-time education for the native and incoming children would be possible by utilising the existing school accommodation to its maximum capacity."[1]

As far as possible, families were to remain united, and therefore secondary pupils would travel with the pupils of a specific primary school, normally that attended by the younger members of their own family. They would be expected to attend the secondary school of the receiving area.

In the south-west, and indeed throughout the country, most of the Catholic population were located in the sending areas, with the remainder in neutral areas. Seventeen of the Catholic senior secondary schools were in like case. Receiving areas were almost totally devoid of Catholic population, and would be terra incognita to evacuated Catholic families.

93

Throughout 1938-39 the repercussions of defence preparations were being felt in the schools. In one receiving area, for example, "on Jan. 19 1939 headmasters were asked to meet to arrange the taking of a census in the town. This would establish how many children could be evacuated there and who would accommodate them...primary teachers would carry out this census...trenches...were being dug in various places, and gas-masks issued."(2) And in a sending area, "on March 20 1939...Air Ministry...began preparations on our playing fields for its inclusion in a balloon barrage area...the headmaster's attendance at the Education Office...to hear details...for the evacuation of children...was another indication that the shadows were deepening."(3)

On Thursday 24 August 1939 a non-aggression pact between Hitler and Stalin was signed, and World War Two, so long awaited so fearfully by so many, erupted. Parliament reassembled six weeks ahead of schedule. France completed mobilis-ation. Teachers in evacuation areas were ordered to report to school on Saturday 26 August carrying gas-masks. On that day, the Anglo-Polish Pact of mutual assistance was signed. Schools reopened after the summer vacation on Monday 28 August for a rehearsal of evacuation procedures. On 31 August the announce-ment was made; "Evacuation takes place on Friday, Saturday, Sunday, 1st, 2nd, 3rd September." On Friday the scheme went into operation, and on Sunday 3rd September 1939 war was declared.

"Altogether 175,812 persons were evacuated in Scotland in September 1939.... From Glasgow 120,000 were removed in three days...about 30,000 Glasgow school children registered for evacuation did not report at the assembly schools.... In Clydebank about a quarter of those not evacuated had registered for evacuation."(4)

First reaction to this massive exercise was to hail it as an outstanding success. On 4 September the Glasgow Herald claimed that "the evacuation of children will be remembered as an example of perfect organisation and grand staff work." The Secretary of State said on the same day "In these last three days more class and caste barriers have been swept away than at any time during the last hundred years."(5) Nevertheless by 9 September the trek back to the cities was under way. By 15 September it was in full flood, and on 19 September a request was made to the Government to allow Glasgow schools to reopen. "30% of the school children evacuated had returned by the end of September, 75% by Christmas...another 15% by Easter.... The supplementary evacuation was a failure.... In February 1940 a new scheme was announced...only if air raids developed on a serious scale...were schools to be evacuated...elaborate arrangements were made...gas-mask drill was repeatedly performed...shelter exercises were rehearsed; in some schools teachers began to wonder when a little time might be salvaged for the education of registered children."(6)

Air-raid shelters were erected in playgrounds and in the neighbourhood of schools, and attendance resumed on a voluntary basis and in limited assembly. By April 1940 attendance at city schools became compulsory to the extent of available accommodation and air-raid protection. The Leaving Certificate examination was held as customary in March, with papers set by local panels and corrected by teachers under the direction of a regional board of assessors. (7)

A moment did arrive when the work of the authorities was put to the test. "Special schemes of evacuation were carried out in Glasgow and Clydeside sending areas after the severe raids in March and May 1941....Under emergency conditions the machinery of evacuation worked more smoothly...."(8)

The following account of the air-raids on Clydebank is taken from a school project held in the local history section of Clydebank Burgh Library:

"At 9.12 pm on Thursday 13 March 1941, the air-raid sirens wailed.... Such warnings were fairly regular and had brought no danger since July 1940 when a lone raider dropped a bomb on a Yoker tenement, killing three people. The night of the 13th was the first full-scale terror Blitz in Scotland.... Havoc was wrought for over nine hours and it was not till 6.00 am the following morning that the "All-Clear" was sounded.... One of the first buildings to be hit by incendiaries was Radnor Park School which was completely destroyed.... Clydebank was still burning when the Luftwaffe returned the following night.... Of the 12,000 homes in the area, only about eight were left untouched, 4,300 being completely destroyed. It is estimated that at least 700 people died. The population dropped from 50,000 to 2,000, mainly due to the evacuation of those who had lost belongings and dwelling houses."

The general disruption of education at the time can be sensed from the recorded experiences of some individual schools and teachers. The following extract is from the Inspectorate's Triennial Report on St. Bonaventure's Junior Secondary School, Glasgow dated 27/10/1943.

"The school was opened in August 1939 with a primary roll of 570 and 244 pupils in the first year of the secondary course. On September 1st evacuation of some 400 pupils took place to Wigtownshire, and during the autumn session groups of 20 pupils attending voluntarily were taught in school. In March 1940 the post-primary classes from St. Luke's School were transferred to this school, and in April compulsory part-time attendance was introduced, all classes except the qualifying being half-time. In November 1940 full-time instruction was given to eight second year secondary classes and to the qualifying class, and half-time to all other classes. In January 1941 full-time was established for all secondary classes. Serious interruption was caused by the raids in March and May. Since Easter 1942 all classes have been on full-time."

The History of St. Mary's Boys' School, Calton, records:

"By October 1939 classes of 20 pupils each on a weekly timetable of 5 hours were being taught.... As the weeks passed...the evacuees drifted back...the need for a closer approximation to normal education facilities became more acute. Air-raid shelters were rapidly erected...by April 1940 the suspension of compulsory attendance was rescinded. In a few months the pupils were back to normal, each coming to school with his gas-mask slung behind him and air-raid drill became a regular and pleasant diversionary measure.... In April 1941 a further evacuation took place as a result of air-raids on the city. This time it was only a handful that went to the new (receiving) areas... By 1942 the school was functioning on ordinary lines (except that)...teachers' summer holidays were curtailed to contrive that their fire-watching duties continued all the year round."(9)

At St. Mungo's Academy a canvass conducted in the first week of October 1939 disclosed that 201 post-intermediate and 565 intermediate pupils were available for instruction out of an approximate 1,000. By the end of October a scheme was operating

"by which 6th Years came in the forenoons, 5th Years in the afternoons and each class of 4th years attended twice a week. By December 100 3rd Year pupils were taking instructions on two half days per class each week, and before Christmas 2nd and 1st Year boys were following a skeleton timetable.   By mid-January, 6th, 5th and 4th Years were on full, and 1st, 2nd and 3rd Years on half-time instruction... The school remained open for half the day during July and August.... The staff staggered the fortnight's holiday that was permitted to them.... After the heavy air-raids on Glasgow on 13 and 14 March 1941, a second evacuation took place...in which 190 pupils took part. This proved to be more successful than the first...largely because the secondary pupils went as a group and were accompanied by their own teachers and taught by them on a sharing basis with the local school."(10)

From St. Ninian's High School, Kirkintilloch, a rare example of a catholic secondary school in a receiving area, comes the following:

"On September 11, 1939, the first day at school of the war, ...97 pupils did not have gas-masks.... Over 600 pupils did have them with them that morning ....on the night of June 24-25 1940 the first air-raid on the town took place... 1941....no meat for (school) dinners, only potatoes, beans or soup. Three hundred and fifty beds allocated to be stored....fire-watching became a necessity...attendance on Friday 14 March about one-third in Primary and less than one-half in Secondary...due to blitz the previous evening on Clydeside area....450 evacuees to be fed communally and sleep here until billeting had been completed....most of Clydebank schools were demolished or useless....24 March....school reopened after having been closed since 14 March....enrolled 93 evacuees from Glasgow and Clydebank Catholic schools....by April 1941 roll had leapt to close on 1,000.... Little is known of evacuees' reaction to the new situation. Headmaster comments on their being backward by as much as half a year."(11)

In 1939 some 70% of the total Catholic population of Scotland was located in the most industrial and congested settlements of the south-west, the majority in Glasgow itself. The main centre of Catholic secondary education was in the schools of the city which, as a port, centre of communications and of industry, was an obvious target for enemy action. The disruption of secondary education as a result of evacuation, which affected all the schools of the sending areas, therefore bore heavily on a major portion of the Catholic sector of the whole nation. It was however probably the case that the more far-reaching consequences for educational standards in general, including those of the secondary schools, resulted from the impact of wartime conditions on the primary schools, which suffered severely especially in the most crowded areas of Clydeside. Of St. John's School in Port Glasgow, for example, it is recorded that "from October 1939 to June 1942 the school was maintained on a half-time basis.. After the Blitz of 1941....many pupils took up residence in safer parts of Scotland."(12) With disruption on this scale the educational attainments at primary level were bound to fall, with predictable consequences for the secondary sector.

The evacuation scheme had inbuilt difficulties for the Catholic sector. Because the vast majority of Catholics were located in the sending or neutral zones, one objective of the scheme "to match householders and evacuees according to social class and religion"(13) was clearly impossible of achievement for them. And since there were few Catholic secondary schools in receiving areas, it was inevitable that the vast majority of Catholic evacuees would find themselves in a scholastic environment very different from that to which they were accustomed. While such an experience need not necessarily have been to their detriment, given time for the emotional, intellectual and curricular adjustment that the situation demanded, the fact is that in the general break-down of the evacuation operation this period of adjustment rarely occurred.(14)

WAR AND PEACE 1942-1945

By the summer of 1942 the war had entered a new phase. Victory at Alamein heralded the end of hostilities in North Africa, and thereafter the main theatre of operations contracted gradually into the heartlands of Europe.

The affects of wartime conditions on schools increased. More male teachers became liable for call-up for national service, as the age of reservation was gradually raised. School staffs were seriously depleted, and retired teachers pressed into service to fill the gaps. Many young women graduates were asked to shoulder burdens formerly carried only by the most experienced men. Single-sex boys' schools were particularly affected. (15) Schools took over allotments and worked at grain and potato harvests. "Pupils from upper classes suspended study periodically to prepare ration books and identity cards.... The debilitating effects of the war - black-out, restriction of food, the worries of evacuation and so on - induced the medical authorities to subject the school population to a periodical examination by radiography." (16) An early casualty was the proposal to raise the school leaving age to 15. Emergency arrangements for the control of the Leaving Certificate Exam-ination were introduced - a consequence of as well as a contribution to a decline in academic standards.

In the catholic secondary sector the impact of war-time conditions was severe, and its leading edge in the more heavily congested areas of Clydeside subjected to maximum upheaval. New schools founded in the years immediately preceding the outbreak of war were disrupted before they had time to become properly established.(17) A high proportion of the Catholic secondary teaching force in 1939 consisted of men who had qualified as teachers in the peak years of the middle and late 'Thirties, and therefore belonged to age-groups liable to be called up for national service as the war progressed. (One result of this was that many who survived war service did not return to teach in Scottish schools. Some sought other careers in Britain, others emigrated).

Many primary schools were closed or kept on a part-time basis for lengthy periods, sometimes to be measured in years rather than months. There was a constant turn-over of staff through call-up as well as through movement to and from evacuation areas. Many schools were bereft of male staff, and many came to rely on the services of elderly retired teachers, some of whom continued in service beyond the age of eighty years. Attendance of pupils was more than usually irregular, and delinquency increased, a consequence also of the reduction in parental control. Attainment in school suffered, and preparation for secondary work was seriously affected. "In spite of the difficulties, great efforts were made in the war years to maintain ordinary standards at least in the basic subjects. It is now clear that this aim was not fully achieved....at the primary stage proficiency in written composition, arithmetic and power to comprehend what is read was not yet (in 1947) up to pre-war standard."(18).

War-time exigencies tended to weaken the barriers that still existed between the Catholic minority and the community as a whole. In all kinds of ways, Catholic people at every level were brought more closely than before into contact with the rest of the nation, with a resultant extension of their mental and social horizons. In the armed forces, many men were provided with a training which opened up for them new vistas of activity on their return to civilian life. Many found wives furth of Scotland. The Catholic population acquired a new sense of "belonging" in the national life, and a new sense of unity with its neighbours. The ghetto mentality, in so far as it continued to exist, suffered a sea-change.

Questions of conscience raised by total war could not be ignored. Within the expanded work-force of Clydeside's revitalised heavy industries, the activity of the British Communist Party increased, supporting or opposing in turn the war effort of the "imperialist and capitalist powers" in obedience to the dictates of the USSR.(19) This evoked a Catholic response in the shape of the Catholic Workers Guild, formed in 1941. "It gained a good representation from the light and heavy industries....anticipated the Young Catholic Workers movement (20) by starting an Apprentice Guild as an antidote to....the Young Communist League.... War service took its toll of members and the movement collapsed.... The need for such an organisation was plain.... It was difficult ....to find any group of men who had not been affected in large or small degrees by the incessant Marxist propaganda, so long a feature of the west of Scotland .... They had been given a first impression of life which remained hard to eradicate. At the same time they were unconscious that the views they held were totally opposed to Catholic doctrine."(21)

During the war years the number of university students dwindled (See Appendix 3) and the number of teachers completing training fell drastically. During the six war-time sessions Downhill Training College awarded 484 teaching certificates, 240 of them for secondary work.

THE EDUCATION (SCOTLAND) ACT 1945

As with the first GREAT WAR, the final year of World War Two saw a major Education Act reaching the Statute Book. The Education (Scotland) Act of 1945 following on the 1944 Act for England and Wales, aimed at bringing the law in Scotland in line with the general policy in Britain, while retaining the distinctive features of the Scottish system. It brought in the following important measures:

"The school leaving age was to be raised to 15 and later to 16 years; adequate and efficient provision of free primary, secondary and further education was to be made; Junior Colleges were to be set up for the compulsory part-time education of young persons of 15 to 18; milk and meals were to be provided in all schools; the Minimum National Salary Scale for teachers would be abolished; marriage would no longer be a bar to the employment of women teachers."

It attempted to define primary and secondary education.

"Primary education means progressive elementary education in such subjects as may be proscribed in the Code, regard being had to the age, ability and aptitude of the pupils concerned, and such education shall be given in primary schools or departments.

Secondary education means progressive courses of instruction of such length and in such subjects as may be approved in terms of the Code as appropriate to the age, aptitude and ability of the pupils who have been promoted from primary schools and departments, and to the period for which they may be expected to remain at school. Such courses shall be given in secondary schools or departments."(22)

Under the Act every Education Authority was required to submit a promotion scheme for approval by the Secretary of State, which would detail the method adopted for promoting pupils from primary to secondary education, and the means employed for ascertaining the kind of courses from which each pupil would be likely to benefit. Primary, secondary and further education would be free, but fees could be charged in a limited number of schools without prejudice however to the prior necessity of adequate provision of free education.

The raising of the school leaving age from 14 to 15 which had been postponed as a consequence of the outbreak of war, was introduced in April 1947. The passing of the Act was one of the last legislative decisions taken by the war-time Government. The General Election of 1945 resulted in a sweeping victory for the Labour Party, by this time the political if not the spiritual home of the majority of the Catholic community.

NOTES

1.   Boyd, Wm. (Editor)   Evacuation in Scotland, SCRE XXII, p.12
2.   Maguire, C.T. and   The Story of a School, p.32. A Short History of St.
          S.V. Murray.   Ninian's High School Kirkintilloch, Deacon Bros.
                                 1974.
3.   Handley, J.E.   History of St. Mungo's Academy, 1858–1958, p.181.
4.   SCRE XXII, p.31
5.   Glasgow Herald, 4 Sept. 1939.
6.   SCRE XXII, pp.33–34.
7.   Handley, J.E.   Op. Cit., pp. 183–4.
8.   SCRE XXII, p.35.
9.   Handley, J.E.   History   of   St.   Mary's   Boys   School,   Calton,
                                 pp.38–39.
10.   Handley, J.E.   History   of   St.   Mungo's   Academy,   pp.190–191.
        See also Sister Francis (NDSA No. 11, p.15), NDSA No. 2 p.16. NDSA
                                 No.6 p.19, NDSA No. 16 pp 13–14, NDSA No. 19
                                 p.7, NDSA No.9 pp.3–4, No.10 pp.10–11.
11.   Maguire, G.T. and   Op. cit., pp.34–38.
          S.V. Murray.
12.   Centenary Brochure Parish of St. John the Baptist, Port Glasgow, p.50.
13.   SCRE XXII   p.74.
14.   Ibid   p.60
        "From only 3 districts out of 76 is it reported that any attempt was
        made to match evacuees and hosts on a social or religious basis, in
        the vast majority of districts it was quite impossible to do anything
        about it. Especially was this true with Roman Catholic children who
        had to be sent to districts that were overwhelmingly Protestant."
        See also A.I. O'Hagan (NDSA No. 9, pp.3–4).
15.   In St. Mungo's Academy 34 members of staff were called up for war
        service.

        In St. Bonaventure's Junior Secondary School:

        "The three-monthly system of evacuation duty has entailed frequent
        changes of teacher. Seven men were called to the Forces, and the number
        of inexperienced teachers is unduly large. Of 28 teachers in the
        secondary division, 19 had only provisional recognition, and of 16
        in the primary staff, 10 were probationers."
        H.M.I. Report S.E.D. 29.10.1943.
16.   Handley, J.E.   History of St. Mungo's Academy, pp.190–191.
17.   See J.J. McKee (NDSA No. 2, p.16) and James Murray (NDSA No. 6, p.19.)
18.   S.E.D. Report   Education in Scotland in 1947.
19.   McShane, H.   No Mean Fighter, p.233.

        "Wm. Gallagher M.P. was a victim of the switch in the party line on
        the outbreak of war.... When Chamberlain was in power, he made speeches
        in the Commons calling for the declaration of war. Then he had to
        change – reluctantly – to opposing the war; in 1941 he had to switch
        to supporting the war again and calling for the opening of the second
        front."
20.   The Catholic Worker was a weekly paper produced for a time by the
        C.S.G. in an attempt to popularise its standpoint. A monthly publication
        The Christian Democrat propagated the theories at a more academic
        level.

21.   Hepburn, A.G.   Scottish Survey
22.   Education (Scotland) Act 1945, Part 1, Section 1.

CHAPTER NINE

CONTEXTS OF CHANGE

On 7 May 1945 the European phase of the second great war of the twentieth
century ended. The Allied Forces were regrouping for the final confrontation
when on 15 August the struggle in the Pacific came to a sudden and terrifying
conclusion.

The years immediately following were marked by confusion and uncertainty.
Hostilities were suspended, but peace was not restored. The fraticidal and
genocidal madness that had dominated the European community for two generations
had yet to be exorcised. From the Atlantic to the Urals the conflict had
left a legacy of material damage and human suffering on an unimaginable scale,
and in Britain for several years the people had to endure conditions of
austerity in some ways more stringent even than in wartime. Young men were
still being called up for various forms of national service; a painful shift
from a wartime to a peace-time economy had to be effected; consumer goods
of all kinds were severely rationed; the 'Black Market' flourished. The severe
winter of 1946-47 brought added hardships, especially to those suffering the
greatest deprivations. Yet, in spite of, or perhaps because of, the appalling
difficulties facing post-war governments, the restoration of the fabric of
the European nations was begun, and proceeded apace, spurred by the frenetic
activity of the people and fuelled by financial and material aid from the
United States.

The years of austerity passed. The world economy entered a phase of prosperity,
(1) and in the general recovery the British people shared. Soon however the
industrial malaise which had long afflicted the south-west began to be
reasserted, and its heavy industries, the traditional providers of mass
employment, went simultaneously into decline. "Clydeside was confronted with
creeping obsolescence on a massive scale."(2) During this period, marked by
an accelerating rate of change in the social order unprecedented in history,
the restructuring of Scottish secondary education following from the Education
Act of 1945 took place. With the remainder of the national system the Catholic
secondary sector was expanded and transformed, a development which, to be
understood, has to be seen in the various contexts of the prevailing economic
climate, ecclesiastical re-organisation and changes in educational theory
and practice as well as in the social mores of the nation as a whole and the
Catholic community in particular.

THE ECONOMIC CONTEXT

Although for some years after 1950 the south-west enjoyed a degree of prosperity marked by a comparatively high level of employment, signs were never lacking of difficulties in store. Coal-mining was in decline. Local iron and steel works were obsolescent, and demand for their products diminishing. Technological advance was stimulating change in a bewildering range of activities, sounding the death-knell of the age of iron and steam. Air and road transport were supplanting carriage by water or rail; electricity, natural gas and oil were ousting coal; and what had survived of the local textiles industry was increasingly threatened by proliferating man-made fibres. Automated devices were beginning to replace a human work force; and new industrial competitors were emerging in various parts of the world, including some which formerly had provided markets for British industry.

The economic performance of the west of Scotland compared with the remainder of the United Kingdom was not good. Whereas during the 'Fifties the rate of unemployment for Britain was less than 2%, the average for the west of Scotland was almost double that figure. The region provided employment for a smaller proportion of skilled men than did the principal industrial areas in the south, and in grading by social class, male operatives in Classes 1 and 11 constituted only 8% of the work force as against a figure of 9.8% overall in England and Wales. In Central Clydeside the corresponding figure was 8.4% and in Glasgow 7.5%.

There was a continuing high rate of emigration which concealed the underlying situation. During the 'Sixties the west of Scotland lost about 75% of its natural increase.(3)

With the passage of time conditions deteriorated. As job opportunities declined, relations between management and workforce became more strained, leading in turn to a sharpening of the image of the region as one where class conflict existed at a more than average intensity. The nature of Clydeside's industrial skills, based on heavy engineering, was a sufficient disadvantage for regeneration without the handicap of a poor reputation in the field of human and industrial relations. The capacity of the region to provide employment on the scale needed to stem the flow of emigrants or indeed to maintain the employment level of those who remained became more and more suspect.

For a time Clydeside received the lion's share of all new economic activity coming to Scotland. In the 1960's this trend was reversed, with Clydeside losing out to the rest of the country.(4) Later still, the development of North Sea oil and the involvement of Britain in a thriving Europe increased further the growing dominance of the east over the west of the country. The importance of Glasgow as a port declined dramatically. Industrial inertia took firm root in the area, clouding the minds of management and unions alike. Although efforts were made to break the vicious spiral of decline, these appear always to have been unsuccessful. The result was "a failure either to regenerate the old or to cause a significant shift from the old to new industries."(5)

The whole region faced an acute housing shortage. The 1951 Census showed that whereas "in very few areas in England was the average above one person per room, in Scotland the national average for all households was 1.04 and in shared houses 1.42........ The tables showed a population of 119,000 in Central Clydeside living at a density of over three to a room. Of these 89,100 were in the city of Glasgow and 11,300 in the county of Lanark." After the hiatus in house-building of the war years, there were between 80,000 and 90,000 families on the waiting list for council houses in the city.

In working out its response to the clamant needs of its citizens for accommodation, Glasgow had to take into account planning recommendations, relevant legislation and local government regulations. The New Towns Act resulted in the designation of East Kilbride in 1947 and Cumbernauld in 1956 as New Towns, the latter specifically to take overspill from Glasgow. Livingstone and Irvine followed in 1962 and 1966 respectively. A 1940 Report (6) had recommended the retention of 'Green Belts' in urbanised areas to preserve amenity and limit urban sprawl, and in 1946 the Abercrombie Plan for the Clyde Valley advocated a planned decentralisation of both population and industry. In addition, the city's approach to a regional planning strategy was affected by the limitations on the powers of the Corporation. Before 1960 its Planning Committee could not buy or lease land, and the Corporation itself was not empowered to build shops, picture houses or other communal facilities. The efforts of the Planning Committee were further constrained by a resolution of 1890, not revoked until 1969, which forbade the locating of public houses on corporation property.

In the event Glasgow produced plans for one of the most ambitious slum clearance schemes in Europe. The project, phased over 25 years, aimed at overspilling large sections of the population into new towns, or into such older settlements as could be persuaded by financial or other considerations to accept them. This process was to be accompanied by the demolition of large sectors of the most congested parts of the city, which would later be re-developed at population densities reduced from about 450 to 160 persons per acre. It was estimated that as a result about 200,000 persons would have to move from Glasgow by 1980. Two major elements required by this strategy were a commitment to a policy of high-rise flats in city centre sites and the development of a new road system with improved river crossings.

Large housing estates sprang up on greenfield sites around the perimeter of the city. Consisting for the most part of rows of three and four-storey flats, modelled on traditional tenements, they gave the impression of transplants unwillingly accepted by a host organism and doomed to rejection. They were in effect working-class dormitory suburbs, having in some cases the population of a good-sized town but lacking communal amenities - no picture houses, libraries, social centres or public houses. In total they absorbed some 10% of Glasgow's population. They were a kind of parody of Glasgow's traditional tenement life (7) incapable of generating their own community spirit, situated miles away from traditional centres of activity and linked thereto only by an undependable and expensive system of public transport. In the central sites however the policies pursued brought some real improvements. Modern facilities in the new homes transformed the domestic scene, and the new road system reduced the traffic congestion which had threatened to bring the pace of cross-city travel back to a victorian crawl. Fresh vistas of Glasgow's magnificent natural setting were opened, the more so when the Clean Air Act came into operation. With coal for domestic heating being replaced by electricity and gas, the fogs characteristic of an earlier era virtually disappeared. Despite these gains however there was no denying the disadvantages which also resulted.

Life in the high flats was unsatisfactory in many ways. Families tended to become isolated. Maintenance of the indispensable lifts, stairs, communal areas and environs generally brought their own problems. All in all, the style of life did not permit the creation of real communities, and the road system which remade Glasgow's internal communications ruptured the classic pattern of the city's urban life.

Between 1961 and 1975 the population of the city fell by more than 20%. New firms did not set up on the scale hoped for, and by 1965 it was accepted that the strategy had been only partially successful. However, parallel with Glasgow's decline went a modest revival in the surrounding region, particularly in Lanarkshire, where the population increased steadily throughout the post-war period. Although coal-mining declined almost to vanishing point, and steel-making showed signs of following in its wake, these were counter-balanced by an influx of light industries, particularly to East Kilbride one of the more successful new towns in Britain. Other parts of the conurbation also benefitted. Port Glasgow-Greenock, Cumbernauld and Irvine all increased in population, industrial diversity and job opportunity at the expense of the city.

The consequences for the educational system were considerable. The new towns drained skilled personnel from the city, leaving behind an undue proportion of the unskilled and semi-skilled.(8) The combination of better housing, better conditions in schools and enhanced career prospects in the expanding settlements proved attractive to many experienced teachers in the city schools, which were subjected to a considerable drain of staff over a lengthy period.

ECCLESIASTICAL RE-ORGANISATION

Of special importance to the Catholic educational system was the major re-organisation undertaken by the Church. Donald Mackintosh, Archbishop of Glasgow from 1922, died in 1943, and was succeeded in 1945 by Donald A. Campbell who had been Bishop of Argyll and the Isles since 1939. In 1948 Glasgow was raised to the status of a Metropolitan Province, and given the new dioceses of Motherwell and Paisley as suffragan sees. A new site was found at Cardross for the archdiocesan seminary formerly at Bearsden (9) which had been destroyed by fire in 1946. Before the end of this episcopate, preparation for the Second Vatican Council had begun.

"(Archbishop Campbell) embarked on a parochial reorganisation designed to break up the older form of the large city parish...he established 41 new parishes, each with a new church, built 13 new churches in existing parishes and instituted 14 new parishes in those parts of his diocese which had been separated in the division of 1947. A new University chaplaincy, Turnbull Hall, was erected and St. Peter's College rebuilt at Cardross".(10) His work was carried on by his successor, James D. Scanlan. During his episcopate which lasted until 1974, 17 new parishes were opened, 7 new churches in existing parishes were added and 9 additional Religious Orders began work in the Archdiocese. A Religious Education Centre was opened, and the policy was introduced of appointing chaplains to the secondary schools. In 1965 a chaplaincy was established at the new University of Strathclyde.

Figure 4 illustrates the burst of energy of the immediate post-war years.

TABLE 10

Growth of Catholic Population in South-West Scotland
1922-1972

| | 1922 | | 1972 | |
	Parishes	Population	Parishes	Population
Glasgow City	31	193,795	78	253,620
Dunbartonshire	19	29,723	24	62,730
Motherwell	35	96,650	72	182,820
Paisley	14	50,668	33	83,510
Galloway	27	16,000	45	44,399
	118	386,836	252	627,079

The above Table summarises the details given in

TABLES 11, 12, 13 and 14.

Between 1945 and 1950 there were established 17 new parishes in Glasgow, 12 in Motherwell and 6 and 3 respectively in Paisley and Galloway. By 1972 the total number of new parishes had risen to 56 in Glasgow, 37 in Motherwell, 16 in Paisley and 13 in Galloway.

MOVEMENT OF THE CATHOLIC POPULATION

This reorganisation followed on the growth in numbers of the Catholic population, and its geographical redistribution as a result of urban renewal. The figures, summarised in Table 10, indicate that in the period covered by this study the total Catholic population of south-west Scotland increased by approximately 60%, in spite of the massive emigrations that followed each of the two World Wars.(11) Along with the numerical increase went a considerable shift in location affecting all parts of the region in greater or less degree.

Re-distribution within the city of Glasgow.

During the inter-war period the Catholic community had shared only in a limited way in the re-distribution of population then taking place. Only 5 new parishes were established, three of them in the new suburbs of Riddrie, Knightswood and Kings's Park, the others in re-housing areas in Possilpark and Royston. The overall population of the older parishes remained relatively stable, and some in the more densely populated districts actually increased. This pattern changed dramatically after World War II. Of the 42 parishes set up between 1945 and 1972, 26 were situated in post-war housing areas on the perimeter, and 4 others were in re-housing areas of the inter-war period. The Catholic population of these parishes amounted to about 130,520, or 51.5% of the city's total. (See Table 11) Of the 12 foundations associated with inner city renewal, 7 were in areas where a parish had been in existence for a long time. In these cases the new parishes resulted from the sub-division of pre-existing units. In others however - Merrylee, Dumbreck, Pollokshields, Bishopbriggs and Jordanhill - no substantial Catholic population had existed between the wars; the need in these cases appeared to result from upward social mobility within the Catholic community, and was an indicator of the growth of an owner-occupier sector within it.

Re-distribution in Dumbartonshire.

In Dumbartonshire in 1922 there were 10 parishes providing for some 30,000 people. During the years of the great depression, this number declined by about 10%, to be followed by a spectacular increase after 1945. In spite of its wartime devastation, the population of Clydebank was restored to a level higher than before. Overall in the older settlements 5 new parishes were set up, and by 1972 together they were accommodating over 40,000 people.

Elsewhere in the county 9 new parishes came into being - 2 in Cumbernauld, 2 in new housing areas at Balloch and Faifley, and 1 in Bearsden, this last clearly attributable to that upward social mobility already noted; the remaining 4 were all small and widely distributed over the county's straggling area.

In 1972 Dumbartonshire accounted for some 17.5% of the archdiocesan population as compared with 15.3% in 1922. (Table 11)

Re-distribution in Motherwell Diocesan area.

From 1922 to 1972 the number of parishes increased from 33, serving 96,650 people, to 72 serving 182,820 - an increase in population of almost 94%. The comparable figure for Glasgow and Dumbartonshire was about 46%.

In 1922 the majority were congregated in three fairly well-defined groupings - Motherwell-Wishaw, Airdrie-Coatbridge and Hamilton-Bothwell-Uddingston, containing in toto about 84% of the population. A further 10% resided in the Rutherglen-Cambuslang area, while the remaining 6% were located in 7 widely separated and relatively small parishes.

In spite of emigration and the catastrophic decline of the traditional heavy industries, the Catholic population almost doubled in 50 years. The explanation for this remarkable outcome is to be found in the establishment of East Kilbride, which by 1972 housed some 13,000 people served by 3 parishes, and by the development of the housing areas at Easterhouse and Garthamlock within Glasgow's civic boundary but in part in the Motherwell diocese, which accommodated a similar number drawn from the city who were now located in the Motherwell diocese.(Table 12)

Paisley Diocesan area.

The population increased by about 70%, from c.50,000 to c.85,000. Geographical stability was a marked feature of this situation. (Table 13) In the Paisley-Johnstone-Renfrew area the 6 older parishes showed a decline in population of about 12%, offset by the founding of 9 new parishes, with a resultant overall increase of 56%. In Port Glasgow-Greenock, the congregations of the 4 older parishes declined by almost half, while the number of parishes increased to 10 and the population rose by 38% to over 35,000. Elsewhere the population more than doubled, and the number of parishes increased from 4 to 7. St. John's Barrhead, the largest in this group, increased to over 5,000. St. Joseph's Clarkston grew from 620 to 2,300, and a small but thriving parish developed at Newton Mearns. These two give a further indication of an upward social trend within the community.

Galloway Diocesan area.

Galloway in 1922 had a Catholic population of about 16,000, roughly equal to that of one very large city parish. The 8 parishes of North Ayrshire which before 1948 were part of the Glasgow Archdiocese, contained a further 11,000 people, the greatest concentration being in the Irvine area. By 1972 the number of parishes in this sector had increased to 14 and the population to 17,000. Elsewhere the greatest concentrations were centred on Ayr, Kilmarnock and Dumfries.

In 1922 the diocese had 29 parishes. By 1972 this number had increased to 45, 27 of which were situated in the areas mentioned. The remainder were small, averaging 450. The population of these dispersed groups probably lay between 5,000 and 6,000, some 17% of the diocesan total. Over the period the balance of population shifted, becoming more urbanised and industrialised in the process. (Table 14)

TABLE 11

Movement of Population in the Archdiocese of Glasgow, 1922-1972

Archdiocese of Glasgow	1922		1972	
	No. of Parishes	Population		
1. Older city centre parishes (pre-1922)	31	192,795	31	94,540
2. Parishes formed between 1922-1939			5	23,360
3. Parishes Post 1940:				
A - In inter-war housing areas			4	9,840
C - In post-war housing areas			26	95,320
D - New city centre			12	28,560
Total within city boundary	31	193,795	78	253,620
Dunbartonshire				
1. Parishes in older areas (pre-1922)	10	29,723	10	25,750
			5	14,500
2. Parishes in new areas			9	22,480
			24	62,730
ARCHDIOCESAN TOTAL	41	223,518	102	316,350

TABLE 12

Population of the Motherwell Diocesan Area, 1922-1972

	Parishes Old	Parishes New	1922 Population	1972 Population	1972 Total
Motherwell-Wishaw	8		28,256	21,000	
		10		24,540	45,540
Airdrie-Coatbridge	10		29,399	25,680	
		9		25,570	51,250
Hamilton-Bothwell	7		23,940	20,560	
		5		12,620	33,180
Rutherglen-Cambuslang	3		9,416	8,080	
		4		7,700	15,780
East Kilbride		3		13,250	13,250
Easterhouse-Garthamlock		3		14,150	14,150
Clydesdale, Monklands, Strathkelvin	7		5,639	5,490	
		3		4,180	9,670
	35	37	96,650		182,820

TABLE 13

Paisley Diocese

	1922		1972	
	Parishes	Population	Parishes	Population
Paisley-Renfrew-Johnstone	St. Mirin	10,000		4,500
	St. Margaret	3,740		3,610
	St. Mary	4,600		3,150
	St. James	1,600		2,500
	St. Charles	1,500		2,500
	St. Conval	1,050		3,500 19,760
		22,490	O.L. of L. Bishopton	750
			St. Fergus	2,500
			St. James	1,650
			St. Peter	3,200
			St. Paul	2,300
			St. Aidan (J)	2,100
			St. Anthony (J)	1,000
			St. Columba (R)	1,950
			O.H.R. (Elderslee)	550 16,000
	6	22,490	15	35,760
Greenock-Port Glasgow-Gourock	St. Mary	10,533		2,000
	St. John	6,000		2,750
	St. Lawrence	5,500		4,850
	St. Ninian	800		2,110 11,710
		22,833	St. Patrick (G'k)	3,000
			St. Mungo (G'k)	4,200
			Holy Family (P.G.)	5,200
			St. Joseph (G'k)	4,500
			St. Andrew (G'k)	5,530
			St. Francis (P.G.)	1,500 23,930
	4	22,833	10	35.640
Remainder	4	5,345	8	35,640
Total	14	50,668	33	12,110
				83,510

TABLE 14

Galloway Diocese

	1922 Parishes	Population	1972 Parishes	Population
North Ayrshire				
St. Palladius	Dalry	931		600
St. Brigid	Saltcoats	3,000		1,700
	Kilbirnie	1,540		1,325
	Largs	310		1,050
	Kilwinning	750		1,300
St. Sophia	Galston	750		850
	Stevenston	1,245		2,100
St. Mary's	Irvine	2,812		2,300
		11,338		11,225
			St. Peter's Ardrossan	2,625
			St. Margaret's Irvine	1,070
			O.L.P.S. Millport	105
			W. Kilbride	240
			O.L.P.S. Beith	400
			St. Brendan Saltcoats	1,880
				6,320
				17,545
Ayr	St. Ann Annbank		St. Quivox Prestwick	610
	St. Margaret Ayr		Good Shepherd Ayr	1,500
	St. Meddan Troon		St. Paul	980
			St. Clara	1,100
				1,750
				1,317
				300
Dumfries	St. Andrew			7,557
			St. Teresa	1,800
				2,850
Kilmarnock	St. Joseph		St. Michael	2,540
	St. Paul (Hurlford)		Carmel	840
				1,850
				2,000
				11,880
Plus 18 small parishes or Mass Centres (Est.)		16,000		7,417
DIOCESAN TOTAL		27,338		26,854
				44,399

SUMMARY

Although the total population of Glasgow decreased, the number of Catholics in the city increased by around 30%. Historic inner-city parishes declined, but some 36% of the people continued to be located within them, and inner city renewal after 1945 resulted in a further 12% being retained in these areas. A very large increase in the numbers of Catholics housed in municipal property occurred, in both inter-and post-war local government housing schemes. The number of Catholic owner-occupiers increased dramatically in some areas. Outwith the city the traditional centres of catholic settlement all showed considerable population increases. The most spectacular growth was in the Motherwell diocese, mainly because of the development of the new town at East Kilbride and of new housing areas on Glasgow's boundary.

RENEWAL: SECOND VATICAN COUNCIL

The Second Vatican Council was called by Pope John XXIII on 25 January 1959, when he had been in office a mere 90 days. It opened on 11 October 1962, after nearly four years of exhaustive preparation, and closed on 8 December 1964. Every important aspect of the life of the Church was examined **(12)**. The master document, The Dogmatic Constitution on the Church, "presents a panoramic and richly biblical view of the Church as the People of God. Concluding the main unfinished business of the First Vatican Council, it formulated with solemn conciliar authority the traditional doctrine of collegiality."..."Taken as a whole, the documents are especially noteworthy for their concern with the poor, for their insistence on the unity of the human family and therefore on the wrongness of discrimination, and for their repeated emphasis on the Christian's duty to help to build a just and peaceful world, a duty which he must carry out in brotherly co-operation with all men of goodwill."**(13)**.

For those engaged in education the Declaration on Christian Education has special importance. In it the Council faces the problems of formal education, but states specifically that it deals only with fundamental principles and that a more developed view is being left to a post-Conciliar Commission and to the Conferences of Bishops. "What is most distinctive about this document... is the insistence upon the integration of Christian Education into the whole pattern of human life in all its aspects.... The contrast is with a form of thinking and acting of another age when it was considered best to keep Christians away from the world lest they be contaminated thereby.... This mentality had generated an idea that catholics were making tremendous sacrifices for a Christian education in order to segregate their children and to protect them.... The Church here states with the utmost clarity that it has no desire to remain away from the world in a form of isolation, but that Christian Education is in the world and in a sense for the world, since man must always work out his salvation in the concrete situation...by contributing to the whole human community of which he is an integral and inseparable part.... We note the strong emphasis on the intellectual values of all education and an appeal for all to strive to achieve the highest development of the human mind...this must be done in the framework of the moral formation of man and in the fullness of his supernatural destiny."**(14)**

For those engaged in the practicalities of the educational process, the work of the Council carries multifarious and varied implications. The Declaration on Christian Education offers guidelines; the implementation of its concepts requires a whole-hearted acceptance of the total conciliar message.

THE EDUCATIONAL CONTEXT

The revolutionary changes in education which were to mark the post-war scene were foreshadowed in the immediate pre-war period. Early in 1939 a revised Day Schools (Scotland) Code abandoned the practice of defining secondary education in terms of types of school (Senior and Junior Secondary) substituting instead the natural divisions of an educational course.(15) "At last secondary education was recognised officially for what it is – a stage in the schooling of every child, not a particular kind of education to be provided for some but not for all. The generous spirit of the revised Code resulted in the attempt to give to education authorities and teachers a considerably greater freedom to devise alternative courses, to introduce new subjects, to try experiments, to plan an organisation appropriate to the special conditions of an area or school and to arrange such schemes of classification and promotion as modern educational theory and experience suggest."(16) This change also marked the beginning of an important process of devolution of power from the Scottish Education Department.

Progress was interrupted by the outbreak of war; but "even before the guns were silent, Parliament had passed an Education Act transcending in its scope even the enlightened provisions of the new Code."(17) The Education Acts (1944 in England, 1945 in Scotland) made education compulsory for children between the ages of 5 and 15; all were required to have a number of years of secondary education in their school career, to be provided out of the public purse; and education authorities had to make provision for the further education of those who had left school.

Before the 1945 Act reached the Statute Book, the Advisory Council on Education had been given a remit "to review the educational provision in Scotland for young people who have completed their primary education and have not attained the age of 18 years...." Its Report, published in 1947, foreshadowed almost in their entirety the changes that were introduced with a sometimes alarming frequency into the Scottish educational system during the next twenty-five years. It made clear that the urge for educational reform stemmed largely from the nation's wartime experience. There was a deep-felt desire to preserve in peacetime the unity realised in war; the dependence of the nation for prosperity and perhaps survival on the practical aspects of education was driven home by that experience, in the light of which it was evident how outmoded was the concept of secondary education as luxury or privilege. The urgent problem was seen to be to "evolve a new type of schooling that will suit the many as well as the old fitted the few."(18)

The problems associated with the ideals of the Act were soon to emerge, the first with the raising of the school leaving age to 15 in 1947.

"It seemed likely that the new measure would add fully 60,000 pupils to the school population... a considerable extension of school accommodation was required...1800 rooms would be needed...nearly all Authorities availed them-selves of the Department's offer to have rooms erected in the form of hutted buildings.... The raising of the school leaving age also produced an increased demand for teachers, thus aggravating the shortage which had grown to serious

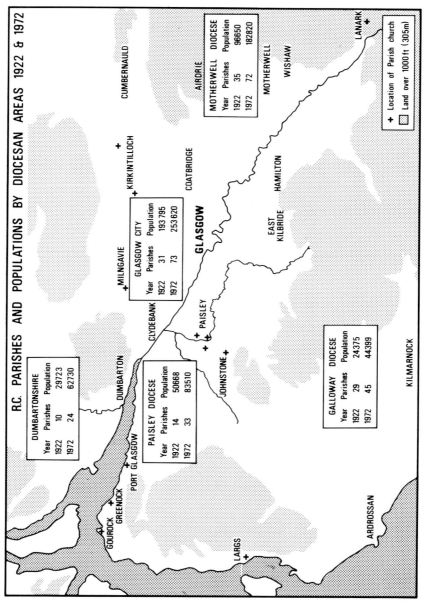

R.C. PARISHES AND POPULATIONS BY DIOCESAN AREAS 1922 & 1972

DUMBARTONSHIRE

Year	Parishes	Population
1922	10	29723
1972	24	62730

PAISLEY DIOCESE

Year	Parishes	Population
1922	14	50668
1972	33	83510

GLASGOW CITY

Year	Parishes	Population
1922	31	193795
1972	73	253620

MOTHERWELL DIOCESE

Year	Parishes	Population
1922	35	96650
1972	72	182820

GALLOWAY DIOCESE

Year	Parishes	Population
1922	29	24375
1972	45	44399

+ Location of Parish church

▓ Land over 1000 ft (305m)

GOUROCK, GREENOCK, PORT GLASGOW, DUMBARTON, CLYDEBANK, MILNGAVIE, KIRKINTILLOCH, CUMBERNAULD, PAISLEY, JOHNSTONE, GLASGOW, COATBRIDGE, AIRDRIE, MOTHERWELL, WISHAW, LANARK, HAMILTON, EAST KILBRIDE, LARGS, ARDROSSAN, KILMARNOCK

Map 3.

dimensions during the war years.... It was necessary to recruit and train under an Emergency Scheme a large group of new entrants to the teaching profession."(19)

The difficulties were exacerbated by the dramatic increase in the birthrate during the immediate post-war years, the effect of which was to be felt in the secondary schools in 1959 and later.(20) An official report in 1951 noted that the shortage of teachers would become progressively more acute because of the large number of new schools being opened, the increase in the number of pupils remaining at school beyond fifteen and developments in secondary and further education.(21) Teachers had also to contend with the curricular changes needed for the vast new school population committed to their care. Some of the related difficulties were outlined in the Memorandum on Junior Secondary Education, applicable to about 75% of the secondary population. Another report expounded concern about the shortage of Mathematics and Science teachers.(22)

A first move to deal with the shortage of teachers had been the introduction of an Emergency Training Scheme. This stop-gap measure went some way towards improving the situation, especially in the primary schools, but for the longer term a more radical solution was needed. In 1958 the Regulations for the Training of Teachers in Scotland were revised, for the first time since 1931. The National Committee for the Training of Teachers was abolished, and replaced by the Scottish Council for the Training of Teachers.(23) Training Colleges were renamed Colleges of Education, and each was given its own Governing Body more widely representative of the interests affected, including those of the teaching profession itself. Between 1964 and 1965 three new Colleges, at Ayr, Falkirk and Hamilton, were established and a beginning was made on the provision of a new building at Bearsden for Notre Dame College.

Before the benefits of these changes could reach the schools, unrest among teachers had grown to such a pitch that in 1961 teachers in Glasgow took strike action, the first such occurrence in the country. Opposition to the Emergency Training Scheme and to the employment of uncertificated teachers (a fairly wide-spread practice forced on the Authorities by the shortages) and to the resulting dilution of the profession were as much part of their dissatisfaction as the inadequacy of their financial rewards. A major outcome of this action was the setting up of the General Teaching Council for Scotland in 1965.(24)

Beyond the logistical problems of staffing and accommodation lay difficulties of an altogether different philosophical order, high-lighted by the Brunton Report in 1963, which noted that progress in Junior Secondary education had been slow and uncertain in the post-war period. Particular obstacles identified were, apart from shortages of teachers and accommodation, conservatism among teachers trained in the traditional manner, and behavioural problems among pupils.(25) The traditional Scottish secondary education course, designed to provide a broad general education with a distinct academic bias, was seen to be suitable as a preparation for the professions, but not for the needs of that 65% or so of the secondary population who might proceed to further education, as the Act required.

One apparently more successful way of approaching the problems involved was to organise secondary schooling along comprehensive lines, with all secondary pupils from one neighbourhood being educated on one campus. This system would, it was believed, at least minimise some of the divisiveness associated with the separate categories of junior and senior secondary pupils. Although it begged the fundamental question of what should be provided for the less academically able children, it seemed to offer a way ahead which as well as being administratively attractive was in keeping with long-standing practice in some parts of Scotland, and acceptable to current political and educational wisdom. In 1965 therefore the Secretary of State asked all Authorities to reorganise their secondary schools along comprehensive lines. The policy had already been instituted in parts of the west of Scotland.

A second set of problems was associated with the content of the curriculum. Prior to 1939 there was little questioning in most secondary schools about what to teach or how to teach it. In the main teachers followed a conventional curriculum regarded as appropriate for the bulk of their pupils. The post-war period saw a complete transformation. The content of every subject was put under scrutiny; new subjects were introduced and old re-written, and methods of organising the work of pupils were fundamentally altered. No subject area or method, however hallowed by experience, was exempt, and elements which had for decades occupied an unchallenged place at the core of the curriculum, began to crumble and disappear. As the classical tradition went into what appeared to be an irreversible decline, the approach to the teaching of languages, native or foreign, was affected, and the capacity of pupils to benefit from their heritage in the languages and literature of European civilisation substantially diminished. In the sciences, vast and rapid change was initiated by an upheaval in the teaching of Mathematics, and continued by the introduction of a wide range of concepts needed to enable the pupil to move with confidence in the world outside the school. In the key area of Physics, the revolutionary theory of Relativity, already half-a-century old made its impact-deadly not only in its incomprehensibility but also in the shadows which it brought in its train. Fresh burdens were placed on teachers specially concerned with the presentation of a world perspective in space and time, to add to those stemming from the frequent re-drawing of the world map. Above all, with the spread of television it became evident that the model of the school as a sheltered environment quietly discharging its function unaffected by the moral and spiritual ferment of the outside world no longer applied, and that the position of the teacher as a dominant authority in the purveying of knowledge and formation of attitudes was under deadly threat.

THE SOCIAL CONTEXT

The extension of government control during the war years, had prepared the nation to assume greater responsibility than before for the general well-being of the people. In 1944 the Beveridge Report laid the foundations of a Welfare State, the principal elements of which were National Insurance, Family Allowances, National Assistance and a National Health Service. The post-war government also embarked on a programme of nationalisation in which the Bank of England, the railways, the iron and steel industry and coal, electricity and gas supplies were brought under government control.

After a period of austerity during the immediate post-war years, standards of living began to rise. Industries became more highly mechanised; working hours shortened and paid holidays lengthened; the people's car became a reality, and the mass media flourished; air travel expanded, and holidays abroad came within the reach of almost every pocket. Although frequent warnings from various sources were issued announcing the imminent extinction by starvation of the human race, the populace ate and drank more than it had been able to do for decades.

With these changes went an alteration in the status of women. The dependence of a nation at war on its pool of female labour continued in time of peace, and with a steadily increasing demand for their labour in occupations which they were well able to undertake, womenfolk were able more and more to take up gainful employment outwith the home.

A new life-style emerged, and with it a phenomenon new at least in its intensity to the people of the west of Scotland - the so-called generation gap. The experience of growth and development of the post-war generations differed so radically from that of their parents that communication between them became more than ordinarily difficult. As the march of progress continued accompanied by a breakdown in established values, the gap between the generations widened, to their mutual loss and bewilderment. Adolescent affluence, unscrupulously exploited and backed by a revolution in modes of communication, stimulated youthful sub-cultures. Parental authority, vitiated by the uncertainties of a society no longer sure of its moral bases, was no match for the conformism demanded by youthful peer groups. For both old and young, freedom from external restraints appeared to be essential; but neither was able to develop the counterbalancing self-control. The result was a permissive society, marked by confusion, rather than by any positive understanding of what could or could not be permitted. The concept of the family as the fundamental unit of society was being eroded by sexual liberty and a growing emphasis on equality for women.

From the mid-Fifties onwards, the consequences became more apparent, in the forms of vandalism, broken homes, single-parent families, and increases in divorces, abortions, drug addiction, crime, alcoholism and mental illness. These symptoms were manifest mainly in major cities where the problems of maintaining standards in housing, education, health, employment and security were having to be faced on a growing scale. The social continuum was affected by the advent of numbers of Commonwealth citizens from Asia, Africa and the West Indies, drawn in to meet the demand for labour in those more menial but necessary tasks that were no longer attractive to the increasingly affluent indigenous population.

With a simultaneous decline in formal church membership and in institutional religion generally, the power of the churches to maintain meaningful contact with the most disturbed sectors of the community decreased. It was however noticeable that the acceptance of commonwealth immigrants into Scotland took place with a relative absence of the kind of disturbances that occurred in conurbations elsewhere in the Kingdom.

With the implementation of the Robbins Report, which had promised an additional 560,000 places in universities and other Higher Education institutions by 1981, a new student class emerged. In Scotland the Royal College of Technology in Glasgow was given university status, with Heriot Watt College in Edinburgh following a year later. At Stirling a third new university was founded, and

Colleges of Technology set up in the major urban centres.   This expansion combined with the reduction of the legal age of adult status to eighteen, had somewhat less dramatic effects in Scotland where the educational tradition was already more egalitarian and democratic than elsewhere in Britain; but itcontributed nevertheless to a decline in traditional attitudes of acceptance of and defence to authority.   Even so, when by the end of the 'Sixties overt revolt among student bodies swept across the campuses of Europe and USA, the repples in Scotland were comparatively slight.

NOTES

1.   Checkland, S.G.   The Upas Tree   p.45
2.   Ibid.   p.47
3.   Ibid.   p.47
4.   Ibid.   p.66
5.   Ibid.   p.46
6.   Report of The Royal Commission on the Distribution of Industrial
         Population.
7.   Checkland   p.69
8.   Ibid.   p.72
9.   St. Peter's Seminary is now (1984) located at Newlands, Glasgow.
10.   W.C.C. 1981.
11.   The increase of 60% over 50 years may be accounted for by (1) a higher
       birth-rate than the national average among Catholics (2) some net
       gain in Catholic population by immigration from Ireland, Poland or
       elsewhere (3) unreliable statistics.
12.   The titles of the official documents are:
         Dogmatic Constitution on the Church.
         Dogmatic Constitution on Divine Revelation.
         Constitution on the Sacred Liturgy.
         Pastoral Constitution on the Church in the Modern World.
         Decree on the Instruments of Social Communication.
         Decree on Ecumenism.
         Decree on Eastern Catholic Churches.
         Decree on Bishops' Pastoral Office in the Church.
         Decree on Priestly Formation.
         Decree on the Appropriate Renewal of the Religious Life.
         Decree on the Apostolate of the Laity.
         Decree on the Ministry and Life of Priests.
         Decree on the Church's Missionary Activity.
         Decree on Christian Education.
         Decree on the Relationship of the Church to non-Christian Religions.
         Decree on Religious Freedom.
13.   Shehan, Cardinal L.   The Documents of Vatican 11, Ed. W.J. Abbott,
                             S.J. (introduction)
14.   Carter, G.E.   Bishop of London, Ontario. Commentary on the
                             Declaration on Christian Education in the
                             Documents of Vatican 11.
15.   Memorandum Explanatory of the Day School (Scotland) Code 1939.
16.   SECONDARY EDUCATION. A Report of the Advisory Council on Education
         in Scotland. Cmd. 7005, p.3.
17.   Ibid.
18.   Ibid.
19.   Education in Scotland in 1947, p.5.
20.   Supply of Teachers. First Report of the Departmental Committee appointed
         by the Secretary of State for Scotland.   Cmd. 8123, 1951.
21.   Report on Measures to Improve the Supply of Teachers in Scotland.
         Cmnd. 644, 1959.
22.   Supply of Teachers of Mathematics and Science in Scotland.
         Cmd. 9419, 1955.
23.   Teachers (Training Authorities)(Scotland) Regulations, 1958.
24.   The Teaching Profession in Scotland. The Wheatley Report, 1963.
25.   From School to Further Education (The Brunton Report)   HMSO 1963.

CHAPTER TEN

THE CATHOLIC SECONDARY SCHOOLS, 1945-1972

In 1939 the provision of secondary places for Catholic pupils was still far from satisfactory, in spite of the progress that had been made. In Lanarkshire for example fewer than 10% of the Catholic schools' population were then able to attain to any form of secondary education. The disparity which had existed since 1918 between the Catholic sector and the national system, still existed, manifested in higher pupil-teacher ratios, poorer accommodation and environmental conditions and lower levels of attainment and aspiration. Some progress towards closing this gap had been made in the inter-war years, but was halted by the outbreak of war.

Because of the concentration of the Catholic community in industrial areas, the impact of war-time conditions on its schools was severe. Although great efforts had been made to maintain ordinary standards, this aim was not fully achieved.(1) For the Catholic secondary sector in particular, a major consequence of the Government's determination to press on with educational reform was a deterioration in working conditions in schools, by far the most serious aspect of which was the shortage of teachers, which, in the eyes of some, could "only result in a lowering of academic standards...and in a general lowering of standards of conduct and citizenship in the body of boys and girls leaving school...overcrowding and understaffing will persist by any acceptable standard...a standard less than that achieved under the pre-war system will be maintained at higher cost in money and effort."(2)

Whether or not the timing was right for a reorganisation of the national system, it was not so for the Catholic secondary sector whose first priority was to try to cope with its enormous backlog of secondary places. The experiences of some schools illustrate the difficulties of the times.

(St. Bonaventure's Junior Secondary School, Glasgow:)

1943   Considerable difficulty experienced in staffing...7 men called to the Forces.... Of 28 teachers in the Secondary division, 19 have only provisional recognition, and of 16 in the primary staff, 10 are probationers.

1948   A recently completed hut has added three more rooms.... When the four rooms at present occupied by the Infant Department have been vacated, the existing deficiency in laboratories will be made good.... Science is taken by boys only.

1951   "Accommodation has recently been improved by the completion of additional huts...a full course can now be offered in all the subjects normally included in the curriculum of a junior secondary school...additional laboratory accommodation made it possible for the first time to give instruction in Science to girls as well as boys."(3)

(St. Mungo's Academy)

"Between 1946 and 1949 the roll rose by 300 to more than 1400.... In 1949 a collection of HORSAS (Huts Operation for the Raising of the School Leaving Age) was assigned to us.... Two years later we were obliged to take over three spare classrooms in St. Mary's Boys School, Calton, thereby adding a fourth annexe to the three of St. Kentigern's, Kennedy Street and Rigby Street, 2 miles away. By the spring of 1953 the roll was more than 1,750."(4)

(St. Mary's Junior Secondary, Calton)

"In 1947...rationing was still on...the school leaving age went up to 15.... Pollok housing scheme had been built...as many as thirteen double-decker buses transported pupils across the city... the roll of the school jumped from something like 500 to 1,000... there was an annexe in St. Mary's Primary School...no dining school on the premises..."(5)

(St. Ninian's High School, Kirkintilloch)

"In 1948...the Education Authority (leased) four rooms in the Church Hall.... Various scattered huts were erected...overcrowding was˙ to become an unwelcome feature for a number of years.... In 1949 the roll was 1,173, the highest ever."(6)

Everywhere the introduction of the school meals system added to the problems of accommodation and to the strains on an already sorely pressed teaching staff.

By the mid-'Fifties the fundamental re-structuring of the secondary systems required by the Act of 1945 could be undertaken. Although the two great measures of 1918 and 1945 seemed to agree in accepting the principle of secondary education for all, there was a profound divergence in their concepts of what that principle entailed. Implicit in the 1918 commitment to "free intermediate and secondary schooling for all children able to profit by it" was the notion of at least two categories of post-primary education, only one of which could properly be designated 'secondary', as well as a limitation on those eligible to receive it; whereas for the framers of the 1945 Act secondary education was to be thought of as a stage in educational experience of all children suited to the age, aptitude and ability of every individual. This latter concept saw educational experience as a totality in which the secondary phase would constitute one stage of an integrated whole. Secondary education would no longer be defined in terms of types of school, and post-primary schooling

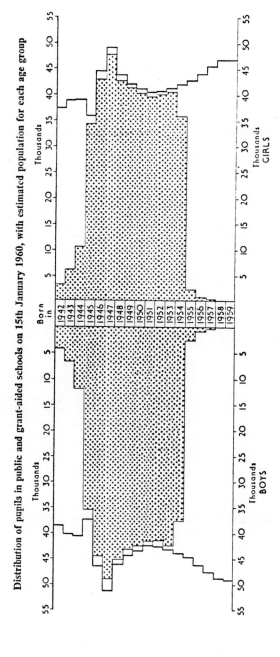

Distribution of pupils in public and grant-aided schools on 15th January 1960, with estimated population for each age group

The whole area represents the estimated population, while the dotted portion shows the numbers who are in public and grant-aided schools

Fig. 5. Number of children born in Scotland 1942-1959
Extracted from: Education in Scotland 1960

would be organised in institutions equipped to meet the needs of all pupils for the period of their compulsory schooling.

Because of the variations in the circumstances of the education authorities, the transition to a new system took place by different routes. Several organisational patterns were tried. In the upshot the all-through six year comprehensive secondary school became the most generally accepted model throughout the region, and was adopted also in the Catholic sector.

In 1947, the number of children born in Scotland was about 100,000, compared with about 71,000 in 1945. The birth-rate in subsequent years remained high. (Figure 5) Birth-rate in the catholic community,although lower than in pre-war years, was above the national average, and followed a similar trend.

EXPANSION IN GLASGOW

The new era of expansion began with the founding in 1954 of St. Augustine's Secondary School in a new housing development at Milton on the northern edge of the city. For more than twenty years thereafter a massive programme of development was carried through, in which the provision of new schools kept pace with rehousing of the people, and established senior secondary and large junior secondary schools were reorganised as comprehensive schools. Small junior secondary schools reverted to primary status, or disappeared. By 1961 there were 12 Catholic schools offering the full range of courses up to sixth-year level, with 5 recently upgraded junior secondary schools building up to that standard. 7 older J.S.schools remained in existence with small rolls, all but one due to be phased out as secondary schools. Between 1961 and 1972 3 more six-year comprehensive schools were established. (see Table 15).

By the end of session 1971-72 the change-over to a system of all-through comprehensive schools was almost complete. Whereas at the beginning of the exercise the great majority of post-primary Catholic pupils had been accommod ated in junior secondary schools, by 1972 almost all of the total roll of c. 25,000 were being educated in comprehensive secondary schools. The co-ordinated movement towards urban renewal and educational reform enabled the Authority to deal simultaneously with the redistribution of population and the backlog in secondary places for the Catholic population.

The completion of the programme resulted in 21 secondary schools (7) providing for a total of 24,843 pupils. 13 had rolls of over 1,000, 5 of them more than 1,500, and the largest 2,400. Of the five schools of the Religious Orders founded before 1981, only St. Mungo's Academy had not experienced sufficient relief of pressure to enable it to adhere to its traditional organisation and style of education. "The Academy had become a bloated scholastic octopus curling its tentacles around fifty classes and 1,800 pupils sucked in from the western and eastern perimeters of the city and almost all the space between, north of the river." (8) Although it had been the wish of the Order that the school be restored approximately to its pre-1918 state, namely, a school of six or seven hundred boys capable and desirous of completing a full academic course, in 1972 the fulfilment of that wish seemed as far away as ever.

TABLE 15

Glasgow Secondary Schools, with Rolls

School	Founded		1961	1972
Our Lady and St. Francis, Charlotte St.	1847		1070	1084
Convent of Mercy, Garnethill	1848		640	700
St. Mungo's Academy, Townhead	1858		1540	1715
St. Aloysius College, Garnethill	1859		500	600
Notre Dame High School, Dowanhill	1897		620	690
Holyrood Secondary, Crosshill	1936		1780	2044
St. Gerard's Secondary, Govan	1937		940	1091
(St. Anthony's Adv. C)	(1928)			
St. Roch's Junior Secondary, Garngad	1928	St. Roch's Secondary	1150	1115
St. Mark's Junior Secondary, Carntyne	1937	St. Andrew's Secondary (1969)	890	942
St. Columba's Junior Secondary, Maryhill	1938	St. Columba of Iona (1968)	480	619
St. Bonaventure's Jun. Sec., Oatlands	1939	John Bosco Secondary (1971)	690	773
St. Bernard's Jun. Sec., Pollok	1960	Bellarmine Secondary (1961)	870	1508
St. Augustine's Secondary, Milton	1953		1480	1846
Lourdes Secondary, Cardonald	1959		1280	1482
St. Thomas Aquinas Sec., Scotstounhill	1960		1320	1420
St. Gregory's Secondary, Cranhill	1960		1340	1594
St. Pius X Secondary, Drumchapel	1961		720	1207
St. Margaret Mary's Sec., Castlemilk	1966			1477
St. Leonard's Secondary, Easterhouse	1964			960
All Saints Secondary, Balornock	1972			920
St. Mary's Junior Secondary, Calton	1926		420	1056
St. Margaret's Junior Sec., Kinning Park			750	
Sacred Heart Junior Sec., Bridgeton			450	
St. Cuthbert's Junior Sec., Possilpark			430	
St. John's (Boys) Junior Sec., Gorbals			160	
St. John's (Girls) Junior Sec., Gorbals			150	
St. Joseph's Junior Sec., Woodside			130	

EXPANSION IN DUMBARTONSHIRE

In Dunbartonshire as elsewhere educational reform brought about substantial increase in the secondary population. The local authority however had also to cope with increases arising from the restoration of Clydebank, and from a movement of population out of Glasgow, particularly into the new town of Cumbernauld. The county's unique disposition, in that it consisted of two geographically separated sections, raised problems which specially affected the growing Catholic communities in the Milngavie-Bearsden and Bishopbriggs areas.

Before 1939, Catholic children in the Milngavie-Bearsden area had ready access to secondary schools in Glasgow. After 1945, the population increased rapidly, and at the same time the Glasgow schools became overcrowded. Dumbartonshire was no longer willing to meet the spiralling cost of the extra-territorial fee demanded by Glasgow. Catholic parents had to choose between sending their children to Dumbarton or Kirkintilloch, or meeting the fee themselves. The difficulty was met by Dunbartonshire Education Authority providing transport for the children resident in Bearsden-Milngavie to St. Ninian's High School in Kirkintilloch.

Parents in the growing Bishopbriggs area were in a somewhat similar position. Bishopbriggs was then part of Lanarkshire, and education for its residents the responsibility of that Authority. As the Catholic population increased accommodation was provided in St. Ninian's High School, by arrangement between the concerned Authorities.

By session 1957-58 increasing numbers of secondary pupils from the Milngavie area began to attend St. Ninian's High School. The roll increased to c. 1400, of whom 615 were secondary pupils. The following year the first few pupils from Cumbernauld arrived and the roll topped 1,500. In 1966 the primary department was transferred to a new school, and St. Ninian's for the first time in its history functioned as a secondary school with no primary department. Pressure nevertheless continued to grow as the children of the post-war 'bulge' moved through the school, and as Cumbernauld continued to attract young families. The opening there of Our Lady's High School in August 1968 seemed at last to promise an end to the problem of accommodation that had so long beset this part of the county.

In the western part of the county major developments were associated with the restoration of war-devastated Clydebank. New housing estates grew up on greenfield sites on the lower slopes of the Old Kilpatrick Hills. Two new Catholic comprehensive secondary schools were opened - St. Columba's, Clydebank in 1961, incorporating the junior secondary department of St. Mary's Duntocher, and St. Andrew's High, in 1970, which replaced the secondary department of Our Holy Redeemer's School.

By 1972 the immediate problems for the Catholic population appeared to have been solved; but already plans had had to be considered for expansion in the Bishopbriggs and Cumbernauld areas.

EXPANSION IN LANARKSHIRE

By 1955 there were still only two Catholic schools in Lanarkshire offering the full secondary course.(9) The three-tier selective system already described operated until 1967, when plans for the reorganisation of secondary education on comprehensive lines were drawn up.

Substantial advance in the provision of secondary places did not begin until the late 1950's. By then the drive for educational reform was increasing in strength; the local economy was healthier than for almost half-a-century; the population was increasing with overspill from Glasgow and the growth of East Kilbride: and the secondary population was increasing under the combined influences of the raising of the school leaving age and high birth-rates.

In anticipation of a further raising of the leaving age to 16, secondary education began to be organised on the basis of four-year and six-year schools. Several new Catholic secondaries were provided. In 1958 St. Margaret's Airdrie and St. Cuthbert's Burnbank opened as three-year junior high schools, and St. Joseph's Blantyre moved into a new building with increased secondary accommodation. In 1961 St. Ambrose High, Coatbridge opened as a four-year secondary, displacing St. Bridget's Junior Secondary Ballieston. In 1964 St. Mary's Whifflet, St. Cuthbert's Burnbank and St. Aidan's (Wishaw) founded in 1963 were upgraded to four-year secondaries; St. Joseph's Motherwell followed in 1968 and St. Margaret's Airdrie in 1970.

By 1964 there were therefore 7 Catholic schols in Lanarkshire able to present pupils for the Ordinary Grade Examination of the Scottish Certificate of Education, viz: Our Lady's High School, Motherwell; St. Patrick's High School, Coatbridge; Elmwood Convent School, Bothwell; Holy Cross High School, Hamilton; St. Mary's High School, Whifflet; St. Aidan's High School Wishaw; and St. Ambrose High School, Coatbridge; of these the first four offered the full Leaving Certificate course. Thereafter it was a relatively short step to a full comprehensive system. Progress to that end is best described separately in a geographical framework.

In the Airdrie-Coatbridge area:-

An extension to St. Mary's Whifflet, which had been provided in 1928, had become an autonomous unit and named St. Edmund's Junior Secondary in 1948. In 1970 St. Mary's High School was reconstituted as a six-year comprehensive secondary incorporating the building and pupils of St. Edmund's, and given the name Columba High School, Coatbridge.(10) Likewise St. Patrick's High, which received full senior secondary status in 1956, was reconstituted in 1970 as a six-year comprehensive school;(11) St. Margaret's Airdrie followed in 1973 and St. Ambrose's, Coatbridge(12) in 1974.

In the Hamilton-East Kilbride-Cambuslang-Rutherglen area:-

Holy Cross High School, Hamilton, founded in 1939, was upgraded to full senior secondary status in 1957, and reclassified as a six-year comprehensive in 1971. St. Cuthbert's Burnbank, opened in 1958, was given four-year status in 1964, and renamed John Ogilvie High School in 1965, with an expanded catchment area including East Kilbride. In 1973 full six-year comprehensive status was accorded.(13) St. Bride's High School in East Kilbride was opened in 1967, and Trinity High School in Cambuslang(14) in 1971, both planned to build up to full six-year status.

In Motherwell-Wishaw-Lanark:-

After the last girls' class was phased out of Our Lady's High Schooll Motherwell in 1945, the school had a selective intake of boys drawn from every part of the county. The roll stood at around 750-800. Boys from the local area who did not follow the full senior secondary course attended St. Joseph's Junior Secondary School. In 1973 Our Lady's High merged with St. Joseph's to form a six-year comprehensive school. The combined roll rose from 1900 to 2,300, accommodated in five different buildings.

St. Aidan's High School Wishaw opened in 1963 with a primary department and 526 secondary pupils. By 1967 the secondary department had risen to c. 900. The school became fully comprehensive in 1971. The following year the secondary roll stood at 1,078, and a separate primary school was provided.(15)

St. Mary's School, Lanark, which had acquired a junior secondary department in 1929, continued to function as a combined primary and secondary school until 1975. Thereafter its secondary pupils were to be accommodated in St. Aidan's High School.

In Uddingston-Bothwell-Bellshill:-

For a number of years after 1945, all Catholic girls in Lanarkshire seeking a full Leaving Certificate course were directed to Elmwood Convent School in Bothwell. Junior Secondary pupils were accommodated at St. John the Baptist School in Uddingston, which opened as a chapel-cum-school in 1882, and at St. Saviour's Bellshill. In 1967 a new school for secondary pupils, St. Catherine's, was opened in Uddingston, and St. Saviour's School acquired four-year secondary status.

Subsequently, in 1977 Cardinal Newman High School opened in Bellshill as a six-year comprehensive school. Elmwood, St. Catherine's and St. Saviour's secondary schools were closed, Elmwood Convent after a life of 99 years, and St. Catherine's after a mere ten. Resultant pressure on accommodation required that the St. Catherine's building be retained as an annexe.

In the working out of this reorganisation, some of the smaller schools which had contributed over the years to secondary education in the county disappeared, absorbed into the new comprehensive schools; others reverted to primary status. Among them were:

St. Aloysius' School, Chapelhall, Airdrie, founded in 1857. Its contribution to secondary education ended in 1973, when all its secondary pupils transferred to St. Margaret's High School.

St. Joseph's School, Blantyre, opened in 1877, reverted to primary status in 1973. St. Mary's Lanark, founded in 1878, acquired junior secondary status in 1929, which continued until 1975, when the secondary roll was about 100.

St. John the Baptist School Uddingston, opened in 1882, had supplementary classes and later non-certificate secondary pupils until 1967.

St. Bridget's Baillieston acquired secondary status only to be displaced by St. Ambrose's High School Coatbridge when it opened in 1961.

St. Saviour's Bellshill, closed in 1971.

Addendum:

By 1972 the comprehensivisation programme in Lanarkshire had not been completed. In 1976 it was proposed that a new secondary school be built for the Blantyre-Cambuslang agea. With the opening of this school,named Trinity High School, it was expected that the roll of John Ogilvie High School, then over 1,400, would stabilise at c. 1,100.

In 1967 St. Bride's High School opened in East Kilbride and acquired full six-year status in 1973.(16)

EXPANSION IN RENFREWSHIRE, AYRSHIRE, DUMFRIESSHIRE

In the Paisley area:

For a period before and during the Second World War, St. Mirin's Academy accepted junior secondary boys and girls as well as the senior secondary boys for whom it had been designed. In 1953 the girls were transferred to St. James's High School in Renfrew which had been upgraded from primary status.(17) St. Mirin's then operated as a comprehensive school for boys only. In 1965, Renfrewshire adopted a two-tier system of Four-ear and Six-Year secondary schools. St. Mirin's became the senior High School for boys, and St. Margaret's Convent the corresponding school for girls.(18) Both would be fed by a complex of Junior High Schools situated throughout East Renfrewshire. The appalling backlog of secondary places for Catholic children then began to be tackled. St. Brendan's High, Linwood opened as a combined primary and junior secondary school in 1964, and reched junior high status in 1973. St. Aelred's High, Paisley opened in 1965 as a junior secondary and was upgraded in 1973. In 1966 St. Luke's High, Barrhead was instituted as a junior secondary, acquiring junior high status in 1971. St. Cuthbert's, Johnstone opened in 1967 with pupils drawn from St. Margaret's Johnstone, which continued to function as a primary school. It became a junior high in 1969. Sacred Heart High, Paisley was purpose-built as a Four Year Junior High School. It opened in 1971 with 359 S.1 pupils.

In Port Glasgow-Greenock-Gourock:

In 1949, St. John's Primary School in Port Glasgow was reconditioned as a primary and junior secondary school.(19) In 1960 the secondary department moved to new premises and renamed St. Stephen's Secondary School, while the primary departmet retained the original name. The first comprehensive intake was received in 1961, and the school acquired full six-year status in 1970.

In St. Columba's High School, Gourock, the roll grew from 700 to 1340 in the ten years from 1960. A new building with accommodation for 1,800 pupils on a site overlooking Cardwell Bay was opened in 1971, and the first comprehensive intake received. The former building was taken over by St. Mary's Junior Secondary School in 1972, renamed Notre Dame High School and given four-year high school status. A year later it was upgraded to a Six-Year Comprehensive with a roll of 950.

In Ayrshire:

Although St. Joseph's High School Kilmarnock had been elevated to full senior secondary status during the war years, it was not until 1956, when a new building came into use, that substantial advance took place. From that date "St. Joseph's would supply educational facilities up to university entrance level, and there would be no need for pupils to leave Kilmarnock at the end of the Third Year to complete their studies in Glasgow."(20) A similar development took place in Irvine, where a new site for St. Michael's was acquired. The new school was opened becoming a six-year comprehensive in 1971 with a roll of c. 1,000. A new purpose-built comprehensive school, St. Andrew's Academy Ardrossan, opened that year to share the provision for the northern part of the county. At the southern end a small junior secondary, St.Conval's High, had been opened in Cumnock in 1961.(21)

In Dumfriesshire:

By virtue of its character as a small boarding school for boys St. Joseph's College Dumfries was somewhat detached from the mainstream of Catholic educational development in the south-west. Over the years its pupils were drawn from many parts of England, Scotland and Ireland and beyond, with Clydeside, Tyneside and Preston supplying the largest proportion for most of the time. It looked to both the Scottish and English educational systems, as well as giving expression to the principles of the Marist Order. Pupils were presented for the English Ordinary Level Examination in Form Four, for the Scottish Leaving Certificate in Form Five and for Advanced Level examinations in Form Six. In the mid-Fifties the College had 310 boarding pupils 70 day pupils and a teaching staff of 25 Marist Brothers.(22)

THE OVERALL POSITION IN 1972

The increase in the number of schools providing the full range of secondary education indicated the remarkable development that had taken place during the post-war period. In Glasgow, the 7 full secondary schools of 1945 had expanded to 21 comprehensives in 1972; Dumbartonshire's 3 had increased to 6; Lanarkshire's 2 old-established senior secondary schools had increased to 12; in Renfrewshire there were 5 six-year and 4 four-year secondary schools; and Ayrshire had doubled its quota from 2 to 4.

This expansion resulted from (1) the Education Act of 1945, (2) the increase in the numbers of the relevant age-groups and (3) the national will for the development of a comprehensive system of education.

In Glasgow the move towards a fully comprehensive system had started soon after the war, and by 1972 was almost complete. Outwith the city the landward authorities, as well as facing the common problems arising from the raising of the school leaving age and the increase in the birth-rate, had to face those stemming from the excessive backlog in provision carried forward from before the war, and from the decanting of population from Glasgow. By 1972 there had emerged a fairly uniform pattern of Catholic secondary education based on the all-through six-year comprehensive school, which was almost complete in Glasgow but still to be completed in the remainder of the south-west.

NOTES

1.   Education in Scotland in 1947, p.7 HMSO Cmd. 7519
2.   Fitzpatrick, T.A. Education in Scotland Tablet 22.2.49.
3.   HMI Reports: 27/10/43 27/5/48 31/10/51.
4.   Handley, J.E. History of St. Mungo's Academy pp. 201-2.
5.   McKee, J.J. NDSA, 2 p. 18.
6.   Maguire GT and SV Murray Story of a School pp. 41-3
7.   Made up of 19 six-year comprehensive schools, 1 junior secondary
        school and St. Aloysius' College.
8.   Handley, J.E. Op. cit. p. 208.
9.   Breen, J. NDSA, 12.
10.   Smith, J.J. 10/12/73. Roll, 1,894; No. of Staff, 86.
11.   Smith, James   /12/73: Roll of St. Patrick's 1,840; Staff 101.
12.   In 1973 the roll of St. Ambrose was 1,510.
13.   In 1973 the roll of John Ogilvie High was 1,270.
14.   Curran, T. NDSA, 20.
15.   The first Sixth Year in St. Aidan's was formed in 1974; roll, 1,327.
16.   For a comprehensive account of the development of catholic secondary
        education in Lanarkshire after 1954, see BREEN J. NDSA 12, pp.
        10-11 and CURRAN, T. NDSA 20.
17.   McCarthy J.J.   Subsequently Trinity High School, Renfrew, which
        opened in 1975 as a Junior High School, superceded St. James's
        school. In its first year Trinity had a roll of c. 800, with 124
        in the post-intermediate department, and a staff of 56. It was
        envisaged that it would grow into a six-year comprehensive school.
18.   Sister Patricia Gallagher FCJ Head Teacher of St. Margaret's High
        School, 12/3/76.
        In 1972 the school with 15 acres of land was sold to Renfrewshire
        Education Authority, with a view to its amalgamation with St.
        Mirin's Academy to form a co-educational school, planned for 1976.
19.   Centenary Brochure 1854-1954 of the Church of St. John the Baptist,
        Port Glasgow.
20.   Souvenir Brochure for the opening of the Church of Our Lady of Mt.
        Carmel, 12/5/63.
21.   By 1972 the roll of St. Conval's had increased to 240.
22.   DJB Vol. 4 No. 4 October 1954.

CHAPTER ELEVEN

THE CRISIS YEARS

The vital element at the heart of the educational process is, in the pregnant phrase of Sir James Robertson, "the slow commerce of person with person." After 1918 this centrality of the teacher acquired a new dimension for the Catholic sector, in that the preservation of the religious character of the schools had come to depend more than ever on the Christian commitment of the teaching staff.

Throughout the post-war period the shortage of qualified teachers was more pronounced in the Catholic than in the non-denominational schools. This gave rise to increased criticism of the separate schools system, which was already seen to be socially divisive and its religious education suspect as a kind of indoctrination. To these recurring charges was added the contention that the system was not viable because of its inability to provide its quota of teachers. It is important therefore that the reasons for the shortage of Catholic secondary teachers be clearly adumbrated. The analysis which follows is based on two premisses:

First, that some of the circumstances which brought about the shortage were unique to the Catholic sector; and second, that of those which operated nationally, some exercised particular force in the Catholic sector.

With regard to the first, five factors peculiar to the Catholic sector can be identified.

Firstly, because of the enormous backlog of secondary places carried forward from before the war, the expansion needed after 1945 was proportionately much greater in the Catholic than in the non-denominational sector. This expansion had to be met from the inadequate base provided by the small group of existing Catholic schools.

It was in the combination of the small base and the massive expansion demanded from it that the uniqueness of the situation lay. In Glasgow for example, when the first new Catholic secondary school of the post-war opened, its supply of teachers had to be drawn mainly from former pupils of the seven pre-existing secondary schools. As other new schools came into being, the supply base could not change until the former pupils of the new establishments could qualify as teachers. In Lanarkshire the base of only two senior secondary

135

schools was even more inadequate to meet the enormous demands imposed on it. Secondly because of the concentration of the Catholic community into a small part of the south-west, there was no other source of trained staff elsewhere in the country on which to draw. Indeed it had traditionally been the role of the south-west to export teachers.

Thirdly war-time experience of the community had introduced many to ways of life previously not open to them. Catholics began to be involved increasingly in the national life in a widening range of activities, and to undertake more of the responsibilities appropriate to their growing numbers. This trend imposed a new demand on that section of the population which could have supplied an increased teaching force.

Fourthly, it nevertheless continued to be the case that the Catholic community was over-represented in the most culturally deprived areas, where schools were unlikely to be able to supply enough teachers for their own needs.(1)

Finally Catholic secondary schools were large, some inordinately so, and made additional demands on the energies of staffs because of their commitment to religious education programmes. As conditions of overcrowding and understaffing persisted, the attractiveness of teaching in them declined. Catholic graduates, many the sons and daughters of teachers, were well-informed on these matters. Of those who did choose to take up a career in teaching, many sought posts in other branches of the educational service, in further education or in non-denominational schools. Many emigrated.

THE SECOND PREMISS

In 1959 a Special Committee of the Advisory Council reported: "The staffing shortage is grave; in the secondary schools it will deteriorate further; and it will still be serious in ten years' time unless present trends are altered." It went on to enumerate the reasons for the crisis, as follows:

"The higher post-war birth-rates and the spectacular decline in infant mortality; the expansion in the number of school places, including about 150,000 in secondary departments; the reduction in the maximum permissible size of classes; raising of the school leaving age to fifteen; the development of Junior Secondary education; the increase in the number of pupils electing to remain at school beyond the leaving age; the expansion of further education; and the reduction in the average age at which children were promoted to secondary departments, because of their earlier maturing."

This analysis made no allowance for any future advances that might be contemplated, such as a reduction in the size of classes, the raising of the leaving age to sixteen, or the introduction of compulsory part-time further education. The Report acknowledged that "if any or all of these advances were to be made, a new crisis would develop."(2)

In the event, the decade of the 1960's saw a worsening of the overall staffing situation, due to a series of radical changes affecting the educational scene. These were:

A general advance throughout the south-west towards a completely comprehensive secondary system; an increase in the number of very large schools, some having upwards of 1,500 pupils; an explosion of knowledge which posed problems of curriculum development; changes in the examination system, first with the abandonment of the Group Certificate of the Higher Leaving Certificate and later with the introduction of the Ordinary Grade of the Scottish Certificate of Education; expansion of higher education; and increased competition for highly qualified personnel in industry and commerce.

It can be argued without invidiousness that the causes outlined above operated at least in some instances with particular severity in the Catholic sector. Birth-rate among the catholic population, although decreasing, was above the national average: the expansion of secondary places was proportionately greater; the raising of the leaving age had a proportionately greater impact because of traditional attitudes to early leaving; a greater backlog of provision for junior secondary education had been carried forward from the pre-war period and the increase in the number of pupils continuing beyond the minimum leaving age was proportionately greater than in the system as a whole. In addition, the Catholic schools were especially afflicted by the problems arising from over-large schools. In Glasgow for example in session 1971-72, there were 22 Catholic secondaries, of which 13 had rolls of more than 1,000, 5 were over 1,500 and the largest 2,044. (In the same session in the city there were 38 non-denominational secondary schools; 13 had rolls of more than 1,000, none was over 1,5000, and the largest had 1,317 pupils).(3)

As the shortage became more acute, Education Authorities resorted to the expedient of employing retired and uncertificated teachers. Two years after the issue of Circular 600 (4), there were 2,579 uncertificated teachers employed in Scottish secondary schools (5). It was estimated that the number of teachers needed to fill vacancies, reduce oversize classes and replace uncertificated teachers and teachers over 70 (6) totalled 3,868, and that the shortage of graduate teachers would increase from 1,500 to 3,500 between 1968 and 1974, and of teachers of practical and aesthetic subjects from 1,500 to 2,900 in the same period. Along with the shortages went the associated problem of instability of staffing, acknowledged to be if anything the more worrying phenomenon. "The almost constant movement of staff in and out of many schools... creates conditions in which progressive education becomes very difficult."(7) "The cumulative effect of all these staffing difficulties was greatest in the most populous areas, especially in the west of the country."(8)

Several steps were taken to combat these difficulties. The Special Recruitment Scheme, introduced in 1951 to attract suitable people into teaching from other walks of life, continued to be supported. The General Teaching Council, set up under the Teachers' Certification (Scotland) Act of 1965 ultimately brought the employment of uncertificated teachers under control. When men were admitted to the 3-year College of Education course for the training of primary teachers, formerly the preserve of women only, a larger proportion of the pool of male graduates became available for the secondary sector.

Nevertheless the shortage of teachers remained acute, tending to obscure other very real difficulties, especially in the Catholic sector.(9) Changes in the content of the secular subjects as well as in the traditional areas of religious education opened up fields of controversy with which many teachers felt themselves ill-equipped to deal; changes in society at large along with the pervasive influences of the media stimulated questioning attitudes in the older and more mature sections of the school population; and parental authority declined as youthful affluence increased. When the Second Vatican Council undertook the first major overhaul of the Church's attitudes since the Franco-Prussian War, the secure base on which the educational system had been erected – the School-Home-Church triangle – was shaken at each of its vertices. Its capacity to adjust to these pressures was affected, not only by the endemic shortage of teachers, but also by the ecclesiastical reorganisation and redistribution of population then taking place throughout the Clydeside conurbation. In all the circumstances the capacity of the schools to fulfil their function was seriously at risk.

THE CATHOLIC SCHOOLS AND COMPREHENSIVE EDUCATION

For a quarter of a century after 1945 the Scottish system of secondary education was reorganised along lines consonant with the great Parliamentary Acts of 1918 and 1945. A far-reaching and often agonising revolution took place, in which the accepted functions and objectives of secondary eduction were subjected to a fierce reappraisal, carried out in the light of two fundamental principles – one, that it is a natural right of all children of whatever ability or social status to receive an education so ordered as to allow him or her to develop to his or her fullest potential; and two, that "a liberal state...will quite properly seek to ensure through education that the creative energies of a new generation are used to direct the forces of change along lines which are socially desirable and in general accord with the nation's traditions and practices."(10)

Contained in this approach which resulted in the emergence of a comprehensive secondary system lay a number of assumptions about the nature of secondary education, the roles of the school, and its power to influence the lives of its pupils and the society in which they live. Whereas justice would concede the right of all children to an appropriate education, as enunciated in the first principle, it does not necessarily or obviously follow that this would be best achieved by sending all children to the same kind of school;(11) while enshrined in the second is an assumption, among others, about the priority of the rights of the state over those of parents in the matter of the education of their children, and for that matter over the rights of the children themselves.(12) It also assumes a consistency between the principles themselves, and yet within them are concealed the conflicting forces which tend to polarise all educational effort, towards the development of the individual person on the one hand and towards meeting the needs of the community to which he or she belongs on the other.

In the application of these principles the following consequences emerged:

Selection procedures for the transfer of pupils from the primary to the secondary stage were abolished, (13) the curriculum expanded the better to meet the needs of individual pupils (14) and the pastoral role of the school in the area of social education was more widely recognised.

Each of these developments implied a need for more resources in schools. Not only would more teachers be required to meet the enlarged spectrum of demand, the skills and attitudes required of them would be of a somewhat different nature than those for which many had been trained and to which their professional experience had accustomed them. The emphasis would shift from mastery of subject content to the development of those capacities which ease interpersonal relationships and foster insight into and sympathy with the problems associated with adolescence.(15) The current shortage of teachers was exacerbated, and even before the comprehensive system was fully established staffing was recognised on all sides as the most serious problem.

Within the Catholic community there was widespread support for the comprehensive approach. In the eyes of many it seemed that the demands of social justice were more likely to be met by a comprehensive than by a selective system; and in the circumstances then existing in the Catholic secondary sector, catering as it did for only a small part of the population, some departure from the established pattern was essential if real advances were to be made. A system based on selection ran the risk of supporting divisions within the community in conflict with the christian view of the value of every individual. It was also the case that theoretical considerations were not seen to be of the first importance. The clamant need was for a major expansion at secondary level, in schools whose character would be determined by their commitment to Christian outlook and practice rather than by their organisational structure.

"We who have been engaged in the work of the Comprehensive School have been less concerned with theories...than with the practical problems. Our philosophy has of necessity been pragmatic, our methods empirical.... We have not set ourselves impossible standards of equality. Equality for us means equality in the sight of God...Justice for all might be nearer to our ideas than equality for all..."(16) As with the non-denominational sector, the Catholic schools had to adapt their outlook to the changed demands which the spirit of the times was imposing on them. From the mid-'fifties onwards, the new schools coming into being were comprehensive in character, and the model of the Catholic secondary school to which the community had become accustomed no longer applied. That model, characterised by single-sex schools managed by religious orders, with well-defined but limited academic objectives steadfastly pursued, was essentially selective in nature, to an extent greater perhaps than those most closely concerned in it were aware. It had fixed in the minds of a generation of Catholic parents and teachers an image of what the Catholic secondary school could and perhaps should be. Among its virtues was a recognition of the need to rely heavily on the influences of home and church to complete the work of education. To some extent it was open to the charge of seeking the "best of both worlds" now and hereafter. As an ideal it had, like the democracy of the Greek city state, much to commend it; but like that ancient ideal left unanswered the question of how to render justice to the helots.

THE CATHOLIC SECTOR AND THE EXPANSION OF THE CURRICULUM

For secondary education in general a range of problems arose from the need constantly to revise curricula in response to pressures from the world outside the school. The practical consequences of meeting within a short space of years the challenges presented, for example, by the introduction of 'new' mathematics, the change-over to a metric system, the re-structuring of the sciences to permit the development of biology and other branches at school level, or the frequent re-drawing of the world map, were in themselves enormous. They were however compounded by the decline of the classical tradition with its implications not only for the teaching of language and literature but also for religious education, by a revolution in physical, aesthetic and technical education in all their aspects, and by the impact of a revolution in systems of communication. Yet beyond these demands in the secular field Catholic teachers had to contend with other pressures. The insights of the Second Vatican Council had profound implications not only for formal religious instruction, but also for all aspects of christian education. Although its recommendations as expressed in its Declaration on Christian Education were confined to a few fundamental principles, in practice these could find implementation only through a properly balanced curriculum which had to be worked out in the schools.

THE CATHOLIC SCHOOLS AND NEW COMMUNITIES

A further aspect of the situation stemmed from the policy of urban renewal and consequent re-distribution of the Catholic population, which resulted in a dramatic increase in the number of Catholic parishes. (See Fig. 4 and Appendix 1). New secondary schools sometimes found themselves acting as catalysts in the formation of new communities, as well as fullfilling their educational role. This was especially so where the schools were situated in new housing areas.(17) In the eyes of some this was seen to be advantageous. "It was a new community...newly housed in new housing with new prospects everywhere. That was the great advantage as the education authorities saw it.... This was a new lease of life people were getting."(18) But experience soon gave rise to the question whether the new housing areas were the best places in which to develop the idea of comprehensive education, evoking a tentative answer from one experienced commentator: "The new housing scheme does not normally include many of the professional classes whose children on the whole are better prepared for the arduous academic courses. The advantage on the other hand is that here there need be no disturbance of existing tradition since the schools will themselves be new. But it is easier to absorb all types into a community which has already established its standards - and the lowly will be more likely to aim high in such circumstances - than it is to establish the school and the tradition together..."(19)

What can be said with certainty is that the institution of new schools in new communities imposed burdens and responsibilities on teaching staff sometimes far in excess of those normally associated with the educational process.

CRISIS

By the mid-1960s Catholic secondary education had entered a critical phase. As the pressures on the schools mounted, their capacity to offer adequate programmes of religious education decreased, as a direct result of the shortage of teachers. As expansion continued, teachers of substantial experience were distributed ever more widely through the new institutions, and replaced by inexperienced or uncertificated teachers or by colleagues drawn from the non-denominational sector. Uncertificated teachers for the most part were not fit to undertake the work of religious education, an inability they shared with some of the least experienced teachers who found the mastery of the teaching of their secular subject sufficiently demanding without the added responsibility of religious teaching. The system of religious education which had operated on the assumption that every member of staff would be willing and trained to share this aspect of the school's life began to crumble. The once central place of religious education was eroded. Religious periods were shortened, their number reduced and their time shared with secular tasks. Even in schools of the Religious Orders, religious programmes were affected. In some instances the strength of the Order so far declined that there was no more than one member active in a school. Such changes put further strains on the lay teaching body, who found that the standards they had been accustomed to expect as the norm now had to be maintained by insufficient staff working in difficult conditions in overcrowded schools. Teachers were deprived of the support and guidance formerly available from the Religious Orders. When to this was added the uncertainties arising from the controversies stimulated by the Second Vatican Council, religious education had entered a critical phase. By the mid-1960's the system of catechetical training of teachers was breaking down, and in 1966 the examination for the Religious Certificate taken by senior secondary pupils was finally abandoned.

The schools experienced a crisis of confidence. Many teachers felt that their competence in the field of religious eduction did not match their own standards in the secular area; many were afflicted by deep uncertainties as to how they should meet the spiritual needs of their charges.(20) Curricular development in religious education did not progress so fast as in the secular subjects. Time and energy for the working out of the integrated programme of secular and religious education which the situation demanded were not available. "The resultant strain...created a weakness which prompted a concerted attack on our schools by political parties, professional bodies, the Church of Scotland and even some Catholics themselves."(21)

RESPONSES

The crisis in moral and spiritual education which reached its height towards the end of the 'sixties was experienced throughout the national system. Reflecting the malaise of contemporary society, it evoked responses from both ecclesiastical and civil authorities.

In the Catholic sector the first took the form of the appointment of full-time chaplains to secondary schools. By 1970 eleven such appointments had been made in the Motherwell diocese, and the post of Organiser of Religious Education had been created.(22) This was followed by the institution of a catechetical centre through which the work of the school chaplains could be co-ordinated and resources made available to teachers. A similar policy was adopted in Glasgow where a catechetical centre was set up, also in 1970, and a start made on the appointment of full-time chaplains to secondary schools. By 1972 four such appointments had been made.(23) A second response was the setting up of the Catolic Education Commission whose remit was to advise and assist the Scottish Bishops in all educational matters. A third was the increased contribution of Notre Dame College of Education to the training of secondary teachers. When male students were admitted to the post-graduate course, it became possible to provide for some at least of the male Catholic teachers the substantial pre-service training in religious education formerly available only to women. By 1970 the College's annual output of secondary teachers had increased threefold from its 1960 level. In 1970-71 a Bachelor of Education degree was introduced with the specific aim of training teachers for secondary work, and a further contribution to the development of religious education was made through programmes of in-service training of teachers. (See Appendix 2).

The response of the civil authority was a broad-based strategy at once radical and imaginative. With the increase in size and complexity of secondary schools at a time of severe staff shortage, it was inevitable that the education of pupils would suffer. Very large schools could be threatening to pupils, especially to those less well-endowed physically, intellectually or emotionally. In them the risk was great that the development of some pupils would suffer such neglect as to have serious consequences. There was seen to be a need for a procedure which would enable teachers to get to know their pupils individually and also help pupils to make the fullest use of the opportunities increasingly becoming available to them.

A two-pronged approach was adopted. The first initiative took the form of the creation of posts of special responsibility for the vocational or curricular guidance of pupils, with the double aim of improving the career structure for teachers and meeting the needs of management in large schools; the second came with the publication of the SED Memorandum "Guidance in Scottish Secondary Schools." This brief but seminal paper which defined guidance in schools as "the taking of that personal interest in pupils as individuals which makes it possible to assist them in making choices or decisions," drew attention to the large size of schools as the source of the need for a change in emphasis in the educational system; it pointed to the increased difficulty of diagnosing the needs of the individual pupil; and finally suggested that guidance could be seen in three main aspects - personal, vocational and curricular - and outlined some possible approaches and forms of organisation.(24)

The number of schools establishing guidance systems increased during 1969-70. Proposals for a fundamental reallocation of duties among promoted staff were put forward in a further Memorandum (25). As a consequence, "guidance was to have a clear place in schools. Subsequently Circular 826 indicated what complements of promoted posts the Secretary of State would normally regard as appropriate... By August 1974 all thirty-five former education authorities had made appointments which were generally in line with the complements recommended."(26)

Partly as a result of its association with the concept of Child Guidance,(27) Notre Dame College was able to contribute vigorously to this developing area from 1970-71 onwards, through its In-Service programmes. (See APPENDIX 2).

RECOVERY

With the overhaul of the promotion structure career prospects in schools dramatically improved - and with it, the supply of teachers. By session 1971-2 the increase in the number of teachers employed in education authority schools was proportionately greater than the rise in the number of pupils. (TABLE 11) "Improvement in the secondary schools was particularly marked in areas with long-standing recruitment problems. Glasgow improved its overall PTR ratio from 17.3 to 16.4:1; Ayrshire from 15.7 to 15.2:1. Shortages persisted in some areas, particularly in Lanarkshire.... Roman Catholic schools continued to be less well staffed than non-denominational schools but their overall ratio improved from 18.4 to 17.7:1, compared with an improvement from 15.7 to 15.2:1 in non-denominational schools."(28) The employment of unqualified teachers in secondary schools was ended.

A further change in the staffing situation resulted from a rapid, continuing and unexpected fall in the national birth-rate. By 1968, the children of the post-war years of high birth-rate were completing tertiary education, and an increasing proportion of these age-groups found posts in secondary schools. As this trend continued the position in the secondary schools steadily improved. The Catholic sector benefited in these ways, along with the non-denominational sector, and experienced a further benefit in that by 1972 the flow of Catholic candidates into teacher-training was being drawn from a greatly enlarged source. (TABLE 17). Nevertheless over the south-west as a whole, progress was uneven. Those areas where the problems of housing and job opportunity were most intractable were also the areas offering the greatest difficulties in the educational field, and in some of these the Catholic community was over-represented. In Glasgow in the autumn of 1971 the PTR in non-denominational secondary schools was 16:1 as against a level in Roman Catholic schools of 19.4:1.

The evidence therefore points to a lingering but decreasing disparity in provision between the denominational and non-denominational sectors, which had its origin in the differences that existed in 1918 between the voluntary and state systems. It would seem that at no time during the following half-century of educational progress were specific steps taken either by Church or State authorities to identify those conditions affecting the Catholic sector which necessitated that its rate of advance would differ from that of the national system. The many major educational advances made were arrived at on the basis of the overall needs of the state system, without regard for any substantial regional or sectional variations that might have existed. In the general advance the Catholic community shared, through the work of its schools, in the benefits conferred by a vigorous and progressive educational system; but it could be argued that by merely following in the wake of the national system the capacity of the Catholic sector to develop its full potential and thereby to confer the maximum benefit on that system was substantially reduced or retarded.

TABLE 16

Secondary Teachers and Pupils in E.A. Schools

Jan.	Pupils(000)	Teachers	PTR	Increase over previous year	
1970	304.0	18,485	16.4:1	632	3.5%
1971	314.4	19,480	16.1:1	995	5.4%
1972	324.4	20,748	15.6:1	1,268	6.5%

TABLE 17

Secondary Schools Attended by Students
Entering Notre Dame College

	1958–59 No. of Schools	% of Intake	1969–70 No. of Schools	% of Intake
Glasgow	5	52.9	17	50.5
Lanarkshire	1	10.6	5	17.5
Dunbartonshire	2	7.7	3	7.3
Renfrewshire	2	10.6	4	11.0
Ayrshire	3	12.5	4	6.3
Stirlingshire	1	1.0	2	1.5
Dumfriesshire	0	–	3	0.9
	14	95.3	38	95.0

In session 1958–59 intake into Notre Dame College consisted of women only. Catholic men students training for teaching attended Jordanhill College. The remaining 5% of students were drawn from catholic schools in other parts of Scotland, from non-denominational schools, or from sources outside of Scotland.

NOTES

1. McKechin, W.J.   Plus or Minus. Local Govt. Research Unit Paisley C. of T. Working Paper No.7, 1976.
2. Report on Measures to Improve the Supply of Teachers in Scotland. Cmd. 644.
3. Corporation of Glasgow Education Committee Handbooks. See also Breen, NDSA 12 and McGinley, NDSA 19 for comments on large schools.
4. 27/10/65 asking Authorities to reorganise secondary education on comprehensive lines.
5. Education in Scotland 1967.   Table B   p.67.
6. There were instances of teachers in Catholic secondary schools remaining in post after attaining eighty years of age.
7. Education in Scotland 1965.   p.28   Cmnd. 2914.
8. Education in Scotland 1966.   p.22   Cmnd. 3216.
9. McGinley, J.   NDSA 19, p.12.
10. Report of the Advisory Council on Secondary Education.
11. The education of mentally or physically handicapped children or of highly gifted children points up this issue in the most obvious way. Equally important are the problems arising from the variety of talents and rates of development of children generally.
12. The second principle opens the questions - Who will decide what is socially desirable? Who will teach the teachers?
13. Education in Scotland 1966.   p.10   Cmnd. 3216.
14. Education in Scotland 1968.   p.15   SED.
15. The Training of Graduates for Secondary Education. Report by the General Teaching Council.   HMSO 1972.
16. Murray, J.   NDSA 6   p.35.
17. Bellarmine(Pollok) St. Margaret Mary's (Castlemilk) St. Leonard's (Easterhouse) All Saints (Balornock) St. Pius' (Drumchapel) St. Augustine's (Milton) and St. Columba's (Clydebank) came into this category.
18. Murray, J.   NDSA 6   p.29.
19. Ibid.   p.36.
20. "One point of general agreement...is that a crisis exists...the Council formulated a new understanding of the church which affected every aspect of its life."   (Hebblethwaite, P.   The Runaway Church, p.229.)
21. McKee, J.J.   Hierarchy Centenary Supplement. The Universe. 3 March 1978.
22. WCC 1969, 1970.
23. WCC 1973.
24. Guidance in Scottish Secondary Schools   pp3-4   HMSO
25. The Structure of Promoted Posts in Scottish Secondary Schools.   HMSO.
26. Guidance in Scottish Secondary Schools. A Progress Report pp.5-6. SED 1976.
27. McAleer, Maureen (Sister Jude SND)   Freedom to grow.
28. Education in Scotland 1972.

CHAPTER TWELVE

END AND BEGINNING

A DISTINCTIVE SYSTEM

When the Church authorities decided in 1918 to transfer their schools into
the State system, they accepted a commitment to develop a secondary sector
distinctive at least to some degree from the national system and on a level
of parity with it for all children up to the age of fourteen. This entailed,
inter alia, their acceptance of state control over a wide area of the
educational process and the concept of secondary education contained in the
Act, as well as the implementation in practice of a view of secular and
religious education as separate and separable processes. There was no accurate
assessment of the demand for secondary education that would arise from the
provisions of the Act. The existing model of catholic education was deemed
appropriate for the new dispensation.

After 1918 control over the quality of the education given in the Catholic
schools depended largely on the right of the Church to provide new schools,
to nominate religious supervisors and to approve the appointment of staff.
When the rights in the matter of accommodation were waived, the role of the
teaching body in the preservation of the ethos of the secondary schools and
therefore of their distinctive character was greatly enhanced.

By 1939 a distinctive but limited Catholic secondary sector had emerged.
The limitations were to be seen in its size, in that it had not yet developed
far enough to serve the needs of the whole community; in its objectives,
in that its principal aim was to provide the educational basis for the
emergence of a professional class; in its curriculum, in that the Catholic
secondary schools restricted their efforts within well-defined academic areas;
and in the relatively slow development of a junior secondary sector. The
distinctiveness rested on its commitment to a view of moral and religious
formation based on the doctrine and sacramental practice of the Catholic
Church. In spite of limitations, the system was able to give expression to
principles fundamental to a truly Christian educational system. These were,
on the one hand, reliance on the personal commitment of teachers to preserve
the religious nature of the education given, and on the other, identity in
outlook and belief with the community which the schools existed to serve.
Through these recognition was given to both individual and community aspects
of the Christian educational ideal.

In their approach to secular education the Catholic schools adopted the model presented by the state sector. The 1918 Act had seen the function of secondary education to be the preparation of a select minority - "those able to benefit from it" - for entry to a higher level of education, and the Catholic sector was shaped by this concept. Schools established before 1945 were selective; offered a curriculum academic in nature, and endorsed the notion of secondary education as a preparation for higher education and careers. They accepted the separation of the religious and secular aspects of education. This convergence with the state system seemed to offer no great threat to the distinctiveness of the Catholic system, which preserved its separate identity in a number of practical ways, as ·for example by the gearing of its holiday pattern to the Church's liturgical year, and generally by acceptance of the Church's discipline in the matter of Mass attendance, observance of fasting and abstinence regulations and so on. There appeared to be no need to elaborate the differences when these were so obvious.

In the fullness of time religious instruction began to take a form very similar to that of the secular subjects. Emphasis was placed on the acquisition of knowledge of doctrine, church history and practice. The system operated on a number of assmptions that were for the most part well-founded, namely, that pupils, parents, and staff were united in faith through their common Baptism; that the teaching given would be reinforcedby practice at home and by participation in the life of the Church; and that the responsibility of the school in religious and moral formation was to be shared with the Church and especially the parents, who carried the prime duty. The methods used were affected by the absence of suitable textbooks as well as by lack of time, but were less inappropriate for pupils conditioned to an academic approach to learning than to a broader spectrum of the community.

Within its limits this system worked well during the inter-war period. There appeared to be emerging a stratum of educated Catholics, unified in outlook, in whom intellectual conviction reinforced traditional loyalty to the Church's teaching and to ecclesiastical authority. Within that group was a growing body of teachers who formed the spearhead of a new cultural force in the community. As the secondary sector expanded, responsibility for the religious as well as the secular elements in Catholic education devolved increasingly on this body of lay men and women.

Perhaps in reaction to this unanimity and to the cohesion which it engendered, the Catholic system of moral and religious education came under attack as being of the nature of indoctrination rather than of true education. While this is a charge which could be brought against almost any educational system, it raises critical questions for one which upholds the primacy of the individual conscience, which identifies the essence of the Godhead with the concept of love, and which points to the free response of the human will, through love of God and neighbour, as the way to salvation. It may be appropriate therefore at this point to give some detailed consideration to this allegation.

If indoctrination means the process of conditioning to which a child is subject through schooling, it would be true to say for all children that this begins before he enters school. Because education is compulsory, parents have already been indoctrinated with a number of ideas before their child is handed over to the schools. These include the acceptance of an authority other than their own in the educational field, and the acceptance of the priorities laid down by it. In his school experience the child is then subjected to a form of conditioning through the curriculum and the ethos of the school, as well as through its hidden curriculum. In a democratic society such a system finds its justification in the fact that parents give their consent in the case of their own children, and are satisfied with the degree of control they are able to exercise through the electoral process. They accept that there is a social aspect to education which requires that they co-operate with the legitimate authority in the matter of the upbringing of their children.

Catholic parents like others accept this situation in the matter of secular education, while retaining the primacy of their own authority. This is not something bestowed on them by the state. It arises by the nature of the parent-child relationship, in which the parents are the authors of the life of the children. In the matter of religious education they claim the right to exercise this authority. The Catholic school derives its right to give a religious education and formation from the parents, who choose to have their children trained in that system, and who accept the doctrines being taught.

The question remains whether the element of parental control reduces simply to an opportunity to choose between alternative forms of indoctrination.

In an ideal system, pupils would be brought to accept or reject propositions, ideas or attitudes through intellectual conviction. In practice they are expected to accept propositions of one sort or another on the authority of the teacher.   The question has to be faced, is it legitimate to teach in this way? What in fact is the essence of 'indoctrination', in the pejorative sense in which it is frequently used? Does it depend on the truth or falsity of the doctrine being taught? Would it constitute indoctrination, for example, to teach that the evolution of species proceeds by a process described as 'survival of the fittest'? Or, does the danger only arise when the doctrine is found to be false, or not proven? Would it constitute indoctrination if a teacher were to propagate a false doctrine which he nevertheless believed to be true? Is the teacher to be the judge in these matters? Again, does indoctrination depend on the extent to which the doctrine (true or false) is accepted?(1) Or on the clarity and conviction with which it is presented? One contributor to the Millar Report attempts to rebut the allegation made against religious education generally by saying that "the confusion and muddle about even the basic facts of the Bible at least puts the lie to the charge of indoctrination."(2)

Teaching cannot proceed without an appeal to authority. Children however are clearly not in a position to judge between one authority and another. In the case of the very young at least, that responsibility must rest with the parents. A point must of necessity arise, however, when the authority of the parent should give way to the right of the child to make his or her own decisions in important areas of living. An educational system should take account of the need to prepare pupils for this critical point in their lives. There must therefore be some difference in approach to the delicate and difficult area of religious education at the secondary as compared to the primary level. It may be that in practice for reasons already adumbrated the Catholic secondary schools for a time did not give sufficient attention to this difference.

If there is any force in the allegation of indoctrination, it might draw its strength from the extent to which the secondary sector relied on methods of teaching more appropriate to the primary schools, namely the system of rote-learning of the Catechism. And yet, if indoctrination it were, many trained that way did not see it as in any way to be denigrated. "The catechism... provided a framework into which mysterious issues could be put in such a way that a child...would see them as acceptable.... It was a formative experience for children...most people would remember their catechism lessons long after every other lesson had been forgotten..."(3)

There remains another aspect of this question to be considered – the position of the teacher, whose demeanour and lifestyle inevitably proclaim his outlook and attitudes, whether deliberately and consciously or not. "The achievement of the specific aim (in the field of religious education) of the catholic school depends not so much on the subject matter or methodology as on the people who work there. The extent to which the Christian message is transmitted through education depends to a very great extent on the teachers. The integration of culture and faith is mediated by the other integration of faith and life in the person of the teacher. The nobility of the task to which they are called demands that...they reveal the Christian message not only by word but also by every gesture of their behaviour. This is what makes the difference between a school whose education is permeated by the Christian spirit, and one in which religion is only regarded as an academic subject like any other."(4)

Whatever their deficiencies of methodology, the Catholic secondary schools of the inter-war period were in fact permeated by the Christian spirit. In the matter of religious education "the paramount impression left on the child was 'this is the most important thing' because of the manner and sincerity and drive which the teachers brought to it."(5)

1945–1972

Because of the changed view of secondary education promulgated by the Act of 1945, closer collaboration between Church and State in the field of education became possible. In the opinion of the Advisory Council on Secondary Education "the chief end of education is to foster the full and harmonious development of the individual...selves can only develop in accordance with their own nature, and their nature is social...one of the major functions of the school is to pass on the moral and social inheritance and to direct the sentiments and habits of young people towards the good life."(6) This may be compared with the view of the Second Vatican Council: "Since every man...is endowed with the dignity of a person, he has an inalienable right to an education corresponding to his proper destiny and suited to his native talents, his sex, his cultural background and his ancestral heritage...young people should be assisted in the harmonious development of their physical, moral and intellectual endowments.... As they advance in years, they should be given positive and prudent sexual education...children and young people have a right to be encouraged to weigh moral values with an upright conscience and to embrace them by personal choice."(7)

Church and State agree in recognising the dignity of persons, the social dimension in education, the importance of moral values and the cultural

Inheritance of groups. Interestingly, in view of the charge of indoctrination, it is the church's statement which stresses personal choice, while the Advisory Council refers to direction. The Council raises the question of the good life, without defining it. Therein no doubt lies the difference between a religious and a secular education.

This philosophical convergence found practical expression in the system of comprehensive schools, which developed more or less in parallel in the denominational and non-denominational sectors. The problems which arose were common to both, and this tended to draw them closer together. This in turn gave rise to increased criticism of the Catholic system as divisive, and to calls for its integration into the national system.

Throughout the period of expansion the Catholic schools strove to maintain their traditional concern for religious and moral formation, a concern shared by many others throughout the country. In a submission to the Millar Committee the Association of County Councils in Scotland said "No society has yet solved the problem of how to teach morality without religion" and saw Christianity as the basis of morality; while the Headmasters Association of Scotland felt that "Moral education without reference to religious belief would be arid, de-personalised and ineffective."(8) Yet these justifications for religious education are less than adequate, in that they propose as reasons for its presence something other than the truth encompassed within it. The Catholic system on the other hand puts forward a view of reality which it holds to be true, from which follows a way of life based on the sacramental practice of the Catholic Church. In this view, moral and religious education are inseparable.

TRANSFORMATION

By 1972 the Catholic secondary sector was completely transformed from its situation in 1922. It had expanded to a size commensurate with the population. Overall, the influence of the Religious Teaching Orders had declined, and all of them, with the exception of the Society of Jesus, operated within the national system. Shortages of staff persisted in certain areas, especially in the practical and aesthetic subjects. The point was being reached where the education of the Catholic people was passing almost entirely into the hands of the laity.

This transformation was accompanied by an equally profound change in the local Catholic community. Between 1922 and 1972, when the Catholic population of Scotland had increased by more than half to c. 823,000, the share of the south-west increased from 67% to 75%, to 628,000. Within the Province of Glasgow the Archdiocese, consisting of the City of Glasgow plus Dunbartonshire, slightly outweighed the combined populations of the Paisley and Motherwell dioceses. Within the city the community was no longer so concentrated geographically, or so unified in outlook and social experience as it had been in the inter-war period.

A professional class had emerged. One of the fruits of this advance was a growing division within the community based on social distinctions. There was no strong tradition of Catholic intellectualism, and an absence of that integration of culture and faith which might be taken to be a hallmark of an educated Catholic community.(9)

Some aspects of these changes have been analysed by Darragh, who reached the following conclusions:

The relationship between the birth-rates of the Catholic and national communities had narrowed from a factor of just under 1.5 in 1900 to 1.3 in the 1970's; between 1961 and 1971 the rate of growth of the Catholic population was only one-fifth of what it had been in the first decade of the century; from 1871 to 1976, net emigration from Scotland had exceeded 2 million; after 1945, emigration probably numbered 900,000, mainly to overseas countries; there was a significant increase in the number of mixed marriages; by 1972, in Glasgow 42%, in Motherwell 32% and in Paisley 45% of all Catholic marriages were 'mixed'; the number of Catholic marriages ending in divorce increased to a level similar to that pertaining nationally; the number of Catholic secondary pupils in Scotland in 1921 was about 3.3% of the Catholic school population; by 1972 this had risen to 31.2%; about 24% of the 3,400 teachers in all Catholic secondary schools in 1971 were not Catholics; a proportion of Catholic children were, by parental choice, attending non-denominational schools in areas where Catholic schools were available; Catholics were not leaving the older city areas in the same numbers as were other sections of the community; leakage from the Church in Scotland was some 52,000 between 1931 and 1951, and 120,000 from 1951 to 1976.

Darragh concludes that at the end of a century of remarkable progress, the Church in Scotland appeared to be losing something of what it had gained. "In 1878, the Catholic community was distinct in practically every respect from the country as a whole, but a century later this was no longer the case." **(10)**

REAPPRAISAL

By 1972 the social and educational context in which the Catholic schools operated was so altered that a complete reappraisal of their situation was needed. The limitations formerly imposed by inadequate accommodation and shortage of staff were disappearing, and no longer constituted a legitimate excuse for avoiding a radical examination of the fundamental aims of the system. The needs of the community had also changed. Hand in hand with the expansion of secondary education had gone a vast increase in the numbers of Catholic students in tertiary education. It has been estimated that the Catholic student community of Glasgow was the largest such in Britain. Preparation of such a group for the heady atmosphere of intellectual freedom should have been a major responsibility of the schools.

The community displayed little initiative in the political or cultural field. Even in education, where its commitment was obviously strong, major developments for the most part emanated from sources elsewhere. There was little urgency to seek a positive and integrated approach to major social or political issues. The community was content to follow or reject the initiatives of others, but not to give a lead. The hope once expressed by C.M. Grieve that future cultural progress in Scotland would come about through the emergence of a new generation of Catholic artists showed little sign of fulfilment. The Catholic Scots-Irish contribution to a literary revival remained depressingly minimal. "Among their many achievements, despite daunting handicaps, they must be acquitted of instigating an artistic upheaval."**(11)** In the political field, no integrated approach inspired by the application of christian principles to major social or political issues emerged. "By the 1950's...Catholics in politics have become part of the 'informal' political establishment in many areas of Scottish life... the sense of Catholic mission, of being a sign of contradiction, may have become less obvious.... The Labour Party...and the Catholic establishment have come to an understanding on the administration of the enormous educational machine.... A situation where no one is too anxious to ask searching questions ...may become one of institutional inertia."(12)

While it would be foolish to attribute too great an influence to the schools for these outcomes, equally it would be wrong to discount it all together. On the positive side, they have been instrumental in laying the foundation for the emergence of an educated laity and a professional class; they have provided, through the expanded teaching cadre and careers structure in schools, a broad economic base for a substantial sector of the Catholic community; they have maintained an integrated approach to religious and moral education, helping to keep alive an awareness of the transcendental nature of existence. On the negative side it could be urged that they have failed to accept sufficient responsibility for shaping their own policies, to be properly self-critical, or to produce an adequate flow of secondary teachers appreciative of the potential contribution that their christian cultural heritage could make across the curricular spectrum.

Some of the questions that might have to be answered would have to do with the attitudes and spirituality of the schools. It could be alleged for example that they were more authoritarian in their mode of operation than their non-denominational counterparts. If so, was this destructive of intellectual effort? Were their products less well prepared to face the liberty of university or adult life? Did a spirituality which emphasised self-denial and withdrawal from the world result, whatever its merits, in attitudes of non-involvement and comparative lack of commitment?

Whatever answers might be given to these or to other related questions, it is clear that the schools cannot by themselves bring about the changes in direction and achievement that the situation seems to require. A concerted effort of the whole community is needed; but it is also clear that in practice the implementation of any policy aiming at educational renewal will rest on the shoulders of the teaching body.

If the Catholic secondary sector is to survive as a separate element within the national system, its distinctive character has to be preserved. This will require, inter alia, a close examination of the manner in which the general principles governing Catholic education apply in the secondary field; exam-ination also of their application in the particular circumstances of the Scottish system; consideration of the interplay of secular and religious aspects of the curriculum, and of the interdependence of the primary and secondary sectors; and a reassessment of the responsibilities of the Catholic secondary teacher particularly in the area of religious education.

Guidelines in these matters were laid down by the Second Vatican Council. In its analysis of christian education it stated with the utmost clarity that christian education is in the world and in a sense for the world, and must achieve its end by contributing to the whole human community. It placed a strong emphasis on the intellectual values of all education and appealed for all to strive to achieve the highest development of the human mind, while recognising that this has to be done in the framework of the moral formation of man and in the fullness of his spiritual supernatural destiny.(13)

The corollary must be that these principles must apply a forteriori to the formation of teachers, who are called upon to show in their personal lives the qualities they are expected to foster in their pupils. The immensity of the challenge which they, and the community, face is adumbrated by the following quotation:

"Today it is more difficult than it once was to synthesize the various disciplines of knowledge and the arts. While the volume and diversity of the elements which make up culture increase, at the same time the capacity of individual men to perceive them and to blend them organically decreases, so that the image of universal man becomes even more faint.(Gaudium at Spes, 61) Any interpretation of knowledge and culture therefore which ignores or even belittles the spiritual essence of man, his aspirations to the fullness of being, his thirst for truth and the absolute, the questions that he asks himself before the enigmas of sorrow and death, cannot be said to satisfy his deepest and most authentic needs. And since it is in the university that young people experience the high point of their formative education, they should be able to find answers not only about the legitimacy and finality of science but also about higher moral and spiritual values - answers that will restore their confidence in the potential of knowledge gained and the exercise of reason, for their own good and for that of society."

Quoted from the address on Education given by Pope John Paul II on the occasion of his visit to St.Andrew's College of Education on 1 June 1982.

NOTES

1.   Millar Report   2.102.
2.   Ibid.
3.   O'Hagan A.I.   NDSA,9 .p.23.
4.   Sacred Congregation for Catholic Education. The Catholic School   V.43.
          Rome, 1971.
5.   O'Hagan, A.I.   Loc.cit.
6.   Secondary Education. Report of the Advisory Council on Education.
          Sections 48,50,90.   Cmd. 7005.
7.   Declaration on Christian Education   pp.639-640.
8.   Millar Report 3.11
9.   The Catholic School   V.43.
10.   Darragh, J.   I.R. XXIX,2
11.   Reilly, P.   I.R. XXIX,2   p.185.
12.   McCaffrey, J.F.   I.R. XXIX,2   pp.152-3.
13.   Declaration on Christian Education.

APPENDIX I/IA

CATHOLIC PARISHES OF SOUTH-WEST SCOTLAND, WITH POPULATION

PARISHES FOUNDED BEFORE 1922

TABLE 18

Parishes of Glasgow City

Index No.	Parish	Location	Date of Foundation	Population 1922	Population 1972
1.	St. Andrew's	Clyde St.	1816	4,500	900
2.	St. Mary's	Abercrombie St.	1842	10,000	2,600
3.	St. Alphonsus'	London Road	1846	5,400	2,800
4.	St. John's	Portugal St.	1846	8,626	2,000
5.	St. Mary's	Pollokshaws	1849	4,085	3,400
6.	St. Mungo's	Townhead	1850	7,600	1,650
7.	St. Patrick's	Anderson	1850	15,000	2,470
8.	St. Paul's	Shettleston	1850	3,000	3,050
9.	Immaculate Conception	Maryhill	1851	6,000	2,600
10.	St. Joseph's	N. Woodside Rd.	1850	7,800	400
11.	St. Aloysius'	Springburn	1856	6,319	5,000
12.	St. Peter's	Partick	1858	10,000	4,000
13.	St. Anthony's	Govan	1861	8,400	1,800
14.	St. Aloysius'	Garnethill	1866	6,500	2,000
15.	St. Francis'	Gorbals	1868	12,150	3,500
16.	Sacred Heart	Bridgeton	1873	12,000	3,000
17.	O.L. & St. Margaret	Kinning Park	1874	10,000	3,000
18.	St. Michael's	Parkhead	1876	5,500	2,030
19.	Holy Cross	Crosshill	1882	4,420	5,870
20.	St. Agnes'	Lambhill	1884	2,600	2,750
21.	St. Joseph's	Tollcross	1893	2,500	2,900
22.	St. Saviour's	Govan	1897	5,300	3,500
23.	St. Anne's	Dennistoun	1898	6,700	3,800
24.	St. Charles'	N. Kelvinside	1899	4,000	4,320
25.	St. Paul's	Whiteinch	1903	3,000	3,000
26.	O.L. of Lourdes	Cardonald	1906	434	5,300
27.	St. Mark's	Carntyne	1906	2,232	2,200
28.	St. Roch's	Garngad	1907	7,279	5,700
29.	St. Columba's	Maryhill	1906	3,800	2,300
30.	St. Luke's	Hutchesontown	1905	6,000	1,000
31.	St. Constantine's	Govan	1921	2,650	5,700
				193,795	94,540

CATHOLIC PARISHES OF SOUTH—WEST SCOTLAND, WITH POPULATION

PARISHES FOUNDED BEFORE 1922

TABLE 19

Parishes of Dunbartonshire

Index No.	Parish	Location	Date of Foundation	Population 1922	1972
32	St. Patrick's	Dumbarton	1830	7,000	2,800
33	St. Mary's	Duntocher	1841	2,574	3,000
34	O.L. & St. Mark's	Alexandria	1859	2,170	2,200
35	St. Joseph's	Helensburgh	1865	1,400	2,200
36	St. Joseph's	Milngavie	1872	683	2,000
37	Holy Family	Kirkintilloch	1874	2,700	2,900
38	Our Holy Redeemer	Clydebank	1888	6,119	1,500
39	St. Martin's	Renton	1899	1,627	1,350
40	Holy Cross	Croy	1902	1,700	2,400
41	St. Stephen's	Dalmuir	1907	3,750	5,400
				29,723	25,750

APPENDIX I/IA

CATHOLIC PARISHES OF SOUTH-WEST SCOTLAND, WITH POPULATION

PARISHES FOUNDED BEFORE 1922

TABLE 20

Parishes of Motherwell Diocesan Area

Index No.	Parish	Location	Date of Foundation	Population 1922	Population 1972
42	St. Margaret's	A Airdrie	1836	2,700	1,700
43	St. Mary's	H Hamilton	1846	5,224	2,000
44	St. Patrick's	A Coatbridge	1848	5,500	2,680
45	St. Athanasius'	C Carluke	1849	500	1,200
46	St. Joseph's	C Carstairs	1851	Served from Lanark	
47	St. Aloysius'	A Chappelhall	1859	2,000	1,950
48	St. Ignatius'	M Wishaw	1859	3,400	3,600
49	St. Mary's	C Lanark	1859	1,250	2,000
50	St. Patrick's	C Strathaven	1859	397	710
51	St. Francis Xavier	M Carfin	1862	3,193	2,340
52	Holy Family	M Mossend	1868	5,392	2,050
53	St. Patrick's	M Shotts	1868	2,300	3,200
54	St. Brigid's	M Newmains	1871	1,268	2,000
55	St. Mary's	H Larkhall	1872	1,650	1,420
56	St. Mary's	M Cleland	1874	2,010	1,460
57	St. Mary's	A Whifflet	1874	3,200	4,750
58	O.L. of Good Aid	M Motherwell	1874	6,913	2,350
59	St. Joseph's	C Stepps	1875	2,022	960
60	St. Joseph's	H Blantyre	1877	4,800	6,600
61	St. Mary's	A Caldercruix	1878	1,319	940
62	St. Bridget's	A Baillieston	1880	2,300	3,300
63	O.L. & St. John's	C Blackwood	1880	750	620
64	O.L. & St. Joseph's	A Glenboig	1880	1,820	1,460
65	St. John Baptist	H Uddingston	1883	3,491	2,500
66	O.L. & St. Anne	H Hamilton	1883	2,223	3,740
67	St. Brides	R Cambuslang	1890	5,000	2,600
68	St. Columkille	R Rutherglen	1851	4,416	5,020
69	St. Patrick's	M Wishaw	1891	4,500	4,000
70	St. Augustine's	A Coatbridge	1892	6,500	3,000
71	St. Cuthbert's	H Burnbank	1893	3,000	2,900
72	St. Charles'	R Newton	1894	1,570	460
73	St. David's	A Plains	1900	1,260	2,100
74	All Saints	A Airdrie	1902	2,800	3,800
75	St. Bride's	H Bothwell	1910	1,982	1,400
76	St. Dominic's	C Greengairs	1893	Served from Plains	
				96,650	80,810

A – Parishes in the Airdrie-Coatbridge area
M – Parishes in the Motherwell-Wishaw area
H – Parishes in the Hamilton-Bothwell area
R – Parishes in the Rutherglen-Cambuslang area
C – 'County' Parishes

APPENDIX I/IA

CATHOLIC PARISHES OF SOUTH—WEST SCOTLAND, WITH POPULATION

PARISHES FOUNDED BEFORE 1922

TABLE 21

Parishes of Paisley Diocesan Area

Index No.	Parish	Location	Date of Foundation	Population 1922	1972
77.	St. Mirin's	Paisley	1808	10,000	4,500
78.	St. Mary's	Greenock	1816	10,533	2,000
79.	St. John's	Barrhead	1841	3,300	5,400
80.	St. Fillan's	Houston	1841	500	820
81.	St. John's	Port Glasgow	1846	6,000	2,750
82.	St. Joseph's	Busby	1880	620	2,300
83.	St. Margaret's	Johnstone	1852	3,740	3,610
84.	St. Laurence	Greenock	1855	5,500	4,850
85.	O.L. & St. Thomas	Neilston	1861	925	1,400
86.	St. Mary's	Paisley	1876	4,600	3,150
87.	St. James's	Renfrew	1877	1,600	2,500
88.	St. Ninian's	Gourock	1880	800	2,110
89.	St. Charles's	Paisley	1897	1,500	2,500
90.	St. Conval	Linwood	1898	1,050	3,500
				50,668	41,390

APPENDIX 1/1A

CATHOLIC PARISHES OF SOUTH-WEST SCOTLAND, WITH POPULATION

PARISHES FOUNDED BEFORE 1922

TABLE 22

Parishes of Galloway Diocesan Area

(a)   North Ayrshire, (Parishes belonging to Glasgow Archdiocese until 1948)

Index No.	Parish	Location	Date of Foundation	Population 1922	Population 1972
91.	St. Palladius'	Dalry	1848	930	600
92.	O.L. Star of the Sea	Saltcoats	1853	3,000	1,700
93.	St. Bridget's	Kilbirnie	1862	1,540	1,325
94.	St. Mary's	Largs	1869	310	1,050
95.	St. Winin's	Kilwinning	1872	750	1,300
96.	St. Sophia's	Galston	1885	600	850
97.	St. John's	Stevenston	1905	1,245	2,100
				8,375	8,925

APPENDIX I/IA

CATHOLIC PARISHES OF SOUTH-WEST SCOTLAND, WITH POPULATION

PARISHES FOUNDED BEFORE 1922

TABLE 22

Parishes of Galloway Diocesan Area

(b) Remainder of diocesan area

Index No.	Parish	Location	Date of Foundation	Population 1922	1972
98.	St. Peter's	Dalbeattie	1814		430
99.	St. Andrew's	Dumfries	1810		1,800
100.	St. Mary's	New Abbey	1815		Served from Dumfries
101.	St. Margaret's	Ayr	1822		1,500
102.	O.L. & St. Ninian	Newton Stewart	1825		220
103.	St. Columba	Annan	1839		500
104.	SS Andrew & Cuthbert	Kirkcudbright	1845		400
105.	St. Joseph's	Stranraer	1846		650
106.	St. Joseph's	Kilmarnock	1847		2,540
107.	St. John Evangelist	Cumnock	1850		1,400
108.	Sacred Hearts	Girvan	1850		920
109	St. Francis Xavier	Duneskin	1860		720
110	O.L. & St. Patrick	Auchinleck	1867		630
111	St. John Evangelist	Castle Douglas	1867		400
112	O.L. & St. Cuthbert	Maybole	1878		520
113	St. Paul	Hurlford	1883		840
114	SS Martin, Ninian	Whithorn	1880		240
115	O.L. & St. Meddan	Troon	1894		980
116	St. Ann	Annbank	1898		610
117	St. Conal	Kirkconnell	1921		160
118	St. Thomas Apostle	Muirkirk	1856		200
119	St. Mary's	Irvine	1862		2,812

16,000(Est.) 18,472

APPENDIX I/IB

CATHOLIC PARISHES OF SOUTH-WEST SCOTLAND, WITH POPULATION

PARISHES FOUNDED BETWEEN 1922 AND 1939

TABLE 23

(a) Glasgow City

Index No.	Parish	Location	Date of Foundation	Population 1972
120	St. Thomas's	Riddrie	1924	3,500
121	St. Ninian's	Knightswood	1927	5,220
122	St. Teresa's	Possilpark	1932	6,700
123	Christ the King	King's Park	1934	4,800
124	St. Philomena	Royston	1939	5,140
				25,360

(b) Dunbartonshire

Nil

(c) Motherwell Diocesan Area

125	St. Catherine of Siena	Harthill M	1924	800
126	St. Isidore	Biggar C	1937	80
127	St. Columba	Viewpark H	1939	5,500
				6,380

(d) Paisley Diocesan Area

128	St. Patrick's	Greenock	1924	3,000
129	O.L. of Lourdes	Bishopton	1926	750
130	St. Mungo's	Greenock	1934	4,200
				7,950

APPENDIX I/IB

CATHOLIC PARISHES OF SOUTH-WEST SCOTLAND, WITH POPULATION

PARISHES FOUNDED BETWEEN 1922 AND 1939

TABLE 23

(e) Galloway Diocesan Area

131	St Peter in Chains	Ardrossan	1939	2,625
132	St. Ninian's	Gretna	1925	190
133	St. Quivox	Prestwick	1938	1,100
				3,915

M, C, H as for Table 22

APPENDIX I/IC

CATHOLIC PARISHES OF SOUTH-WEST SCOTLAND, WITH POPULATION
PARISHES FOUNDED BETWEEN 1940 - 1972

TABLE 24
Glasgow City

Index No.	Parish	Location	Date of Foundation		Population 1972
134	St. Robert Bellarmine	Househillwood	1941	C	6,850
135	Immaculate Heart of Mary	Balornock	1946	C	1,400
136	St. Matthew's	Bishopbriggs	1948	D	4,250
137	St. Simon's	Partick	1945	D	1,000
138	St. Vincent's	Thornliebank	1942	C	6,150
139	St. Brendan's	Yoker	1946	A	3,500
140	Good Shepherd	Dalbeth	1948	C	2,500
141	O.L. & St. George's	Penilee	1949	C	5,000
142	St. Conval's	Pollok	1949	C	4,600
143	St. James's	Crookston	1949	C	2,550
144	St. Catherine's	Balornock	1950	C	3,300
145	St. Bernadette's	Carntyne	1950	A	2,600
146	St. Barnabas's	Shettleston	1950	C	1,700
147	O.L. of Fatima	Dalmarnock	1959	D	3,500
148	St. Bonaventure's	Oatlands	1952	D	2,000
146	St. Augustine's	Milton	1953	C	3,200
150	St. Jude's	Barlanark	1954	C	2,640
151	St. Lawrence's	Drumchapel	1954	C	4,200
152	O.L. of the Assumption	Ruchill	1952	C	3,080
153	St. Maria Goretti	Cranhill	1953	C	4,000
154	St. Philip	Ruchazie	1954	A	2,200
155	St. Pius X	Drumchapel	1954	C	4,200
156	St. Joachim	Carmyle	1954	D	1,160
157	St. Bartholomew	Castlemilk	1955	C	3,800
158	St. Brigid	Toryglen	1955	C	4,000
159	St. Gabriel	Merrylee	1955	D	2,000
160	St. John Ogilvie	Easterhouse	1957	C	2,400
161	St. Margaret Mary	Castlemilk	1957	C	5,950
162	St. Martin	Castlemilk	1958	C	6,000
163	St. Bernard	Nitshill	1960	C	3,000
164	St. Benedict	Drumchapel	1960	C	3,500
165	St. Leo	Dumbreck	1962	D	1,300
166	O.L. of Perpetual Succour	Jordanhill	1962	D	2,500
167	St. Albert	Pollokshields	1965	D	2,250
168	St. Gregory	Wyndford	1965	C	4,000
169	O.L. of Good Counsel	Dennistoun	1965	D	2,400
170	O.L. of Consolation	Govanhill	1966	D	4,400
171	St. Helen	Langside	1966	D	1,800
172	St. Stephen	Sighthill	1968	C	1,900
173	All Saints	Barmulloch	1969	C	3,500
174	Corpus Christi	Scotstounhill	1969	A	1,540
175	St. Monica	Milton	1969	C	1,900
					133,720

A - New parishes in inter-war housing areas - total population			9,840
C - Parishes in post-war housing areas	-		95,320
D - New Parishes in Older areas	-		28,560
B - Old parishes of inter-war housing areas - (from Table 25)			25,360

APPENDIX I/IC

CATHOLIC PARISHES OF SOUTH—WEST SCOTLAND, WITH POPULATION

PARISHES FOUNDED BETWEEN 1940 AND 1972

TABLE 25

Dunbartonshire

Index No.	Parish	Location	Foundation	1972
176	St. John of the Cross	Twechar	1945	580
177	St. Patrick's	Old Kilpatrick	1946	670
178	St. Michael's	Dumbarton	1946	4,500
179	St. Eunan's	Clydebank	1946	2.500
180	St. Flannan's	Kirkintilloch	1948	3,500
181	St. Gilda's	Rosneath	1951	270
182	St. Kessog	Balloch	1952	2,700
183	SS Peter & Paul	Arrochar	1953	260
184	St. Joseph	Faifley	1957	3,200
185	Sacred Heart	Cumbernauld	1958	4,700
186	St. Peter	Dumbarton	1966	3,000
187	St. Joseph	Cumbernauld	1967	2,000
188	St. Andrew	Bearsden	1967	2,300
189	St. Margaret	Clydebank	1969	3,400
190	St. Lucy	Cumbernauld	1973	2,000
191	St. Ronan	Bonhill	1973	1,400

| | | | | 36,980 |

APPENDIX I/IC

CATHOLIC PARISHES OF SOUTH-WEST SCOTLAND, WITH POPULATION

TABLE 26

Motherwell Diocesan Area

Index No.	Parish	Location	Date of Foundation		1972
192	St. John Bosco	New Stevenston	1946	M	3,400
193	St. Bride	East Kilbride	1946	E	4,400
194	St. Barbara	Muirhead	1947	C	1,850
195	St. Kevin	Bargeddie	1947	A	1,000
196	Corpus Christi	Calderbank	1948	A	1,110
197	St. Cadoc	Cambuslang	1949	R	2,100
198	O.L. of Scotland	Uddingston	1949	H	
199	Sacred Heart	Bellshill	1949	M	4,570
200	St. Bernadette	Motherwell	1950	M	3,090
201	St. Andrew	Airdrie	1950	A	2,410
202	St. Monica	Coatbridge	1950	A	4,720
203	St. Bartholomew	Coatbridge	1950	A	3,900
204	St. Peter	Hamilton	1953	H	3,140
205	St. Luke	Motherwell	1954	M	1,450
206	St. Mungo	Garthamlock	1954	G	2,900
207	St. Paul	Hamilton	1954	H	1,200
208	St. Ninian	Hamilton	1955	H	2,780
209	St. Teresa	Newarthill	1956	M	3,000
210	St. Thomas	Wishaw	1957	M	2,700
211	St. James	Coatbridge	1956	A	4,700
212	St. Mark	Rutherglen	1956	R	2,750
213	O.L. of Lourdes	East Kilbride	1958	E	5,100
214	St. Benedict	Easterhouse	1958	G	6,250
215	St. Clare	Easterhouse	1959	G	5,000
216	St. Edward	Airdrie	1960	A	2,820
217	St. Michael	Moodiesburn	1960	C	2,250
218	St. Aidan	Wishaw	1960	M	2,300
219	St. Serf	Airdrie	1961	A	3,210
220	St. Brendan	Motherwell	1965	M	1,930
221	St. Anthony	Rutherglen	1965	R	2,500
222	St. Leonard	East Kilbride	1966	E	3,750
223	St. Gerard	Bellshill	1967	M	1,300
224	St. Francis of Assisi	Baillieston	1970	A	1,700
225	St. Dominic	Craigend	1972	R	350

95,630

E – Parishes in the East Kilbride Area.
G – Parishes in the Easterhouse – Garthamlock area.
A, M, H, R, C as for Table 22

APPENDIX I/IC

CATHOLIC PARISHES OF SOUTH-WEST SCOTLAND, WITH POPULATION

PARISHES FOUNDED BETWEEN 1940 - 1972

TABLE 27

Paisley Diocesan Area

Index No.	Parish	Location	Date of Foundation	1972
226	Holy Family	Port Glasgow	1946	5,200
227	O.L. of Lourdes	Bishopton	1946	750
228	St. Joseph	Greenock	1947	4,500
229	St. Fergus	Paisley	1948	2,500
230	St. James	Paisley	1948	1,650
231	Christ the King	Howwood	1948	430
232	St. Andrew	Greenock	1951	5,530
233	St. Peter	Paisley	1954	3,200
234	St. Paul	Paisley	1960	2,300
235	St. Aidan	Johnstone	1960	2,100
236	St. Cadoc	Newton Mearns	1966	930
237	Our Holy Redeemer	Elderslie	1969	550
238	St. Anthony	Johnstone	1969	1,000
239	St. Francis	Port Glasgow	1969	1,500
240	St. Columba	Renfrew	1969	1,950
241	SS Joseph & Patrick	Wemyss Bay	1971	80
				34,170

APPENDIX I/IC

CATHOLIC PARISHES OF SOUTH—WEST SCOTLAND, WITH POPULATION

PARISHES FOUNDED BETWEEN 1940 - 1972

TABLE 28

Galloway Diocesan Area

Index No.	Parish	Location	Date of Foundation	1972
242	O.L. of Perpetual Succour	Millport	1939	105
243	St. Bride	West Kilbride	1947	240
244	O.L. of Perpetual Succour	Beith	1947	400
245	St. Michael	Kilmarnock	1953	1,850
246	Good Shepherd	Ayr	1957	1,750
247	St. Teresa	Dumfries	1958	2,850
248	St. Joseph	Catrine	1960	430
249		Langholm	1960	65
250	O.L. of Carmel	Kilmarnock	1963	2,000
251	St. Clare	Drongan	1965	
252	St. Brenda	Saltcoats	1965	1,880
253	St. Paul	Ayr	1967	1,317
254	St. Mungo	Lockerbie	1968	200

13,087

APPENDIX I/ID

CATHOLIC PARISHES OF SOUTH-WEST SCOTLAND, WITH POPULATION

TABLE 29

Rate of Foundation of Catholic Parishes in
South-West Scotland 1800 - 1972

	Glasgow City	Dunbartonshire	Motherwell	Paisley	Galloway	Total
1800–1840	1	1	1	2	6	11
1840–1859	11	2	9	5	8	35
1860–1879	6	3	11	3	8	31
1880–1899	6	2	11	4	5	28
1900–1919	6	2	3	0	1	12
1920–1939	6	0	3	3	5	17
1940–1959	29	10	24	8	5	76
1960–1972	13	4	10	8	7	42
1800–1972	78	24	72	33	45	252

APPENDIX I/ID

CATHOLIC PARISHES OF SOUTH—WEST SCOTLAND, WITH POPULATION

TABLE 30

Parishes and Populations in South—West Scotland
1922 and 1972 : By Diocesan Areas

	1922 Parishes	1922 Population	1972 Parishes	1972 Population	1972 Total Parishes	1972 Total Population
Glasgow City	31	193,795	31	94,540		
			5	25,360		
			42	133,720	78	253,620
Dumbartonshire	10	29,723	10	25,750		
			14	36,980	24	62,730
	41	223,518	102	316,350	102	316,350
Motherwell	35	96,650	35	80,810		
			3	6,380		
			34	95,630	72	182,820
Paisley	14	50,668	14	41,390		
			3	7,950		
			16	34,170	33	83,510
Province of Glasgow					207	582,680
Galloway	22	16,000	22	18,472		
			3	3,915		
			13	13,087		
N. Ayrshire	7	8,375	7	8,925	45	44,399
South—West Scotland	119	395,211			252	627,079

APPENDIX II

THE CONTRIBUTION OF NOTRE DAME COLLEGE TO
THE DEVELOPMENT OF CATHOLIC SECONDARY EDUCATION IN
SOUTH-WEST SCOTLAND 1894-1972

Until the last quarter of the nineteenth century, formal higher education of women in Scotland did not exist. In Glasgow it started in the 1870's, when women began to attend a series of Occasional Lectures given by members of staff of the University. This led eventually to the formation of the Glasgow Association whose main objective was the provision of teaching for women, in a limited number of subjects, by lecturers of the Arts Faculty, at standards aproximating to those accepted for male students. In 1883 the Glasgow Association constituted itself under the Companies Act as a College for the exclusive education of women, and took the name of Queen Margaret College. In 1892 the Scottish Universities were opened to women, and in the same year the University admitted women to the examinations of the Medical Faculty. It is of interest that one of the first women to graduate with a medical degree, Dr. Marion Gilchrist (1) who took the degree of MBCM in 1894, had previously been recognised as L.L.A.-Lady Literate in Arts-this being the precursor for the ladies of the M.A. degree. The attitude of the University authorities towards the admission of women was less than enthusiastic; according to one writer, they "had no desire to see university standards debased by the transfer of large numbers of women students."(2)

At this time the aspirations of the Catholic population for higher education for men or for women were not great. Before 1900 only a tiny minority attained to any form of secondary education. What was to become the main provision of post-primary education for them before 1918, namely the system of supplementary classes in primary schools, only began to take effect in 1903 in the reorganisation which followed upon the raising of the school leaving age to 14 in 1901.(3) When the Education (Scotland) Act of 1918 was passed, there were in Glasgow, then by far the largest concentration of Catholics in the country, 22 Catholic elementary schools with a total of 32,785 pupils, and in the Govan Parish 5 schools with 7,828 pupils. Further education for the products of these elementary schools was catered for by 4 intermediate and one secondary school with a total of 1,201 pupils.(4) Less than 3% of Catholic pupils went on to receive some form of secondary education.

The Catholic schools of these days were severely handicapped, by the poverty of the population and the lack of a teaching staff qualified at the higher levels. For the supply of trained Catholic teachers in the whole of the United Kingdom there then existed three training colleges: one for male students at St. Mary's Hammersmith, and two for female students -Wandsworth, under the direction of the Sacred Heart Nuns, and Mount Pleasant College run by the Sisters of Notre Dame in Liverpool. "Slowly over the years these three colleges built up the professional body of Catholic teachers, and up to 1894, when Notre Dame Training College was opened at Dowanhill, Glasgow, they had trained some 1,500 teachers for Great Britain."(5)

The then plight of Catholic education in Scotland should be seen in the context of higher education for Catholics in Great Britain as a whole. Although the Catholic Emancipation Act had been put on the statute book in 1829, there was a considerable time-lag before the Catholic population awoke to the necessity of, and began to strive seriously for, higher education at University level. Indeed, throughout the nineteenth century Catholics were discouraged from attending universities in England because the Church authorities of the day feared that university life might be a threat to faith. In England, the situation was altered in 1895 when Cardinal Vaughan lifted the ban on attendance at the universities. From that time forward, the Catholic presence steadily increased, with the Society of Jesus leading the way. At Oxford, a Private Hall, the fore-runner of Campion Hall, was opened in an annexe of St. John's College, in 1896. In Scotland, the first element of change came after the restoration of the Scottish Hierarchy of the Roman Catholic Church in 1878. (The English Hierarchy had been restored in 1850). Archbishop Charles Eyre, the first occupant of the restored See of Glasgow, in 1894 brought to his Archdiocese the Sisters of Notre Dame de Namur, to play a leading part in his plans for the development of the education of his people. His choice of this Order was no doubt influenced by the considerable experience it had already acquired, since its foundation in 1804, of teaching and teacher-training in France, Belgium, England and America.

His first objective in bringing the Sisters to Glasgow was to provide a teacher-training college to meet the needs of the under-privileged and growing Catholic population of the area. The first move of the Order therefore was to open such a college, at Dowanhill. Until then Scottish Catholic women teachers had been trained in Mount Pleasant College or on the pupil-teacher system.

Accommodation was found in two commodious villas, in Victoria Circus, close to the University and to places of cultural interest, and with easy access to city schools for teaching practice. The site immediately to the north was at that time occupied by the Observatory of Glasgow University's Department of Astronomy.

The College began as a private concern, staffed and managed by the Sisters of Notre Dame de Namur, under the direction of the Scottish Catholic Hierarchy. From its beginning all the students were residential. Within a remarkably short space of time the Sisters had opened, in 1897, a High School for Girls, in a fine purpose-built red sandstone building on a site neighbouring to the College, and soon afterwards, a primary school. In the course of years the University Observatory left its site for new facilities and better visibility at Killermont, and Glasgow Corporation provided a new building for Notre Dame High School on the old Observatory site. The primary school population moved into the building thus vacated, and the site of the original primary school became available for extension of the College.

From its beginning the College had to fulfil a dual purpose- namely, to cultivate the personal qualities of its students to a level for which there was no provision elsewhere within the local Catholic educational system, and to prepare them for the herculean task which lay ahead of assisting in the education of the Catholic population. "Since students came from some of the poorest sections of the community, there was no question of their paying their way...From 1898, selected students attended university classes and by 1900 the College was training post-graduate students. The task was colossal: the building up of standards within a depressed Irish community which was still largely illiterate."(6)

However, it would be possible to paint too black a picture. Writing about the first women students at Glasgow University, Gilbert Murray says: "The women students were a select few, all with strong intellectural tastes, and generally more eager to learn than the average of the men's class."(7) Given the prevailing attitudes towards higher education for women, and the poverty, cultural standards and educational opportunities of the Catholic population, it is likely that mutatis mutandis a statement somewhat similar to Gilbert Murray's could be accurately applied to the first women students at Notre Dame College. Though they were being prepared for careers in primary education they were, like their contemporaries at Glasgow University, pioneers in the field of higher education for women.(8) And while their preparation over the then customery two years of training was directed towards a professional commitment to children at the early stages of their growth and education, in the course of their teaching lives many of them, and perhaps the majority, had to strive to meet the ever-increasing demands for the education of a developing an expanding Catholic population, in circumstances in which the educational system itself was undergoing profound change. When, in 1903, the system of supplementary courses was introduced, it was largely upon the diplomates of Notre Dame College that the duty fell of serving in an embryonic Catholic secondary school system.(9)

Of the 22 pioneers who made up the first class possibly the most interesting was Lucy Carter, who is recorded as having gone on at a later date to graduate with a B.Sc.(Hons.) degree; and, later still, as Sister Bernardine S.N.D. to have taken a Ph.D. degree. Her achievement in a scientific field is undoubtedly to be attributed to the influence of Sister Monica Taylor S.N.D. D.Sc.(10) who joined the staff in 1901 and taught there until her retiral in 1946. The science laboratories at Bearsden bear her name as a memorial to her work.

Progress in the production of trained teachers from 1896 until 1904 is shown in Table 33. All of these are recorded as having followed a two-year course of training; one, in 1900, went on to be awarded the qualification L.L.A.;(11) one was later, in 1911, awarded an M.A. degree with Honours; three others graduated M.A. and one, in 1905, as B.Sc. It may be that the marked increase in the numbers completing the course from 1900 onwards was due to the fact that Notre Dame High School, founded in 1897, had begun to add its quota to the numbers going on to teacher-training.

During its early years the College accommodated about 50 residential students divided between the two years of the training course. In addition classes were provided for pupil-teachers. At this stage the professional training of women students in attendance at the University, came under the supervision of local University Committees. In 1905 however, Provincial Committees responsible to the Scotch Education Department took over the local provision and direction of Teacher Training. Although the universities no longer provided directly the professional training of teachers, each Provincial Committee was connected with a university, through representation on the Board, and students from Training Centres and Training Colleges were able to follow

TABLE 31

Number of Students Completing the Two-year Course of
Teacher Training at Dowanhill Training College: 1896-1904

Session	No. Completing two-year Course	Graduating later	
1895 - 1896	22		2 (Hons.)
97	22		
98	29		
99	29		
1899 - 1900	37	2 L.L.A. M.A	
1900 - 1901	42		
02	50	1	1
03	43	1 (Hons.)	
04	52	1	
TOTAL	326	5	3

In 1905, Provincial Committees responsible to the Scotch Education Department
took over the local provision and direction of teacher-training.

some university courses. The Presbyterian Training Colleges were taken over and incorporated into regional Teacher Training Centres managed by the Provincial Committees, but the Episcopal Training College in Edinburgh and the Catholic Training College at Dowanhill were able to opt out of this scheme and to continue as denominational colleges under their own committees of management. "Indeed the Principal of Dowanhill was anxious to remain outside the Provincial Committee scheme. Racial and religious friction was such that she had good reason to prefer direct dealing with the Central Department rather than submit to any form of local control."(12)

After 1905 the pattern changed. In that year, 55 students completed the two-year course, and 4 a three-year course. Of these, one went on to gain an M.A. degree; and two of the three students who completed the three-year course the following year also graduated in Arts, indicating that the system of concurrent teacher-training and study at the University had been introduced into the College. Also in 1906 a Junior Student Centre was established, and the following year the pupil-teacher system finally came to an end in Scotland.

Tables 31 and 32 record the progress made from the foundation of the College until session 1921-22. The picture that emerges is one of steady growth in the number of two-year trained primary teachers, with small numbers of three - or four - year trained people, and a tiny trickle of university graduates. Two sessions, 1909 and 1916, stand out as providing exceptional numbers. Perhaps not surprisingly there was no diminution during the war years of 1914-1918, but the immediate post-year period shows an increase in the numbers completing longer courses of training, possibly because the improved career prospects for Catholic teachers resulting from the 1918 Act were already being recognised.

The system of teacher-training changed again in the wake of the Act, when in 1920 the administration of Teacher Training in Scotland was centralised. There was set up a National Committee for the training of teachers, consisting entirely of members elected by the Education Authorities. The Provincial Committees became the managing bodies of the Training Centres. At this point the three denominational colleges - the Episcopal College and the new Catholic College at Craiglockhart, both in Edinburgh, and the College at Dowanhill - became part of the national system under the direction of the National Committee; they were not however under the control locally of the Provincial Committees, but had their own Committees of Management.

One condition of the transfer was that the Principal of Notre Dame College should always be appointed from among the Sisters of the Institute of Notre Dame de Namur.

Shortly afterwards the College was recognised for the training of Honours Graduates. The Practising School became known as the Montessori School, and in 1931 a Child Guidance Clinic was opened. Other changes during this period were the rulings that male teachers should henceforth be university graduates, or diplomates in the practical or aesthetic subjects; and that the two-year Certificate course for women only should be extended to three years.

Table 33 covers the period from 1922 to 1958, when the next major revision of regulations covering teacher - training in Scotland took place. This shows

TABLE 32

Number of Students completing Teacher-Training Courses
Sessions 1904-05 till 1921-22

Session	Primary 4-Year Course	Primary 3-Year Course	Primary 2-Year Course	Primary 1-Year Course	Secondary Arts	Secondary Science
1904-05		4	55 (1 M.A.)		1	
-06		3 (2 M.A.)	56 (1 M.A.1911)		3 (2 in 1906)	
-07			57		1 (Hons. 1913)	
-08		1 (1 M.A.Hons.)	73	2	1	
-09		3 (2 M.A.1909) (1 M.A.1912)	103 (1 B.Sc.Hons. 1913)		3 (2 in 1909)	1 (Hons.1913)
-10	1 (B.Sc.1912)	1 (1 M.A.)	79 (1 M.A.Hons. 1913)	2	2 (1 Hons.1913)	1 (1912)
-11		2 (1 M.A.1913) (1 M.A.Hons.)	81		2	
-12	1 (1 M.A.Hons. 1914)		85 (1 M.A.)	2 (1 M.A.Hons.)	3 (2 Hons.)	
-13	1 (B.Sc.Hons.)	5	63 (1 M.A.Hons.)	3 (3 M.A.)	4 (1 Hons.)	1 (Hons.)
1913-14		1	69			
-15			82	1		
-16	3 (M.A.Hons.)		102		3 (Hons.)	
-17	2	1	90	1		
-18	2 (1 B.Sc.) (1 M.A.)		93 (2 M.A.)	2	3	1
-19	4		81	1		
-20	7		80	1 (1 M.A.)	1	
-21	5	6	71	3 (3 M.A.)	3	
1921-22	5	1	70	1		
TOTAL	31	28	1,390	19	30	4

that in session 1925-26 there began a substantial production of graduate teachers for secondary schools, which increased steadily until session 1940-41, when the number of both graduates and diplomates dwindled. But whereas the production of primary diplomates, boosted by an 'emergency' crop of 45 in session 1946-47 shows a more or less steady and continuing increase thereafter, the rate of production of graduates continued to fall in the post - World War II period, reaching its nadir in session 1951-52, when only 11 secondary teachers completed training at Notre Dame College.

The Teachers (Training Authorities) (Scotland) Regulations 1958 brought about a further transformation of the administration of teacher training. The National Committee was replaced by the Scottish Council for the Training of Teachers. Governing Bodies were constituted for each training college, which were to be renamed Colleges of Education. The Governing Body was to provide, administer and conduct the college entrusted to it, and would therefore be responsible for the provision of courses as required by the Teacher Training Regulations, including shortened and In - service courses, the appointment of Principal and staff, the maintenance and extension of lands, buildings and facilities, and the administration of demonstration schools. Each Governing Body was to have among its members representatives of the Local Education Authorities, and of the religious denomination concerned. The main sources of revenue at the disposal of the Governing Bodies would be students' fees and grants from the Secretary of State. An important innovation under these Regulations was the creation of a Board of Studies in each college, consisting of members of the teaching staff, with the Principal as chairman; and it became a duty of the Governing Body to see that a Students' Representative Council elected by the student body be set up.

At Notre Dame College of Education the new Board of Governors was faced with the problem of an overcrowded and inconvenient college building, at a time when an increase in the number of students was to be expected. At this time there were over 300 resident students in a building intended to house 220.(13) Expansion at Dowanhill seemed impossible. The fifty - acre site of the former St. Peter's College at Bearsden (14)was put at the disposal of the Board of Governors by Archbishop Donald Campbell, and a new building was planned to house around 500 students - the official estimate of the peak number of future Notre Dame students - with hostel accommodation for 350.

It was intended that the new college should be ready for occupation by October 1963. Progress however was interrupted through labour difficulties. By 1961 it had become obvious that estimates of the future roll were far too low, and that extensions would have to be added to the new building as soon as it was completed. As an interim measure three Medway buildings were erected at Dowanhill to ease the situation. When the new college building came into use in October 1967, pressure on accommodation continued at such a level that it remained necessary to occupy the buildings at Dowanhill, which were now the property of the Scottish Education Department.

Development in the period from 1958 to 1972 is shown in Tables 33 and 34. During that period the student population rose from just over 300 to more than 1,400. Expansion at first was most marked in the primary area, partly through the operation of the Special Recruitment Scheme, and again when male students were admitted, in 1967, to the three - year course in Primary Education. In

TABLE 33

Number of Students Completing Teacher-Training Courses
Sessions 1922-23 till 1957-58

Session	Primary 4-Yr.	3-Yr.	2-Yr.	1-Yr.	Total Prim.	Art	Music	Secondary M.A. degree Hons.	Ord.	B.Sc Hons.	Ord.	Total Sec.
1922-23	9	1	75	2	87				1			1
23-24	11	7	77	3	98							
24-25	8	11	73	1	93				2	1		3
25-26	10	–	82	–	92			1	14	3	2	20
26-27	–	–	94	–	94			1	15	2	2	20
27-28	–	1	98	–	99			6	13	–	1	20
28-29	–	–	76	–	76			–	20	–	3	23
29-30	–	–	100	–	100			2	16	1	–	19
30-31	–	–	93	–	93			3	51	–	3	57
31-32	–	9	78	–	87			3	42	–	1	46
32-33	–	75	–	–	75	2	1	3	33	2	6	47
33-34	5	69	–	1	75	1	–	4	42	–	1	48
34-35	1	54	–	–	55	–	1	6	37	–	6	50
35-36	3	52	–	–	55	1	1	2	42	1	2	49
36-37	–	49	–	–	49	1	1	2	42	1	8	55
37-38	–	52	–	–	52	7	2	4	36	–	3	52
38-39	1	49	–	–	50	–	1	4	36	–	9	50
39-40	–	41	–	–	41	6	1	8	33	–	5	53
40-41	–	43	–	–	43	4	1	1	22	2	5	35
41-42	–	31	–	–	31	1	2	3	27	–	2	35
42-43	–	52	–	–	52	3	–	2	38	2	2	47
43-44	–	38	–	–	38	2	–	3	33	1	–	39
44-45	–	32	–	–	32	4	1	1	32	–	–	38
45-46	–	50	–	3	53	–	3	1	23	–	2	29
46-47	–	80	45 (Emergency)			1	3	–	19	–	2	25
47-48	–	64	1	–	65	–	1	1	26	–	2	30
48-49	–	47	7	–	54	3	5	1	10	–	–	19
49-50	–	77	1	–	78	2	1	2	17	–	–	22
50-51	–	74	–	2	76	4	4	–	16	–	–	24
51-52	–	59	–	1	60	–	1	1	8	–	1	11
52-53	–	66 + 6 S.R.	–	–	72	1	4	2	11	–	4	22
53-54	–	47+9	–	–	56	3	3	4	15	–	4	29
54-55	–	78+6	–	–	84	–	3	1	13	2	2	21
55-56	–	71+11	–	3	85	1	4	4	17	1	2	29
56-57	–	56+12	–	2	70	2	6	1	15	1	5	30
57-58	–	90+12	–	1	103	–	1	–	14	1	7	23
TOTAL	48	1,581	900	19	2,548	49	51	77	831	21	92	1,121

N.B. 1. Most graduates and diplomates in Art of Music trained for primary as well
       as for secondary education.
      2. Totals given for 1952-53 and subsequent sessions included teachers
         trained under the Special Recruitment Scheme.
      3. The 10 students listed as completing a 4-year course in 1925-26 had taken
         the concurrent course. 8 graduated M.A.(Ord.), 1 as M.A.(Hons.) and 1 as
         B.Sc(Hons.).
      4. New Regulations governing teacher-training were promulgated in 1958.

that year 96 male students were accepted, more than half of them through the Special Recruitment Scheme. In the following year a course leading to the award of a College Diploma in Music was introduced. This course, which extended over three academic sessions, aimed at qualifying teachers for both primary and secondary sectors. It was open to men and women, and because of its special nature was established on a non-denominational basis, as also were the various courses of training for teachers - in - service which were introduced during the same session. A major expansion of the College's contribution to secondary education began in 1969 when male Catholic graduates, who until then had followed the post-graduate teacher - training course at Jordanhill College, were admitted. In that year 29 came to Notre Dame, 6 of them being Special Recruitment admissions. About the same time the number of women graduates began to increase. (15) By session 1971-72, the total number of men and women following the post-graduate course had increased to 183, of whom 104 were men. It should be noted however that this was an exceptional year. Because of the coincidence of an economic recession with a continuing shortage of secondary teachers, an opportunity had been provided for suitably qualified graduates to transfer from industry into teaching through a Special Recruitment Scheme. So many wished to take advantage of this that the post-graduate course at Jordanhill College was over-subscribed, and some of the surplus was accommodated at Notre Dame College.

Finally, in 1970-71, a Bachelor of Education Degree, a four-year concurrent course of qualification and training validated by the Council for National Academic Awards, was introduced, the first such course under C.N.A.A. auspices to be established in the United Kingdom. Because of the continuing shortage of secondary teachers which was felt most acutely in the Catholic sector, this course was designed specifically for the training of Catholic secondary teachers. It was open to men and women, and the first graduates, 30 women and 15 men, were certificated at the end of session 1973-74. (16)

The development of the secondary sector was accompanied by a spectacular increase in the number of Primary Diplomates, from an annual average of 60-70 in the early 1960's to more than 400 by the end of the period.

With the advent of male students into a college which had been entirely a feminine preserve, changes also took place at the staff level. From 1966 onwards, men were recruited on to the college staff. In that year, the academic staff consisted of 5 men and 68 women, of whom 17 were Sisters of the Institute of Notre Dame. By session 1971-72, the number had grown to 45 men and 69 women, of whom 8 were Sisters of Notre Dame.

During this period further developments of the national system of teacher-training came into being. A General Teaching Council was established through which the teaching profession was given a greater degree of control over admission to its membership and over the maintenance of standards; the power to award Teaching Certificates was removed from the Secretary of State and placed with the Colleges of Education; (17) and, in 1967, the further training of teachers in service was made a statutory responsibility of the Scottish Colleges of Education, (18) and a National Committee for the In - service Training of Teachers was set up to provide resources and stimulate development in that area.

TABLE 34

Number of Students completing Teacher-Training Courses
Sessions 1958-59 till 1971-72

Session	Primary 3-Yr.	1-Yr.	Total Prim.	Art	Music	Secondary M.A. Hons.	Ord.	B.Sc. Hons.	Ord.	Total Sec.
1958-59	85	–	85	4	1	4	15	1	5	30
59-60	87	1	88	–	4	5	18	1	2	30
60-61	99	1	100	2	5	2	24	1	7	41
61-62	108	–	108	–	3	4	26	1	6	40
62-63	110	–	110	2	5	3	18	1	6	35
63-64	130	–	130	2	3	4	17	1	9	36
64-65	179	–	179	4	3	6	18	2	15	48
65-66	276	–	276	–	2	6	23	3	6	40
66-67	244	–	244	1	1	9	26	2	11	50
67-68	294	–	294	1	1	7	27	2	13	51
68-69	258	–	258	2	1	7	36	1	21	68
TOTAL	1,870	2	1,872	18	29	57	248	16	101	469

N.B.   1. The Bearsden complex came into use at the beginning of session 1967-68.

2. Male students were accepted into College in October 1967. A small
number were certified in session 1968-69 in accordance with
arrangements approved by the Genral Teaching Council.

3. A college Diploma in Music was introduced in session 1968-69.

TABLE 35

Number of Students completing Teacher-Training Courses
Sessions 1969-70 till 1974-75

Session	Primary W.	Primary M.	(Prim.Grads.) W.	(Prim.Grads.) M.	Total Prim.	Art W.	Art M.	Music W.	Music M.	M.A. Hons. W.	M.A. Hons. M.	M.A. Ord. W.	M.A. Ord. M.	B.Sc. Hons. W.	B.Sc. Hons. M.	B.Sc. Ord. W.	B.Sc. Ord. M.	B.Ed. W.	B.Ed. M.	Music W.	Dip. M.	Total Sec.
1969-70	331	78	6	1	416	1	2	1	–	5	6	46	9	4	6	20	4	–	–	–	–	104
70-71	355	58	4	–	417	1	1	1	–	7	5	40	9	2	5	13	11	–	–	2	–	97
71-72	355	56	7	4	422	–	3	–	3	10	22	39	12	4	20	26	44	–	–	5	3	191
72-73	352	42	5	2	401	1	1	1	–	10	5	39	12	9	20	13	25	–	–	6	1	143
73-74	324	74	7	4	409	1	1	1	3	10	9	35	17	3	18	14	30	30	15	–	2	176
TOTAL	1,717	308	29	11	2,065	4	8	4	5	42	47	199	59	22	69	90	98	30	15	13	6	711

CONTRIBUTION OF NOTRE DAME COLLEGE TO THE DEVELOPMENT OF
CATHOLIC SECONDARY EDUCATION

The Early Role

Prior to 1918, the role of the College was clear. As well as providing the
training of the teachers then so desperately needed, it had to assist in filling
the gap in provision then existing between the Catholic primary and secondary
sectors. Its concern was not so much with primary or secondary education as
such, but rather with a more fundamental commitment to the full development,
intellectual, moral and spiritual, of its students and through them to the
generations of pupils for whom they would become responsible. The first
principal, Mary Adele Lescher (Sister Mary of St. Wilfred) expressed the philosophy which informed the approach: "To be worthy of the name, education must
be directed to the development of the moral character of the child more than
to the development of its intellectual faculties. 'Manners makyth Man', and
the Catholic Church knows no other means of development than the christian
religion with its sanctions and its practices."(19)

From the foundation of the College till the passing of the Education (Scotland)
Act of 1918, little progress was made in expanding the provision of secondary
places for Catholic children. Such advances as were made, were for girls.
From 1909, St. Mary's School in Greenock developed a Higher Grade department,
and n 1912 the Notre Dame Institute founded a Convent School at Clerkhill
in Dumbarton; but no comparable advances were made in the provision for boys.
For the bulk of the population it continued to be the case that the only
post-primary education available to them was that offered in the supplementary
classes of some primary schools. The College's main effort therefore was directed
towards the production of primary teachers.

The enactment of the 1918 Act brought about a dramatic change. As the flow
of Catholic students through the existing secondary schools, to the University
and to the Training College increased, so did the commitment of Notre Dame
College to secondary education. By session 1925-26, 20 women graduates were
following the post-graduate course, although in the immediately preceding years
there had never been more than 3 graduate trainees in any year, and in no
preceding year at any time had there been more than 8 graduates associated
with one session.(20)

Tables 31, 32, 33, 34 and 35, show the rates at which the number of students
qualifying in each of the courses changed. Table 36 summarises their findings.
Although any interpreting of these figures can only be tentative, it may be
that the following conclusions can be properly drawn:

1.   The imbalance in number of primary and secondary teachers, a legacy from
the early years of the College's history, appears to have persisted longer
than was desirable.

2.   There was for many years a marked imbalance in the numbers of graduates
in Arts and Science. Whereas the number of Arts graduates increased considerably
in session 1925-26, there was no corresponding increase in the Science side

TABLE 36

Students Completing Teacher-Training Courses : 1896-1974
Summary of TABLES 31, 32, 33, 34, 35

Table	Period	Primary Certificate	Aesthetic Subjects	Secondary Certificate Arts	Science
33	1895-1904	326	–	5	3
34	1904-1922	1,468	–	30	4
35	1922-1958	2,548	100	908	113
36	1958-1969	1,872	47	305	117
37	1969-1974	2,065	40	347	279
		5,279	187	1,595	516

N.B.   Many students awarded the Secondary certificate were also awarded a Primary
Certificate.

until the decade of the '60's. If in the period 1925-26 till 1950-51 the number of Science post-graduates is expressed as a percentage of those qualified in Arts Subjects, the average is approximately 10%. The period 1951-52 to 1967-68 produces an average of 34%; but for the three years after the admission of male graduates the corresponding percentages become 51, 50 and 113; the last being the figure for 1971-72, an exceptional year.

3.   There was a remarkable and persistent paucity of applicants in the two aesthetic subjects in which the College was able to give a secondary certificate to suitably qualified students. For a College so long dedicated to the education of women and girls, the absence of opportunity to develop in needlecraft and associated activities at secondary level was a distinct disadvantage.

Since the College depended on the schools for its supply of students; the above conclusions must relate at least in some degree to the attainments at school level.

CONTRIBUTION THROUGH NON-QUALIFYING COURSES

The Religious Education Certificate

As a denominational institution operating within the national system, the raison d'être of Notre Dame College was to train teachers for the Roman Catholic schools of Scotland at both primary and secondary levels.

Teachers who wished to be considered for an appointment in a Catholic school had to satisfy conditions laid down by the Scottish Catholic Hierarchy, in addition to meeting the requirements of the civil authority. To comply with these, all Roman Catholic students at Notre Dame College followed a course in Religious Education, leading to the award of a Certificate of Religious Education, necessary for appointment to a Catholic school in Scotland. (21) The course involved the student in about 4 hours per week of lecture or seminar time during in-college phases of his course, covering aspects of Scripture, Theology, Moral Philosophy and Catechetics. During periods of school experience, students were expected to be associated with the religious education given in school, through observation or by participation in the teaching under supervision. During such phases students were visited by members of staff of the Religious Education Department, as well as by tutors in specialist subject areas. A further spiritual dimension to he training experience was added through the liturgical life of the College, which was sustained by the College chaplain and Sisters of the Notre Dame Orders, as well as by the staff and student community as a whole.

The operation of the system involved the students in a considerable amount of work beyond that required by the civil authority. It also added to the burdens of lecturing and administrative staff, mainly because of the added complications of time-tabling for in-college phases, and of travelling and supervision during teaching practices.

Before the transfer of the Roman Catholic schools to civil control in 1918, the Catholic educational system was essentially primary in character. A total

change set in after 1918, and with the subsequent expansion of the secondary
sector new problems arose particularly affecting religious education. Syllabuses,
textbooks and courses suitable for intellectual, moral and spiritual nourishment
of an adolescent school population which was simultaneously being offered new
and attractive realms to explore in every secular subject, did not exist. The
gap was filled by continuing the system that functioned in the primary sector,
strengthened by material adapted from text-books and courses designed in the
first instance for use in seminaries.

Because of the faith and commitment of the teachers, the strength of the bonds
between school, home and church, and the selective nature of the Catholic
secondary schools, this system was able to serve well enough, for a time. By
virtue of their small size, the Catholic secondary schools were of the 'grammar'
school type, in which the pupils followed courses leading to the Higher Leaving
Certificate, and were therefore able to cope with a presentation of Religious
Studies which called for a high degree of linguistic ability as well as a
considerable capacity for abstract thinking. But the system could not long
survive the stresses to which it was soon subjected. As the numbers coming
forward for secondary education increased, so the need for some modification
or restatement of the conceptual framework within which religious knowledge
was presented, also increased. The secondary school system was not, and could
not be, geared to the parish structure in the manner of the primary schools.
Divisions tended to grow up, even within the family circle, between those who
had an opportunity of receiving a secondary education, and the others; and
to these stresses were to be added others arising from the upheavals consequent
on a World War, a redistribution of population which broke down long-established
communities, and an explosion of secular knowledge upsetting to those whose
minds and consciousness had been formed within the framework of an earlier
cosmology. After the Second World War the need for new development in the field
of religious education became even more urgent. In the massive expansion of
the Catholic secondary sector that then took place, accompanied by a programme
of comprehensivisation and an apparently endemic shortage of teaching staff,
religious education in the secondary schools was one of the major casualties.
Instead of holding an honoured and fixed place at the centre of the curriculum,
Religious Knowledge was downgraded almost to the level of an optional extra
in the curriculum. The 'RK' period became a 'floater' like that of any secular
subject; the Religious Certificate examination, once highly regarded as providing
along with the 'Highers' the climax to a school career, disappeared. In the
absence of Religious Education Departments, there was no one within the staff
of the school, other than the head teacher, with the responsibility or authority
to defend the subject from the inroads of other disciplines. The secondary
school as a praying and prayerful community lost something of its character.

These changes in the Scottish scene reflected to a certain extent the upheavals
being experienced in the whole christian community, in response to which Pope
John XXIII in 1963, called the bishops of the world to attend the Second Vatican
Council whose findings are still reverberating throughout the world.

It is against this general background that the contribution of Notre Dame College
to religious education in the period under review has to be traced. In the
pre-World War 1 period the College, a close-knit, small community of Sisters,
staff and residential students, was a clearly-identifiable part of the west
of Scotland Catholic community, with a clearly defined role in it. The students
grew up, flourished and served in an atmosphere of stability and spiritual

unity. "In certis, unitas" was the appropriate motto for the day. In the post-World War 2 period however, stability and unity were replaced by uncertainties and division; and the second part of that mediaeval triptych "In dubiis, libertas" came more and more to apply. Responding to the spirit of the times, the Church in a general movement sought to renew itself by returning to its apostolic origins, and in so doing introduced a re-scrutiny of all its attitudes and practices, including some which, although associated with christian practice over the centuries, were nevertheless not of the essence of the faith.

For all involved in religious education, these developments were the source of profound and sometimes traumatic re-appraisements. During the post-World War 2 period, and particularly as staff and resources began to increase in the post-conciliar period, Notre Dame College strove to play an even more significant part in the restoration and updating of religious education. Increasing efforts were apparent especially in the areas of liturgical practice, catechetical methods and scriptural study. In each of these areas highly qualified specialists were added to the staff of a large religious education department.

In her contribution to the Notre Dame Sound Archive, Sister Francis, who became Principal of the College in 1965, makes the following statement:

> "I still see the need for Catholic colleges of education...for the specific purpose of christian commitment. Because of the many counter attractions of our modern world we can't to the same extent count on the family life for inculcating in children this commitment...I see a need for it to be done in other ways, through the schools and through the teachers, and if the teachers are to become committed Catholics they must learn this commitment themselves....But I would see them as being of service not only to the Catholic community but to the community as a whole specifically the christian community, to these committed christians...because they too look for some sort of lead; some sort of support in keeping alive the christian faith in this age. So I would like to see our Catholic colleges open to other christians as well as to catholics... provided that they remain specifically Catholic themselves."
> (NDSA NO.11, p.11)

CONTRIBUTION TO SECONDARY EDUCATION THROUGH IN-SERVICE TRAINING

In 1967 the further training of teachers in service became a statutory responsibility of the Scottish Colleges of Education.

In spite of the heavy administrative demands on an institution simultaneously undergoing metamorphosis from an all-female to a mixed community and burgeoning new courses on two sites some five miles apart, a start was made in session 1967-68 on the development of in-service activities. 7 in-service courses were offered that year, 3 of them for secondary teachers. (Table 40)

From 1966 onwards, a massive expansion in student numbers took place, always in advance of the necessary corresponding increase in academic or other staff.

In these circumstances only minimal resources could be spared for in-service training.   In 1968 a post of Adviser to Men Students was created, carrying the added responsibility of promoting activity in the in-service area.(22)

Rapid expansion followed.   From the outset, the policy adopted was to involve all academic departments, and thus to maintain links between the pre- and in-service programmes. No separate department of in-service training was instituted.   In the particular circumstances of Notre Dame College, it was thought desirable to exploit the different potentialities of the Dowanhill and Bearsden sites as in-service centres, Dowanhill for short one-day, week-end or evening courses, and Bearsden for vacation and residential courses.

These policies were soon implemented. On 27-28 October 1969, the first major event, a 2-day conference entitled Modern Studies in the Christian Context, attracted an attendance of 140 teachers and others concerned from a wide scatter of education authorities throughout Scotland. This venture was   followed by several others covering a diversity of subjects.

In session 1970-71 the programme was increasingly diversified. By then all departments of the College were contributing to in-service activity; a Geography Working Party was set up under in-service auspices, which went on to make a significant contribution (23) to the further development of the subject at secondary level; and at the end of this session the first of many major conferences on Guidance in Secondary Schools, took place. By 1971-72 the possibility of further expansion within the existing framework was very limited. Short courses were offered after school hours at Dowanhill. This had the advantage of allowing teachers within easy travelling distance to take part in additional training exercises without having to seek release from school duties.

In-service courses were offered on a non-denominational basis, thus bringing greater numbers of Catholic teachers into closer association with colleagues from the non-denominational sector, in professional activities, than had formerly been the case.

Contribution to the Development of Religious Education

Within secondary education however, the College had a particular contribution to make in the field of Religious Education. Its first major contribution was the introduction of an Advanced Diploma of Religious Education, in session 1971-72. This was planned in anticipation of the introduction of a Specialist Qualification in Religious Education for Secondary Teachers, which in the event did not come about until session 1974-75. This initiative derived from an awareness of the need for a reappraisal of current practices in religious education, some of which had become outdated by the work of the Second Vatican Council, and for a fresh approach to the catechetical and other problems associated with religious education at the secondary level in the changing school environment. These problems were compounded by the shortage of fully qualified Catholic teachers in the secondary schools.

The Advanced Diploma Course therefore was designed for secondary teachers, who were interested in and had experience of Religious Education. They were required to attend 20 meetings per session over each of three sessions, and to submit a dissertation on a subject related to the work of the course. The first group to complete the course, in March 1974, consisted of fully registered teachers, some very highly qualified, some in senior positions of responsibility, and all having experience of and commitment to the arduous task of providing religious education in schools. When later the decision to introduce the category of Specialist Teachers of Religious Education was reached, it was open to those who had gained this Advanced Diploma, who so wished, to apply to the General Teaching Council for Exceptional Admission to the Register as Specialist Teacher of Religious Education.

Contribution of Notre Dame College to the Development of Guidance in Secondary Schools

The expansion of comprehensive secondary education in the quarter-of-a-century after World War II, occurring as it did at a time when the post-war 'bulge' in the school population was advancing into and through the secondary schools, resulted in an increase - some would say an inordinate increase - in the rolls of many secondary schools. One response to this was the introduction of Guidance structures into the secondary school system. After a period of experimentation and study the Scottish Education Department initiated a major movement in this direction in 1968, when the Memorandum 'Guidance in Scottish Secondary Schools' was published.

The concept of Guidance had been associated with Notre Dame College at least since the setting up of the Notre Dame Child Guidance Clinic by Sister Marie Hilda in 1931. The College was therefore predisposed to enter with vigour into this area of development, and ready to approach with a measure of optimism what was a major innovation in the Scottish schools system.

During session 1970-71, an Ad Hoc Committee (24) was set up to direct and develop the provision which the College might make in this delicate and potentially controversial field. The first fruit of its work was a residential course, held at Bearsden from 1 - 10 July, 1971, which was attended by 140 teachers drawn from 15 Education Authorities throughout Scotland. Of them, 92 were from the non-denominational sector. This was the first of what proved to be a series of such conferences, held annually at the beginning of the summer vacation. As the number of teachers appointed to this work increased, so did the demand for a basic course of training. The material and approach developed in the 1971 conference provided a satisfactory basis for future progress. Eventually there was also manifest a demand for a more advanced course of training from staff who were gaining experience through practical work in schools. In session 1971-72 therefore two courses were offered, Course A at basic level, which was attended by 104 teachers from 18 Education Authorities, and Course B at a more advanced level, suported by 117 teachers from 19 Authorities.(25)

Contribution to Secondary Education through In-Service Publications

The First Decade, 1967-77.

Models in Human Geography.   Proceedings   1970

Georgraphy and the Environment.   Proceedings 1972

Alternative Higher Geography.   Some Resources   1975

Contribution of Geography to the Curriculum, and its Assessment.1979

Guidance and Conselling   Proceeding of Summer Vacation Course.
                                 July 1972.

                                 Proceedings of Renfrewshire Conference.
                                 May 1973.

                                 Proceedings of Summer Vacation Courses.
                                 July 1973.

Organisation and Training of the Guidance Team. Proceedings of
                                 National In-service Course.
                                 March 1975.

Coherence in the Curriculum The Complementary Roles of Guidance
Staff and Subject Teachers. Proceedings of National In-Service course.
                             April 1979.

Sex Education and the Catholic Secondary Schools.
Conference Proceedings: Sept. 1976; Oct. 1977, May 1980.

Human Sexuality in the Light of the Gospel and Reason. Feb. 1978.

Education in a Social Work Context. Conference Proceedings. April 1978

Specialised Learning - Provision for Alienated Children in Secondary Schools.
Conference Proceedings. April 1981.

TABLE 37

Attendance of Guidance Conferences 1970-72

	No. of Teachers	Authorities	Denom.	Non-Denom.
1970-71	140	15	48	92
1971-72 A	104	18	34	70
B	117	19	49	68

TABLE 38

In-Service Training at Notre Dame College, 1967-72

	No. of Courses and Conferences	No. for Sec. Teachers	No. of Teachers	No. of Sec. Teachers
1967-68	7	3	200	118
1968-69	12	6	266	119
1969-70	29	12	1,158	600
1970-71	36	11	1,472	767
1971-72	40	17	1,420	770
TOTAL	124	49	4,516	2,374

NOTES

1.   College Courant, Vol. 9.
2.   Cruickshank, M.   Teacher Training in Scotland, pp.114-5
                                        SCRE.
3.   Wade, N.A.   Post-Primary Education in Scotland
                                        Elementary Schools, pp.102-3, SCRE.
4.   Skinnider, Sister M. (SND) SCRE No. 54, pp.63
5.   Anon   DBJ 1962.
6.   Cruickshank, M.   op. cit. p.123
     See also Sister Francis (NDSA No. 11, p.11)
     "Between the twenties and thirties...the Training Colleges still
     had the function of providing the academic content to education
     as well as the professional training for teachers."
7.   College Courant, Vol. 6, p.106
8.   Sister Dorothy Gillies,   Gives a list of the first group of 22
                                       diplomates trained at Notre Dame College.
                                       Six of them afterwards entered the
                                       Institute of Notre Dame, and one of them,
                                       Mary Agnes Quinn, became the Superior of
                                       Dowanhill.
     A Pioneer of Catholic Teacher-Training in Scotland, p.37
                                       NDA Vol. 1, No. 1, 1978.
9.   Many examples could be quoted: one is Jane B. Lomax, who completed the
     2-year course in 1907; graduated M.A. with Honours in 1913; later had
     a long career in secondary education, with service in Notre Dame High
     and Holyrood Secondary Schools.
10. Sister Monica Taylor SND, a sister of Professor Sir Hugh S. Taylor FRS,
     Lectured in Biology at Notre Dame College from 1901 to 1946. She was
     awarded the Honorary Degree of LI.D. by Glasgow University in 1953.
     See Cruickshank, op.cit., p.156, footnote; also Sister Francis Ellen
     Henry SND, N.D.S.A. No. 11, p.10; and Sister Dorothy Gillies, op.cit.
     pp.52-53.
11. For some details of the L.L.A. award (Lady Literate in Arts), see Josephine
     Small, N.D.S.A. No.1.
12. Cruickshank, M.   op.cit. pp.138
     Sister Dorothy Gillies   op.cit. pp.51-57 outlines some of the
                                       opposition which the Sisters had to face.
13. Sister Francis SND   NDSA NO.11, p.9
14. St. Peter's College, Bearsden, the Archdiocesan seminary for the training
     of priests, had been destroyed by fire in 1946. The seminary was transferred
     to Kilmahew, at Cardross.
15. Sister Francis   NDSA NO.11, pp.12-13 comments on the advent
                                       of male students.
16. Ibid.   pp. 14-16 contains lengthy comment on the
                                       introduction of the B.Ed. degree, contact
                                       with the Council for National Academic
                                       Awards, and the concurrent system of teacher
                                       -training.
17. The Teaching Profession in Scotland. Wheatley Report. 1963.
     The Teaching Council (Scotland) Act. 1965.
18. Teachers' (Colleges of Education)(Scotland) Regulations 1967.
     Part 11 and 13.

19.   S.N.D. Sister Mary of St. Philip 1825–1905 (Frances Mary Lescher)
      Longmans 1920.

20.   NDSA No. 11, p.14.

21.   It has to be noted that the Certificate of Religious Education was a
      College award, it did not give recognition to the holder as a Specialist
      Teacher of Religious Education. This latter was a qualification which
      came into being at a later date.

22.   The first holder of this post was T.A. Fitzpatrick.

23.   The efforts of the Working Party resulted in a second major conference
      'Geography and the Environment', in 1972. The Proceedings of this
      conference were made generally available to schools at cost as a College
      Publication. The Working Party went on to produce a study of the
      Alternative Higher Geography Syllabus, in 1974.

24.   Composition of the Ad Hoc Committee was as follows:
      T.A. Fitzpatrick,   Organiser of In-service Courses.   Convener.
      C.A. Forbes,   Assistant Principal.
      J.J. Murray (retired Head Teacher of St. Gregory's Sec. School)
                            Course Director.
      A.H. Ferguson, H.M.I. Assessor.

25.   Proceedings of these conferences were made available as College
      publications.

APPENDIX III

THE CATHOLIC CHAPLAINCY OF GLASGOW UNIVERSITY IN THE 'THIRTIES

The Chaplaincy for Catholic students of Glasgow University was opened in 1930 at the direction of His Grace Archbishop Mackintosh, in a large terrace house, at 53 Southpark Avenue. In later years it moved to its present premises in Turnbull Hall, Southpark Terrace.

On the occasion of the official opening of Turnbull Hall in 1956, the G.U. Catholic Society produced a commemorative brochure which gives some account of the development of a Catholic presence in the University in the modern period.

According to that account, the number of Catholic students had begun to show a steady increase from about 1911. Before that, numbers had been very small and consisted mainly of former pupils of St. Aloysius College. There were few women students. The doors of the University had been opened to them in 1892, but by the end of the first decade of the present century their number was still very small, and of Catholic women miniscule.(1)

Early in the century an Old Boys' Sodality was founded by a Jesuit priest, Father Parry, to provide for the spiritual needs of former pupils of St. Aloysius College who had proceeded to the University. After 1913, membership was opened to all male Catholic students at all the institutions of higher education in Glasgow, and the name changed to 'The University Students Sodality'. It is a fair assumption that the total number of Catholics studying at all of these institutions, which would include the Anderson College of Medicine, the Veterinary College, the Glasgow School of Art, the Academy of Music and the Royal Technical College, was still small, and that a majority would be former pupils of St. Aloysius College.

In 1915 the Sodality was given a tremendous boost when Professor J.S. Phillimore (2) who then occupied the Chair of Humanities became its Honorary President. In 1919 its existence was officially recognised by the University and thenceforth its name appeared in the University Calendar and Students' Handbook, and the scope of its activities increased. At a meeting in February 1920 at which Fr. J.H. Pollan S.J. delivered a lecture on 'Early Scottish Jesuits and the Reformation Settlement', the chair was taken by Dudley Medley then Professor of History, and Professor Rait of Scottish History, later Principal of the University, delivered the vote of thanks. In 1925 the Sodality again changed its title, and became officially established as the Glasgow University Catholic Men's Society.

In keeping with the temper of the times, the provision for women followed a separate route. Women students had been admitted to the University from 1892, but although they were allowed to qualify for degrees they were taught in separate classes, many of which were held in the Queen Margaret College building (now occupied by the B.B.C.). By about the end of the First World War Catholic women students, among whom former pupils of Notre Dame High School were in the majority, became numerous enough to form an association of their own. This was set up by the Sisters of Notre Dame with the title of The Glasgow University Catholic Women's Association. The first spiritual director was Monsignor Forbes, Rector of St. Peter's College, Bearsden, the senior seminary in Scotland for the training of priests.(3) Meetings of G.U.C.W.A. were first held in Notre Dame Training College at Dowanhill, and after 1930 in the Chaplaincy in Southpark Avenue.

By the latter date the Education Act of 1918 was bearing fruit, and former pupils of the Catholic secondary schools of the west of Scotland were reaching the University in ever - increasing numbers. No accurate record of these numbers is easily obtainable. One indication of the trend however can be reached from a scrutiny of the numbers of women graduates who entered teacher-training at Notre Dame Training College. In session 1925-26 20 women graduates followed the one - year post-graduate course, although in the immediately preceeding years there had never been more than 3 graduates in any year, (See Appendix II). The rate of flow continued at about the same level until session 1930-31, when it leapt to 57, and a somewhat comparable level was maintained until the outbreak of World War 2.

The number of Catholic men undergraduates, already much greater than the number of women, probably increased at a similar or even faster rate. In the 1930's, many Catholic parents were still chary of allowing their daughters to embark on a university career, and preferred the safe alternative, open to them but not to men students, of the College training.(4) For men, entry to teaching was mainly by the graduation route. This was especially so for Catholics, who for a variety of reasons among which the absence of job opportunities took a high place, were very slow to seek qualification in the aesthetic or practical subjects.(5) In any case, men were more ready than women to take advantage of university education and the wider range of career opportunities which it offered. In addition, by the early 1930's, the male former pupils of the developing Catholic schools, in Motherwell, Paisley or Dumbarton, were coming forward to swell the numbers of Catholic undergraduates. Girls from these areas who decided to pursue a university career were much fewer in number.(6)

It was at this critical period in the life of the community that the Rev. W.E. Brown was appointed as chaplain to the Catholic students of Glasgow University. It would be difficult to over-emphasise the importance of this event. William Eric Brown had come to Glasgow in 1920 as Lecturer in British History at the University. He was born in Kent in 1893, of non-catholic parents. He joined the Catholic Church in 1919, chiefly as a result of his contact with the Church and with Catholics during his service with the Royal Artillery in the Great War of 1914-18. He already held a Bachelor of Science Degree of London University, where he had specialised in Mathematics. After the War, in which he was wounded and gassed and awarded the Military Cross, he went up to Oxford to study History, gaining a First at St. John's, of which College he became an Honorary Scholar. He then served as a lecturer on the staff of the History Department of Glasgow University from 1920 until 1924, when he resigned to study at Scots College Rome for the diocesan priesthood. On Easter Sunday 1929 he was ordained priest in the Basilica of St. John Lateran in Rome, and in the summer of that year took the degree of Doctor of Theology with ease and distinction. While in Rome he also took the Diploma of the Vatican School of Palaeography. In 1930 he became first chaplain to the Catholic students of Glasgow University, and in 1934 chaplain to the Don Bosco Guild of Catholic Teachers, which was inaugurated in that yearby Archbishop Mackintosh. Under his unobtrusive leadership the Catholic Societies flourished until the outbreak of World War II. As the war progressed the number of male students dwindled, and the activities of the

Catholic societies came to depend more and more on the women students. Eventually in 1943 the G.U.C.M.S. and G.U.C.W.A. were united, to form the G.U. Catholic Society. It would appear that it needed a world war to bring them together.

While in Rome Fr. Brown took a leading part in the preparation of the evidence for the beatification of John Ogilvie, and also found time to produce a book on The Achievement of the Middle Ages, and another on Bishops for a series on 'Pioneers of Christendom'. On his return to Glasgow he lectured on Church History at St. Peter's College, and contributed the long section on 'Christianity to the Edict of Milan' to the second volume of Edward Eyre's European Civilisation: Its Origin and Development, and the chapter on 'The Reformation in Scotland' to the fourth.

In 1945 he was compelled to retire through ill-health, the result of the gassing he suffered in the first World War, and on medical advice he went to South Africa in the hope that its dry climate might restore him to health. There he interested himself in the state of the church and, in spite of his invalid state, composed the first history of the Catholic Church in South Africa (7) His last years were spent mostly in a sanatorium. He died November 1957 at the age of 64.

More than any other single individual, Father Brown enriched the life of the Catholic community of Glasgow. His obituary notice contained the following comment:

> "All that had gone before (his appointment as G.U. chaplain) was a preparation for a magnificent apostolate, an apostolate that ought to make his name live in perpetuity. This kind of statement may surprise the many who never had a chance of knowing Father Brown, especially the younger generation; but they should know that they are the product of schools and indeed of homes that owe a debt to his personal efforts... Large numbers of graduates were needed to staff the new secondary schools of the future...they came without any tradition of learning behind them...Father Brown undertook the larger and more difficult task of shaping the Catholic student body into the mould of a higher culture."

The following tribute by Colm Brogan underlines this theme:

> "If, as I am told, the present generation of Catholic students in Glasgow University are, on the whole, more enterprising, more self-confident and more open-minded than their predecessors of 30 years ago, that change must be credited to a man who is no more than a name to them. Father Brown decisively altered the atmosphere of Glasgow Catholic university life...He was able to do so because of qualities which few men indeed possess to the same degree. The first of these was a genial tolerance that carried not the faintest trace of condescension....He asked nobody to abandon his prejudices. He asked only that young men of exceptional ability and liveliness of mind should cultivate clear, dispassionate thinking and should be anxious acquirers of knowledge in many directions." (9)

Above all, Father Brown gave to the local Catholic student body – graduate and undergraduate alike – a quality of which they were in dire need: confidence in the fact that it was possible to profess the traditional Catholic faith and still hold an intellectually respectable position. His devotion to and grasp of the Summa Theologica of St. Thomas, his comprehensive historical background with a particular appreciation of the Middle Ages, his early scientific training and essentially mathematical mind, his experience of men and affairs in war and in peace, his wide contacts and universal vision: all these combined with his cheerful, relaxed, tolerant and genial disposition to initiate or stimulate radical changes in the cultural bases of the educated Scottish Catholic community.

Simple, direct personal contact was possibly the most important part of his apostolate. Apart from this, his influence was specially exerted through innumerable study circles, and, in the world of education, through his service as chaplain to the Don Bosco Guild of Catholic Teachers, through the various series of lectures on Church History which he delivered to seminarians at St. Peter's College at Bearsden and to prospective Catholic teachers who then had to follow a prescribed course, through visitation often with Dr. P. McGlynn of the Humanities Department to upper forms of schools to give guidance on university matters generally, and through his sponsoring and editing the Catholic Student Magazine.

Lest it should seem that this is a picture of Superman and therefore untrue, perhaps it should be noted that Father Brown was less successful with women than with men students; that as a golfer the best that could be said of him was that he was dogged; and that he had absolutely no ear for music and was in fact tone-deaf.(10)

The pre-war generations of Catholic graduates were of special significance in the development of the Catholic secondary schools system, in that it was mainly from their ranks that teachers were found to meet the demands of the expanding Catholic schools system in the post-war period. By 1939 the supply of Catholic graduates had more than overtaken the demand for teachers, with the exception of some subject areas. Many were unable to obtain teaching posts on completion of their training; and in the post-war period many did not return to teaching in Scotland, some seeking other careers, some emigrating. Their numbers however were sufficient to sustain at least for a time the expanding demands of the schools, and through them a degree of continuity was provided in the Catholic sector that otherwise might well have been missing. Perhaps more importantly, they provided to a very considerable extent the promoted and senior staff required when the Catholic secondary sector experienced its fullest expansion as a result of 'comprehensivisation' in the 1950's. This was the group most profoundly influenced by W.E. Brown, before the combined effects of ill-health and a fresh outbreak of war began to take their toll.

In 1952 the present Chaplaincy, Turnbull Hall, was opened in conjunction with the quincentenary celebration of the founding of the University, and so named in memory of Bishop Turnbull, founder and first Chancellor of the University. (The official opening ceremony which took place in 1956 awaited the completion of the building of the St. Mungo Chapel).

With the increase in numbers of Catholic students at universities generally during 'thirties, a movement had begun to form a federation of University Catholic Societies. From this arose the Newman Association, a United Kingdom organisation of Catholic graduates, and in due course branches were established in Glasgow and Edinburgh, which gathered strength as ex-servicemen and women returned to civil life. In 1949 the Glasgow and Edinburgh branches combined to mount a history conference, at Polmont, which resulted in turn in the setting up of the Catholic Historical Association, the fons et origo of the Innes Review,

NOTES

1.   Small, Josephine   N.D.S.A. No. 1, p.14
     also Shannon, F.J.   N.D.S.A. No. 14, pp.2-7

2.   Pierre   College Courant   Martinmas 1970, p.53
     "The other great influence was J.S. Phillimore, most entrancing of
     of professors, to have known whom was a liberal education. His classes
     were a delight...Belloc and Phillimore were of course close friends."

3   The former site of St. Peter's College is now occupied by St. Andrew's
     College of Education. St. Peter's College was destroyed by fire in 1946.

4.   Even in the mid-1930's there was considerable opposition among Catholic
     parents to university education for their daughters. In 1934 fewer than
     10 former pupils of Our Lady and St. Francis Secondary School went
     on to Glasgow University in that year, according to a joint statement
     made by two members of that group. The main source of Catholic women
     undergraduates was Notre Dame High School. The intake of Catholic
     women from the West of Scotland was probably of the order of 40-50 per
     year.
     See Murray, M.P.   N.D.S.A. No. 16, pp. 8-10; and Curran, T. N.D.S.A.
     No. 20 p.6.

5.   See Murray, M.P.   Loc.cit, re entry of Catholic girls
                                         into College of Domestic Science or
                                         College of Physical Education; also
                                         Curran, Loc.cit.
     The dearth of Catholic teachers qualified in the Chapter VI subjects
     would have been much greater but for the work of the Ommer School of
     Music, which operated in the Crosshill area after World War.1. The school
     was managed by three sisters of a German Catholic family, and was well
     supported by the local Catholic community. Many of its alumni gained
     there the basic qualification in Music for entry into teacher-training.

6.   Murray, M.P.   Loc.cit.

7.   The History of the Catholic Church in S. Africa. Burns & Oates, 1960.

8.   Western Catholic Calendar 1958.

9.   Brogan, C   Glasgow Observer 1958.

10. McEwan, Canon Sydney   On the High 'C'S, pp.106-109.
     This light-hearted autobiography contains some personal reminiscences
     of Fr. Brown.

APPENDIX IV

THE GUILD OF CATHOLIC TEACHERS

Prior to 1918 there had been a number of organisations which existed and campaigned for the professional and political interests of Catholic teachers. "The Catholic teachers at that time had no security of tenure. They were subject to arbitrary dismissal. They were miserably paid, but notwithstanding their poor conditions they were unselfish, self-sacrificing, zealous and wholly devoted to their charges...they played no small part, by precept and example, in and out of school, in the religious training and fervour of the older Catholics in the more populous districts of this country."(1)

"In such conditions of penury, poor buildings and teaching equipment, huge classes to cope with and many unqualified teachers... the teachers of those days hankered after a professional consciousness and sought to better their conditions and status by banding themselves together in associations to achieve their purposes....Their efforts understandably lacked cohesion and uniformity, so much so that at one time three organisations often at cross purposes were functioning at the same time. Each did some useful work but all had the fatal weakness of being confined to a section of Glasgow teachers."(2)

Gradually the futility of these unco-ordinated efforts was realised, and the result was the gradual formation of the Scottish Catholic Federation comprised mainly of the teachers of Dundee, Edinburgh and Glasgow. This more or less national organisation was granted representation on the Scottish Catholic Education Council and was recognised by the Scottish Education Department, and thus had some say in the negotiations which led to the passing of the Education (Scotland) Act, 1918.

With the passing of this measure, most of the teachers' economic grievances were removed. The Catholic teachers then turned to the Educational Institute of Scotland, and the Catholic Teachers Federation suffered a gradual decline.

As conditions in the schools improved, it began to be felt that although the professional and material interests of teachers were being looked after, something else was needed. By the early 1930's the Catholic schools then mainly in the primary sector were staffed by an ever-increasing number of young men and women, well qualified academically and professionally, but having no association with their Catholic colleagues other than through the E.I.S. Some other organisation was needed to cater for their religious, cultural and social activities and to weld them together as a professional body. W.S. Moore,(3)F.E. Davis and others of the moribund Federation, realising that there were many purely Catholic educational problems with which the E.I.S. could not deal, enlisted the aid of Dr. P.G. McGlynn, then a member of staff of the Humanities Department of Glasgow University, and Rev. Dr. W.E. Brown, chaplain to the Catholic students of the University, and formerly lecturer in the History Department. The idea of a Guild for teachers on the model of the mediaeval vocational guilds began to take shape. The project had to be regularised by the official dissolution of the Federation, and the approval of the Hierarchy also had to be obtained.

On 16 September 1934 a meeting was called by Archbishop Mackintosh of Glasgow in the City Hall. A personal invitation to attend was issued to every Catholic teacher in the Archdiocese, and 2,000 attended. The Guild of Catholic Teachers was formed with a membership in 1934-35 of 2,300, almost 100% of Catholic teachers in the Archdiocese, and chose as its patron the recently canonised St. John Boso.(4)

Although much of the energy of the Guild went into activities of a social nature, its principal enthusiasms at least in its early years were directed towards cultural or educational objectives. Some idea of the range of interests may be gained from the study groups which were set up immediately: to examine, inter alia, the recent Papal Encyclical on the Christian Education of Youth,(5) Scholastic Philosophy, Plain Chant, history textbooks, the use and misuse of films, and to compile a book list for school libraries.

The notion of a Guild attracted attention in other parts of the country and beyond, and during session 1935-36 a similar organisation was established in the Archdiocese of St. Andrew's and Edinburgh, and a joint committee was formed with a view to co-operation between the two.

In spite of the inevitable decline in activities during the war years, the Guild was able to maintain its progress in several directions, particularly in the establishment of Regional Districts in Aberdeen, Dundee, Edinburgh, Glasgow and Dumfries. In 1947 when the membership was at the high level of 2,100 teachers in the Archdiocese of Glasgow, the first of a series of National Congresses took place in Edinburgh, the principal speaker being Mr. Frank Sheed. (6) That year, which may have marked the high point in Guild activity, also saw the appearance of the first number of the Don Bosco Journal, which continued to appear at first on a quarterly and later on a twice yearly basis until November 1966.

During the quarter-of-a-century after the end of World War 2, the fortunes of the Guild declined. Among the many factors contributing to this change, the most significant may have been the following:

1. With the subdivision of the Archdiocese of Glasgow in 1948 and the subsequent establishment of separate Guilds in Glasgow, Paisley and Motherwell, the euphoria associated with the large membership of the early years began to subside.

2. The strength of the Guild from its beginning was in the staffs of the primary schools, which in pre-war days accounted for the vast majority of Catholic teachers. In the post-war period the expansion of Catholic secondary sector altered this balance. The needs and interests of the primary and secondary teachers diverged. Shortage of Catholic teachers, particularly in the secondary sector, imposed very considerable strains on the teaching staffs, sufficient to reduce significantly the energies available for voluntary work.

3. Demands imposed on teachers by the rate of change in society generally as well as in the educational system itself had the effect of directing energies and interests towards national rather than regional or denominational issues. Catholic teachers began to look outward to the national professional organisations. This experience of the Teacher's Guild was shared by other Catholic organisations.

4. The Second Vatican Council sent shock waves through the Catholic comunity,

particularly affecting the teaching body, which was beset by uncertainties and divisions connected with the difficult task of Religious Education.

5.   With the expansion of educational opportunity, increasing numbers of young Catholic men and women made their careers outwith teaching.   The status of the profession in the eyes of the Catholic community declined.

The fluctuation in the fortunes of the Guild were paralleled by those of its little review, the Don Bosco Journal, possibly its major achievement.   The first number appeared in 1947, edited by Frank MacMillan, a Glasgow graduate in Modern Languages, teacher, headmaster and free lance journalist.(7) The journal devoted itself to educational matters of special interest to the Catholic sector. It drew some of its inspiration from 'The Catholic Student', which had been sponsored and edited by W.E. Brown, University Chaplain and first chaplain to the Don Bosco Guild.

NOTES

1.   Barry, W.   DBJ   May 1955

2.   Moore, W.S.   DBJ   October 1955

3.   W.S Moore was the first head teacher of St. Gerard's Secondary School, and a president of the Guild of Catholic Teachers.

4.   On Easter Sunday, 1934, Don Bosco, a man who had spent practically all his life teaching, working among under-privileged boys, the founder of a Religious Teaching Order (the Salesians) and the originator of a system of education aimed at curing the problem of juvenile delinquency, was canonised in Rome as St. John Bosco. When choosing a patron in the manner of the mediaeval guilds, it seemed appropriate that the Teachers' Guild should select this modern recently canonised educator.

5.   Pius XI   The Christian Education of Youth.

6.   Frank Sheed, director of the publishing firm Sheed & Ward, author of 'A Map of Life' and many other publications, was an outstanding Catholic lay apologist and theologian. He died in 1981.

7.   Frank MacMillan taught in St. Aloysius College and Holyrood Secondary School before being appointed headmaster of Don Bosco Secondary and later Lourdes Secondary School. As a free lance journalist he contributed among other journals to The Tablet, The Mercat Cross (in which he edited a regular column), Round the World and the Glasgow Observer. He was succeeded as editor of the Don Bosco Journal by Joseph McConnell, then Principal Teacher of Classics in Holyrood School and later to become the first headmaster of St. Thomas Aquinas Secondary School in Glasgow. In his turn he was succeeded by John McShane, a Glasgow teacher and journalist, noted particularly for his regular contributions to The Scottish Field.

BIBLIOGRAPHY

ABBREVIATIONS

A.U.P.	Aberdeen University Press
C.E.C.	Catholic Education Commission
C.T.S.	Catholic Truth Society
C.U.A.	Catholic University of America
D.B.J.	Don Bosco Journal
H.C.S.	Hierarchy Centenary Supplement
H.J.	Historical Journal
I.R.	Innes Review
N.D.A.	Notre Dame Archive
NDSA	Notre Dame Sound Archive
O.U.P.	Oxford University Press
S.C.H.C.	Scottish Catholic Historical Committee
S.N.D.	Sister of Notre Dame
S.S.T.A.	Scottish Secondary Teachers Association
U.G.P.	University of Glasgow Press
TT	Tablet
U.L.P.	University of London Press
W.C.C.	Western Catholic Calendar

BOOKS

Abbott, Wm. (Ed.)	The Documents of Vatican 11	Chapman 1966
Anderson, R.D.	Education and Opportunity in Victorian Scotland	O.U.P.
Anson, P.F.	The Catholic Church in Modern Scotland	Burns, Oates 1937
Belloc, H.	The Servile State	Foulis 1913
Bone, T.R. (Ed.)	Studies in the History of Scottish Education 1872-1939	SCRE No.54
Boyd, W.	Evacuation in Scotland	SCRE
Boyle, J.	A Sense of Freedom	Pan Books
Brogan, C.	The Glasgow Story	Muller 1952
	The Educational Revolution	Muller 19--
Bryant, Barbara & Richard	Change and Conflict	A.U.P.
Checkland, S.G.	The Upas Tree	U.G.P. 1976
Cruickshank, M.	History of the Training of Teachers in Scotland	SCRE
Dealy, Sister MB	Catholic Schools in Scotland	CUA Press Washington DC 1945
Fletcher, A.	Guidance in Schools	A.U.P. 1980
Gillies, Sister D.	A Pioneer of Catholic Teacher Training in Scotland (Mary Adela Lescher)	NDA 1978

Handley, J.E.	The Irish in Scotland	Cork Univ. Press 1945
	The Irish in Modern Scotland	Cork Univ. Press 1947
	History of St. Mungo's Academy	J. Aitken (Paisley)
	History of St. Mary's Boys School Calton	J.S. Burns
Hebblethwaite, P.	The Runaway Church	Collins 1975
Hirst, P.H.	Moral Education in a Secular Society	ULP 1974
Humes, W. & Paterson, H. (Eds.)	Scottish Culture and Education 1800-1980	John Donald 1983
Hutchison. H.	Scottish Public Educational Documents 1570-1960	SCRE 1973
Jackson, J.A.	The Irish in Britain	
Jude, Sister SND	Freedom to Grow	J.S. Burns
Konstant, Bishop D.	Signposts and Homecomings	St. Paul Pubs. 1981
Linscott, Sister M.	Quiet Revolution	J.S. Burns 1966
McEwan, Mons. H.G.	Henry Gray Graham	J.S. Burns
McEwan, Canon S.	On the High 'C's	J.S. Burns
McShane, H.	No Mean Fighter	Pluto Press 1978
Maguire,G.T. and S.V. Murray	The Story of a School 1874-1974	Deacon Bros.
Martindale, C.C.	Charles Dominic Plater	Harding and More 1922
Meehan, P.	Innocent Villain	Pan Books
Middlemas, R.K.	The Clydesiders	Hutchison 1965
Miller, R. and J. Tivy (Eds.)	The Glasgow Region	British Association 1958
Murray, W.	The Old Firm	John Donald 1984
O'Connor, K.	The Irish in Britain	Gill and MacMillan 1972
Paterson, A.C.	Educational History of Clydebank	Clydebank Burgh Library
Roxburgh, J.M.	The School Board of Glasgow 1873-1919	SCRE 1971
Scotland, J.	A History of Scottish Education	
Smith,J.V. and D. Hamilton	The Meritocratic Intellect	A.U.P.
S.N.D.	Sister Mary of St. Philip. 1825-1905 (Frances Mary Leacher)	Longman 1920
Wade, N.A.	Post-Primary Education in the Primary Schools of Scotland 1872-1936	SCRE 1939
Ward, M.	Gilbert Keith Chesterton	Sheed and Ward
Woodham-Smith, C.	The Great Hunger	Hamish Hamilton 1964
Whyte, J.H.	Catholics in Western Democracies	Gill and MacMillan 1982

ARTICLES IN PERIODICALS

Anderson, W.J.	Education for Scottish Children in pre-Emancipation Days	IR XIV(I) 1963
Archer, A.	Ghetto Education	TT 13.3.82
Barry, W.	Catholic Schools after 1918	DBJ 1955
Coggan, Archbishop	Christian Believing and Public Life	TT 5.8.78
Darragh, J.	Catholic Population of Scotland since 1680	IR IV(I) 1953

	James Edmund Handley	IR XXII(I) 1971
	Catholic Population of Scotland	
	1878–1977	IR XXIX(2) 1978
	David McRoberts 1912–1978	IR XXX 1979
	Hierarchy Centenary Supplement	Universe 3.3.78
Dilworth, M.	Religious Orders in Scotland	IR XXIX(I) 1978
	1878–1978	
Edwards, O.D.	The Catholic Press in Scotland	IR XXIX(2) 1978
	since the Restoration of the	
	Hierarchy	
Fitzpatrick, T.A.	Education in Scotland	TT 22.1.1949
Gilfillan, J.B.S. and	Industrial and Commercial	The Glasgow Region
H.A. Moisley	Developments to 1914	
Goodwin, W.	The Sociology of Religion	TT 6.12.80
Handley, J.E.	French Influence on Scottish	IR I(I) 1950
	Catholic Education in the	
	Nineteenth Century	
Hornsby-Smith, M.P.	Catholic Opinion 1–1V	TT 2/9/16/23.2.80
Hume, Cardinal B.	The Catholic School	TT 26.5.79
Jackson, D.A.	A Catholic Curriculum	TT 30.5.81
Kenneth, Bro.	The Education (Scotland) Act	IR XIX(2) 1968
	in the Making	
	Catholic Education	DBJ 1962
McElligott, T.J.	The Role of the Laity	TT 29.8.81
McCaffrey, J.F.	Politics of the Catholic	IR XXIX(2) 1978
	Community since 1878	
	The Irish Vote in Glasgow in	IR XXI(I) 1970
	the late Nineteenth Century	
	Glasgow 1858 (Introduction)	UGP
McClelland V.A.	Curriculum Development	TT 28.11.81
	Sixth Form Curriculum 1 and 2	TT 26.5.79, 4.8.79
McGloin, J.	Catholic Education in Ayr 1823–	IR XIII(1,2) 1963
	1918	
	Some Refugee French Clerics and	IR XVI(I) 1965
	Laymen in Scotland 1784–1814	
	The Abbe Nicolas	IR XIV(I) 1963
McKee, J.J.	The Struggle to Maintain	Universe 3.3.78
	Catholic Schools	
McRoberts, Mons.D.	The Restoration of the Scottish	IR XXIX(I) 1978
	Hierarchy in 1878	
Nichols, Mons.K.	Towards a Theology of Education	TT 4.8.79
O'Riordan, M.	Comprehensivisation	TT 29.1.77
Phillimore, J.S.	The Prospects of the Catholic	Dublin Review 171
	Church in Scotland	1922
Quinn, J.	Ecumenism and Scottish Catholics	IR XXIX(2) 1978
Reilly, P.	Catholics and Scottish	IR XXIX(2) 1978
	Literature 1878–1978	
Roberts, A.F.B.	The Operation of the Ad Hoc	SCRE 54
	Education Authority in Dumbar-	
	tonshire between 1919 and 1930	
Ross, Anthony O.P.	Development of the Scottish	IR XXIX(I) 1978
	Catholic Community 1878–1978	
Skinnider, Sister M.	Catholic Elementary Education	SCRE 54
	in Glasgow 1818–1918	
Solzhenitsyn, A.	A World Divided	TT 29.7.1978

Smith, R.A.L.	Religious Education in Scotland	Dublin Review July 1943
Treble, J.H.	The Development of Roman Catholic Education in Scotland 1878-1978	IR XXXI(2) 1972
	The Working of the 1918 Education Act in the Glasgow Archdiocese	IR XXXI(I) 1980
Turner, G.	Catechesis and Theological Education	TT 30.8.80
	Theology in the Classroom	TT 28.2.81
Walker, W.M.	Irish Immigrants in Scotland; Their Priests, Politics and Parochial Life.	H.J. XV,4(1976)
Wood, I.S.	John Wheatley, the Irish and the Labour Movement in Scotland.	IR XXXI(2) 1980
	Irish Immigrants and Scottish Radicalism 1880-1906 Essays in Scottish Labour History I. MacDougall(Ed.)	

PAMPHLETS, BROCHURES, UNPUBLISHED MATERIAL

Catholicity in Greenock   Star Publishing Company 1909.
Centenary Brochure 1854-1954 of the Church of St. John the Baptist, Port Glasgow, 1954.

Commemorative Brochure: Glasgow University Chaplaincy   1956.
Golden Jubilee Brochure: St. Augustine's Church Coatbridge   1949.
Golden Jubilee: Notre Dame College   1895-1945.
Souvenir Brochure: Church of Our Lady of Mount Carmel, Kilmarnock.
Hierarchy Centenary Supplement: The Universe   3.3.78.
The Catholic School   Sacred Congregation for Catholic Education   CTS
The Franciscan Nuns in Scotland 1847-1930   Glasgow Observer 1930.
The Catholic Student   1933-1940   J.S. Burns.

Brown, W.F.	The Case for Catholic Schools	CTS(London) 1943.
Durkan J. et al.	The University of Glasgow and the Catholic Church 1450-1950.	S.C.H.C.
Graham, Bishop H.G.	The Church in Scotland	CTS(London) 1927.
Kenneth, Bro.	Catholic Schools in Scotland 1872-1972.	C.E.C. 1972.
McKechin, W.J.	Plus or Minus Local Govt. Research Unit Working Paper No.7	
Pope Pius XI	The Christian Education of Youth	CTS
Robertson, J.G.	The Education (Scotland) Act 1918	CTS
Robertson, J.J.	The Scottish Solution: Religious and Moral Education in the schools of Scotland.	Church of Scotland Commission on Education 1954.
White, J.	Our Lady's High School, Motherwell.	Typescript.

REPORTS

Education in Scotland.   Annual Reports 1922-39; 1947-72.
Primary Education   Advisory Council   Cmd. 6973 1946
Secondary Education   Advisory Council   Cmd. 7005 1947
The Supply of Teachers   Cmd. 8123 1951
Junior Secondary Education HM Inspectorate   1955
The Teachers (Training Authorities)(Scotland) Regulations   1958
Report on Measures to Improve the Supply of Teachers in Scotland. Cmnd. 644 1959
The Post-Fourth Year Examination Structure in Scotland   Cmnd. 1068 1960
From School to Further Education   Brunton Report   1963
The Teaching Profession in Scotland   Wheatley Report   1963
The Teaching Council (Scotland) Act.   1963.
The Schools (Scotland) Code Amendment Regulations Cir. 584.   1965.
The Teachers (Colleges of Education)(Scotland) Regulations   1967.
Guidance in Scottish Secondary Schools HM Inspectorate   1968.
The Structure of Promoted Posts in Secondary Schools in Scotland
                                                    HM Inspectorate 1971
Moral and Religious Education in Scottish Schools   Millar Report. 1972
Guidance in Scottish Secondary Schools   HM Inspectorate   1976
The Training of Graduates for Secondary Education   GTC   1972
Working Conditions in Scottish Secondary Schools   SSTA   1948
Teacher Shortage in Sessions 1945-6 and 1946-7   SSTA   1948
Scottish Educational Statistics   HMSO
Third Statistical Account of Scotland: Glasgow, Lanark, Dumbarton, Renfrew, Ayr.
Education Committee Annual Handbooks   Glasgow Corporation Education Department.

CHURCH REPORTS

Scottish Catholic Directory   Annual
Western Catholic Calendar   Annual
The Approach to Religious Education in the Catholic Secondary Schools
Signposts and Homecomings. The Educational Task of the Catholic Community.
          A Report to the Bishops of England and Wales.
The Easter People   1980.

YEARBOOK OF EDUCATION

Effects of War   1948
Moral Education and the Scottish Solution   1951.

INDEX